Problems in Public Utility Economics and Regulation

Problems in Public Utility Economics and Regulation

Edited by
Michael A. Crew
Rutgers University

LexingtonBooks
D.C. Heath and Company
Lexington, Massachusetts
Toronto

Library of Congress Cataloging in Publication Data
Main entry under title:

Problems in public utility economics and regulation.

"This collection of papers arose of two seminars held at Rutgers University's Graduate School of Business Administration. The first of these, 'Public utility regulation and performance,' was held on June 9, 1978, and the second, 'Recent developments in public utility pricing,' on October 27, 1978."
Bibliography: p.
1. Public utilities—Congresses. 2. Public utilities—Rates—Congresses. I. Crew, Michael A.
HD2763.P75 338.4'3 78-20608
ISBN 0-669-02775-8

Published simultaneously in Canada

Printed in the United States of America

International Standard Book Number: 0-669-02775-8

Library of Congress Catalog Card Number: 78-20608

Contents

Acknowledgments

This collection of papers arose out of two seminars held at Rutgers University's Graduate School of Business Administration. The first of these, "Public Utility Regulation and Performance," was held on June 9, 1978, and the second, "Recent Developments in Public Utility Pricing," on October 27, 1978. The seminars were made possible by financial support provided by five of New Jersey's leading utilities: Elizabethtown Gas Company, Jersey Central Power and Light Company, New Jersey Bell, Public Service Electric and Gas Company, and South Jersey Gas Company. They are not, of course, responsible for the views expressed in the papers, which represent only the positions of the individual authors.

In addition to the financial support that they provided, the utilities contributed to the success of the seminars through their advice and counsel. Utility executives who gave generously of their time include George Baulig, Bert J. Blewitt, Lawrence R. Codey, Russell Fleming, Jr., John Graham, Donald P. Marione, and Paul Preis.

I also acknowledge the assistance I have received from Fred S. Grygiel, chief economist of the New Jersey Board of Public Utilities, who was a constant source of good ideas on the project.

I would like to thank the individual contributors for providing a lively presentation of their papers and for their efforts in preparing them for publication. I would especially like to thank my long-time co-author, Paul Kleindorfer, for his willingness to discuss the project and for his helpful advice on numerous occasions.

I am grateful to Shelley Bauer, Kathleen Harkin, Pat Rotonda, and Lenore Rutz for typewriting assistance.

Finally, I would like to thank Horace J. De Podwin, dean of the Graduate School of Business Administration, for his constant interest in the project. I am grateful to him for making school facilities and services available for the project.

Michael A. Crew

1 An Introduction to Current Problems in Public Utility Economics and Regulation

Michael A. Crew and
Paul R. Kleindorfer

This chapter introduces some of the current problems in public utility pricing and regulation and hints at the extent to which the contributions that follow deal with these problems. We concentrate on two major problems, peak loads and regulation, and accordingly will devote much attention to these areas. We have divided the chapter into three sections. Section I introduces the welfare framework, briefly examines the contribution of peak load pricing, and discusses some unresolved problems. Section II introduces regulation and raises some current regulation questions. Section III introduces the contributions made in subsequent chapters of the book.

I. The Simple Theory of Peak-Load Pricing

The peak-load problem arises from the economic nonstorability of the product produced and the periodic fluctuation of the demand for the product over time.[1] In the case of electricity and telecommunications, the demand fluctuates according to the time of day or the season. For electricity in the United States, it is usually lowest on a winter's night and highest on a hot summer's day. This peak demand means that capacity has to be built to meet the demand. This capacity is not used fully at other times. Its idleness (with its accompanying costs) is the basis of the peak-load problem.

The peak-load problem in utilities first became evident when electricity was used mainly for lighting. Daily peaks occurred at nightfall when everyone turned their lights on. It was not long before pricing principles were enunciated to curb this peak demand. Indeed, the grandfather of electricity rate making, John Hopkinson, urged the use of maximum demand tariffs as early as the 1890s, and the so-called Hopkinson tariff, with a kwh charge as well as a charge per kw of maximum demand, has since become the basis for electricity rate making almost worldwide.

Economists became interested in the peak-load problem only relatively recently, with major contributions by W. Arthur Lewis (1941), Marcel Boiteux (1949), H.S. Houthakker (1951), I.M.D. Little (1953), and Peter

Steiner (1957). The approach they have suggested is to base prices on marginal costs. By exactly matching marginal costs with consumers' willingness to pay for additional output, a balance is achieved between the social costs of increasing production and the consumer satisfaction such increased output would generate. Aside from these economy-wide efficiency aspects, marginal-cost pricing also has intraindustry efficiency advantages in that the determination of long-run marginal costs is forward looking in contrast to pricing based on recovery of historical accounting costs, and requires a rational evaluation of future trends in such matters as inflation and factor prices, and the utility's planned response to such trends. One consequence of marginal-cost pricing is that peak-period consumers will have to pay a higher price than off-peak users, since marginal increases in peak demand entail expanding capacity in the long run, whereas increased off-peak demand simply incurs incremental production costs on existing units. The simple logic of this theory has not escaped practitioners, but there are many problems in applying marginal-cost pricing, as the ongoing Electric Utility Rate Design Study has documented.

The generally accepted approach in the economics literature to the peak-load problem stems from Boiteux (1949) and Steiner (1957). Steiner has been perhaps more frequently cited because of his use of diagrammatic methods, but Boiteux' earlier contribution contains essentially the same solution.

Steiner adopted a welfare-maximizing approach of setting prices to achieve "the maximization of the excess of expressed consumer satisfaction over the cost of resources devoted to production" (1957, p. 485). This involves assuming that the utility attempts to maximize welfare as measured by

$$\text{net benefit } W = \text{total benefit less total cost} = TR + S - TC, \tag{1.1}$$

where TR = total revenue, S = consumers' surplus, and TC = total costs.

The producers' net benefits are clearly $TR - TC$. Consumers' net benefits are represented by consumers' surplus as measured by the area under the usual Marshallian demand curve and above the price line. Thus, for the firm peak case in figure 1-1, the consumers' surplus at price $p_2 = b + \beta$ is the area of the triangle P_2LC, which measures the difference between what consumers would be willing to pay for output x_2 over and above what they actually pay (what they actually pay is Op_2Cx_2). For example, consumers would be willing to pay OL for the first unit of consumption, whereas they only pay p_2. Their surplus from the first unit consumed is thus $OL - p_2$. Looking at the second and further units consumed and adding their surpluses, one obtains the triangle p_2LC as total surplus.

The welfare measure (equation 1.1) is neutral with respect to which group of consumers (or producers) benefits. Everyone's dollars of net bene-

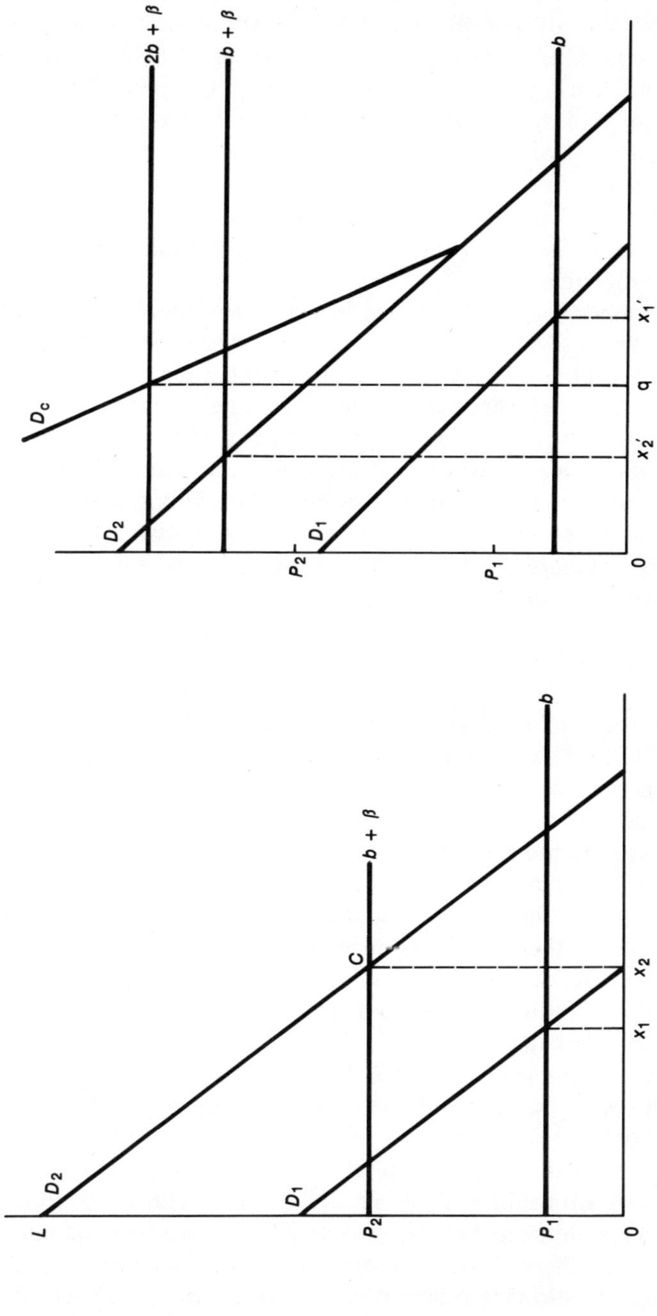

Figure 1-1. Firm Peak and Shifting Peak

fits count the same here. As a related point, the welfare function considers only aggregate social benefits, not the welfare of any specific group. What lies behind this line of reasoning is the assumption that public utilities should act in general to achieve a maximum aggregate benefit, leaving refinements in the distribution of benefits to other public policy instruments, such as taxes and social insurance programs. In this way, the distribution and efficiency aspects of public utilities planning are separated. If we make this assumption and maximize the welfare function W, prices should be set equal to marginal costs. This conclusion can be argued in a more general setting than that embodied in equation 1.1, though we shall continue to use W as our welfare indicator.

Steiner assumes a typical day divided into two equal-length periods, each governed by its own independent demand curve: $D_1(p)$ and $D_2(p)$. The peak-load problem here results from the assumption that one of these two demand curves lies everywhere above the other. The demands are independent in the sense that the price charged in one period has no effect on the quantity demanded in the other period. Costs are assumed linear: b is operating cost per unit per period; β is the cost of providing a unit of capacity. Thus, a unit demanded in a period will cost b if the capacity already exists to supply it, and $b + \beta$ if additional capacity has to be installed. Once a unit of capacity is installed (at cost β), it is available for meeting demands in both periods.

The solution to the two-period problem is given in figure 1-1, where the demand curves D_1 and D_2 are drawn. The left-hand part of the figure illustrates the firm peak case and involves pricing at $p_2 = b + \beta$ and $p_1 = b$, with period outputs $x_2 > x_1$, and with capacity $q = x_2$.

In the firm peak case, the peak period revenue (p_2x_2) covers the clearly identifiable peak period costs, both capacity (βq) and running costs (bx_1), and the off-peak period revenue (p_1x_1) covers only running costs. Since it follows directly from our welfare function that no price less than b or greater than $b + \beta$ is warranted, charging the highest feasible price in the peak period and the lowest feasible price in the off-peak period is something of a polar case. Steiner's analysis implies that as long as these prices can be charged while still leaving spare capacity $q - x_1 > 0$ in the off-peak period, such prices are in fact optimal.

By contrast, if the prices ($b + \beta$, b) are charged in the shifting peak case, quantities of $x'_2 < x'_1$ result. The peak has apparently shifted in that what was the off-peak demand (x_1) has now become the larger quantity demanded and thus the determinant of the amount of capacity required. This solution appears odd and, in fact, fails to maximize welfare. The correct solution is obtained by adding vertically the two demand curves D_1 and D_2 to get D_c. Where D_c cuts the horizontal line drawn at $2b + \beta$ gives optimal capacity q, allowing prices to be read off as p_1 and p_2, which, as in the firm peak case, satisfy $p_1 + p_2 = 2b + \beta$. Peak users pay a higher price than off-peak users even though the quantity supplied is identical in both periods.

In the shifting peak case, both demands contribute to capacity cost (β), and capacity is fully utilized in both periods. There is no precise rule for allocating capacity costs between peak and off peak; it depends on the relative strength of these demands. Thus if peak demand increases relative to off peak, optimality would require that the peak period consumers pay relatively more of the capacity cost β. It is not just the relationship between the demands that determine whether it is a firm or a shifting peak. The size of capacity costs relative to demands is also important. Thus, in the right-hand part of the figure 1–1 if β were to fall sufficiently, this case would become a firm peak; and if β were to rise by a large enough amount in the left-hand part of figure 1–1, this would become a shifting peak. It is apparent why this happens. If capacity costs are relatively large, any failure (as in firm peak case) to utilize capacity fully is expensive and encourages better utilization or a switchover to a shifting peak. In both the shifting peak and firm peak case, profit at optimum equals zero, a consequence of our welfare function, and the assumed constant returns to scale.

When increasing returns to scale obtain, the welfare optimal solution of marginal-cost pricing can be shown to lead to deficits, as Mohring (1970) discusses in detail. Under these circumstances, achieving a normal (nonnegative) profit in welfare-optimal fashion requires adjusting the marginal-cost pricing solution so as to distort the optimal demand pattern least. For example, if the utility analyzed in the Steiner framework incurred additional fixed costs R beyond the total capacity costs q, then marginal-cost pricing yields a net deficit of R. To recover R in welfare-optimal fashion, prices can be shown to satisfy the following profit-margin constraint in the firm peak case,

$$\frac{p_1 - b}{p_1} = -\frac{M}{\eta_1}, \qquad \frac{p_2 - (b + \beta)}{p_2} = -\frac{M}{\eta_2}, \tag{1.2}$$

where $\eta i \leq 0$ is the demand elasticity in period i and where $M \geq 0$ is adjusted upward until fixed costs are recovered at the resulting prices. From 1.2, we see that the more elastic demand is in a particular period, the less the welfare-optimal breakeven price in that period will deviate from marginal costs. The resulting demand pattern is therefore least distorted from the marginal-cost pricing demands when prices are set as in equation 1.2.

The simple peak-load problem has provided the basis for considerable extension to situations closer to those faced by the utilities. For example, the assumptions have been relaxed to allow unequal-length demand periods (Williamson, 1966), increasing returns (Mohring, 1970), multiple plant types (Crew and Kleindorfer, 1971, 1975a, 1975b), stochastic demand (Crew and Kleindorfer, 1976; Sherman and Visscher, 1978a), time-varying demand (Dansby, 1975; Crew and Kleindorfer 1979b), and combinations of these relaxed assumptions. All of these solutions reinforce the Boiteux-Steiner results that, in principle, prices and technology should be chosen so that efficient productive operations obtain (long-run cost minimization at the output provided) and so that a balance between consumers' willingness to pay and social costs of additional output are equated at the margin (marginal-cost pricing to the extent to which this is possible). These two conditions are slightly more difficult to characterize when one relaxes the Steiner assumptions, but the conditions themselves remain intuitive.

In summary, then, the theoretical literature to date has found under a wide variety of assumptions that prices on marginal costs maximize the welfare function (equation 1.1). There are, of course, several objections to marginal-cost pricing as well. Aside from departures from marginal-cost prices to achieve financial targets (as in equation 1.2) and, possibly, to achieve income redistribution goals (for example, through life-line rates), there is also the fundamental problem of whether optimizing prices and resource allocations in a single sector (the partial equilibrium approach used above in maximizing in equation 1.2) is appropriate when there may be distortions in other sectors of the economy. We are, however, beginning to make some progress in understanding these matters (Hatta 1977); the emerging philosophy is to use marginal-cost pricing as a benchmark, which is then adjusted to achieve financial targets, and income redistribution aims and to account for significant price distortions elsewhere in the economy. Altogether, the weight of the theoretical argument for marginal-cost-based pricing, together with initial successes in Europe in achieving increased efficiency through tariffs based on marginal-cost (in particular peak-load pricing), have led to a gradual and cautious introduction of such tariffs in the United States.[2] A number of problems remain in implementing peak-load pricing, however, and we now turn our attention to these.

Some Unresolved Problems

Although many of the problems of implementing peak-load pricing are common across utilities in various sectors, there are also great differences among sectors as a result of product and technology differences. To be concrete, we will concentrate on the electricity supply industry. The very ambitious *Electric Utility Rate Design Study* (EURD Study) has considered in great detail the implementation of peak-load pricing in the electricity supply industry and has suggested the following preliminary conclusions concerning areas where additional research is needed in improving rate-making procedures:[3]

1. The appropriate accounting and economic definition(s) of marginal costs need further research. In addition, linking accounting (history-oriented) and economic (future-oriented) costs in relation to revenue requirements and tariff design remains an unresolved practical and theoretical question.
2. The need to understand consumer decision processes and reactions to peak-load pricing remains an important research issue. European experience, as reported by Mitchell et all. (1978), indicates that substantial shifts in demand can be expected with the introduction of peak-load pricing and load management controls. Providing a practical framework for evaluating these demand shifts, and associated consumer and producer costs and benefits, is one of the critical research issues highlighted in the EURD Study.

In addition to the above research topics, we would like to speculate on some further problems, which seem to be important issues for peak-load pricing in electricity supply: peak loads and energy conservation; peak loads and regulation; and maximum demand charges and peak loads.

Peak Loads and Energy Conservation

The relation between peak-load pricing and energy conservation has become a topic of increasing interest recently. Peak-load pricing and time-of-day rates have been seen as promoting energy conservation from several quarters, including the present administration and key congressional advocates of new energy legislation.

Our previous work (Crew and Kleindorfer 1975b), first indicated that the capacity saving benefit traditionally attributed to peak-load pricing from the early days (by Steiner 1957 and Hirshleifer 1958, for example) might be of much less significance in the case of multiple plant types than savings in running cost. For example, under fairly realistic assumptions on technology, it is easy to show that when demands in each period are linear (but not necessarily independent between periods), peak-load pricing always provides a running cost saving when compared with a (welfare-optimal) uniform price schedule. However, depending on the cost parameters, capacity costs might be increased or decreased as a result of peak-load pricing.

The basic rationale for energy savings from peak-load pricing is simple.

By flattening the effective demand schedule, a more efficient plant mix can be used on average. This may be at the expense of additional capacity costs, however, because the flattened demand schedule will also call for replacing some peaking plant with base-load or intermediate-load plant. The magnitude of capacity and running cost changes depend on the demand structure and, in particular, on interperiod substitution possibilities. Estimating these cost changes remains an interesting empirical question.

It is not always the case that peak-load pricing leads to running cost savings. To illustrate, assume a plant mix consisting of two plants with per-unit running costs (b_1 and b_2) and per-unit capacity costs (β_1 and β_2), where[4]

$$b_1 = 1.4, \qquad b_2 = 2; \qquad \beta_1 = 3, \qquad \beta_2 = 2; \tag{1.3}$$

and with demands for two equal-length periods given by

$$p_1(x_1) = 100 \exp(-x_1/4) \tag{1.4}$$

and

$$p_2(x_2) = 200 - 10x_2, \tag{1.5}$$

where $\exp(x) = e^x$ is the exponential function. It can be shown for this two-plant, firm-peak case[5] that the welfare-optimal (marginal-cost) prices are

$$p_1 = (2b_1 + \beta_1) - (b_2 + \beta_2) = 1.8; \qquad p_2 = (b_2 + \beta_2) = 4, \tag{1.6}$$

with resulting outputs of

$$x_1 = 16.07; \qquad x_2 = 19.60. \tag{1.7}$$

The welfare-optimal uniform price, on the other hand, can be shown (by a comparative area analysis) to be $\bar{p} = 2.68$. Outputs under this uniform price are therefore

$$\bar{x} = 14.47; \qquad \bar{x}_2 = 19.73. \tag{1.8}$$

We note that x_1 increases substantially, and x_2 decreases only by a small amount with peak-load pricing. Given the cost characteristics (1.3) of the available plants, it is straightforward to show that the optimal amounts of each plant, q_1 and q_2, to construct are

$$q_1 = x_1; \qquad q_2 = x_2 - x_1; \tag{1.9}$$

with plant 1 being operated to full capacity in both periods and plant 2 being used only in the peak period. Given this and the outputs (equation 1.7 minus equation 1.8), we can compute running costs and capacity cost changes, denoted *RC* and *CC* below, resulting from peak-load pricing as follows:

$$RC = 2b_1(x_1 - \bar{x}_1) + b_2(x_2 - \bar{x}_2) = 1.02, \tag{1.10}$$

and

$$CC = \beta_1(x_1 - \bar{x}_1) + \beta_2(x_2 - x_1) - (\bar{x}_2 - \bar{x}_1) = 1.34. \tag{1.11}$$

Thus, the net effect of peak-load pricing in this case is to raise both capacity and running costs. Consumers, of course, gain more than these losses in the additional surplus, which peak-load pricing entails.

More generally, equation 1.10 can be arranged to show that *RC* is negative (peak-load pricing saves energy) in this two-period, two-plant case whenever

$$\frac{2b_1}{b_2} < \frac{\bar{x}_2 - \hat{x}_2}{x_1 - \bar{x}_1}. \tag{1.12}$$

In particular, 1.12 is likely to hold unless peak demand is very inelastic relative to off-peak demand as in the above example.

It would be interesting to extend the above results, following Wenders (1976) and Crew and Kleindorfer (1979b), to deal with more general demand patterns and changes as captured in a load duration curve. In any case, there is at least a theoretical possibility that both energy and capacity costs may increase in changing from uniform to peak-load pricing. Additional theoretical and empirical work to assess who would bear what burdens under peak-load pricing therefore is of interest.

A further matter of practical importance in this regard is the extent to which primary energy costs reflect their marginal social costs, given the role of the regulatory apparatus in determining these costs. Assessing the energy conservation impact of peak-load pricing would appear to require a detailed system planning effort for each utility.

Maximum Demand Rates and Peak-Load Pricing

Traditionally economists have considered maximum demand rates as generally inferior to time-of-day rates.[6] Our argument here is that there may be reasons for considering maximum demand charges along with time-of-day rates because of the problem of splitting discretely the time periods when the various rates apply. The problem can be illustrated by a simple case. Imagine that there are three equal-length periods, but that constraints require that only two prices for two equal-length periods be used. This situation is illustrated in figure 1-2. The solid line shows demands given uniform pricing. The effect of, say, charging a peak price for 0-12 hours is to reduce peak demand and increase off-peak demand in kw, shown by the dotted line in the figure. By having an off-peak price in period 12-24 hours, we get an increase in off-peak demand from 12-16 hours and an increase in shoulder demand from 16-24 hours. A slight miscalculation of demand elasticities or the presence of other uncertainties could, in fact, lead to the situation depicted in figure 1-2 where the prices chosen lead to a shift in the timing of the peak period. In addition to this moving-peak phenomenon, a further problem of concern to utilities is needle peaking, where a peak of short duration within the peak period occurs. It is concern with problems like this that has prompted the Virginia Electric and Power Company (VEPCO) to introduce maximum demand rates into its tariffs. VEPCO argues:

> as to the inclusion of a demand charge in to prototype rate, such a charge is theoretically desirable for two reasons; first, the cost-causation element of load factor should be recognized, and second, without such a charge, the per-kilowatt-hour "inclusive rate" would be so high as to foster needle-peaking, i.e., reducing peak-season usage without materially reducing peak demand on the hot, hot day.[7]

The demand charge thus causes consumers to self-impose quotas on their consumption. The consequence is that demand is less variable in the peak period, which has obvious benefits for capacity and revenue planning. In effect, the consumer is assuming a greater portion of the risks associated with uncertain events (such as the weather) under a maximum demand charge, while the utilities bear the major risks under peak-load pricing. Indeed the argument for the efficiency of maximum demand charges may rest more on risk-sharing properties than on mean allocative effects.[8]

To gain some further insight into maximum demand charges, we analyzed some particular cases in detail (Crew and Kleindorfer, 1979b). These examples were concerned with a utility facing several different customer groups, with demand for electricity over a daily cycle having three periods (with flat demand within each period). We assumed that the same kwh price would be charged in both the second and third periods, with a possibly different price for period 1 and, additionally, a maximum demand charge. By maximizing a weighted sum of consumers' utilities and company profits a Pareto-efficient price schedule was obtained. For reasonable assumptions on the parameters involved, these efficient price schedules entailed positive demand charges. The reason was intuitive. Without demand charges, needle peaking occurred within the second pricing period

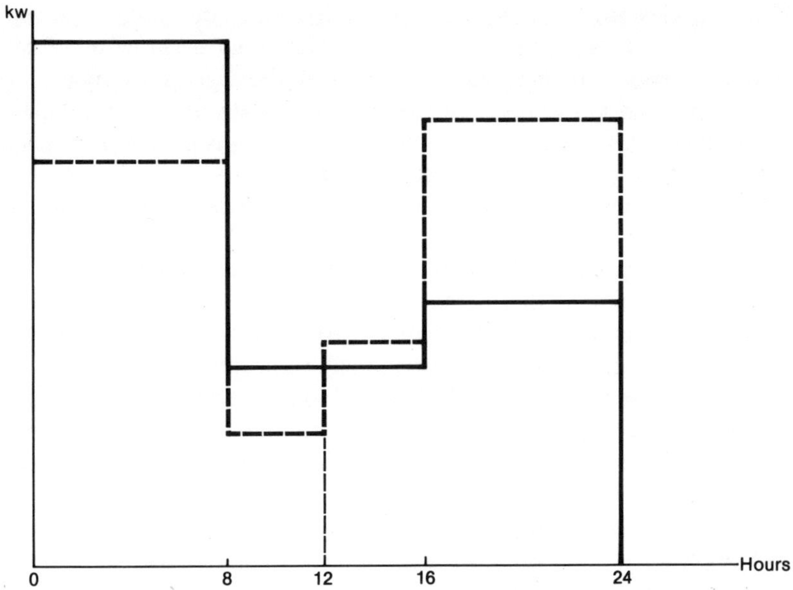

Figure 1–2. Effect of Time–of–Day Rates

(comprising the second and third demand periods). Demand charges, on the other hand, allowed each customer group to self-select its own peak period while still paying its fair share of capacity costs.

In summary, then, the long-standing use of maximum demand charges in practice and our preliminary theoretical results suggest that there is scope for the efficient use of maximum demand tariffs, either alone or in conjunction with time-of-day rates. We still have much to learn here, however. To mention just a few concerns, no results seem to be known concerning the structure of either welfare-optimal or profit maximizing maximum demand tariffs. Nor do we understand what level of interperiod demand substitutivity and diversity would make simple maximum-demand tariffs preferable to simple peak-load pricing. These are interesting questions, which seem long overdue for research.[9]

II. Some Aspects of Current Research in Regulation

Increasingly research in the economics of public utilities has become more concerned with consideration of the efficiency consequences of the regulatory process. This concern with efficiency has led to a much more critical and broader view not only of the nature of efficiency but also of the regulatory process itself. No longer is the research just concerned with the simple neoclassical aspects of inefficiency implied by the divergence of price and marginal cost and at the heart of the early rationale for much regulation. The concern now is much broader encompassing aspects of X-inefficiency, transaction costs, market and hierarchical failure, and a much deeper view of allocative efficiency required in situations where demand and supply are not deterministic.

While Leibenstein (1966) was first to draw attention to the notion of X-inefficiency, the idea that firms or organizations might not be operating at least cost—that is, not producing a given output at minimum cost—Averch and Johnson (1962) had previously indicated how internal inefficiency (in this case, excessive capital intensity) might actually be induced by rate-of-return regulation. The A-J thesis, rapidly seized upon by economists, still dominates regulatory economics, although other aspects of efficiency are increasingly being considered.

Williamson (1975), in his study of markets and hierarchies, has argued convincingly for a broader and deeper consideration of the nature of efficiency. He provides a framework for comparison of the efficiency of completing a related set of transactions through the market or through a firm (or hierarchy). His analysis therefore concentrates on transaction costs. These costs may be affected by a number of factors, such as the limited capacity of decision makers (bounded rationality) and the ability of a contractual arrangement to limit strategic and dysfunctional behavior on the part of the other party to the contract (attenuation of opportunism). Thus whether the markets or a hierarchy performs a given set of related transactions depends upon the transactions costs associated with each alternative. In short, the contracting mode employed will depend upon the extent to which it economizes a bounded rationality and attenuates opportunism.

The approach can be extended to the study of regulation as Williamson (1976) has to compare the efficiency consequences of regulation and franchise bidding to CATV. By further consideration of transactions costs, the approach can be extended to compare alternative methods of regulation. Given that some kind of regulation is required—for example, for political reasons, like the need to make monopoly acceptable—then the Williamson approach suggests new ways for evaluating various alternative regulatory schemes. One possibility of interest is the quantification of transactions costs of the existing regulatory system. These include the transactions costs of the companies in preparing for rate cases, plus the costs of operating commissions, and the costs of consumer groups in making their views known at hearings. Because of the increased frequency of hearings, this process might place too great a burden on the regulatory process relative to the benefits of regulation. Assessing the magnitude of these transactions costs should prove to be fruitful area for research in the future.

Current research in regulation is not just concerned with a broader view of the nature of efficiency. Baumol (1977) and Panzar and Willig (1977) have raised fundamental issues on the nature and sustainability of natural monopoly prices.[10] They proceed from the traditional definition of natural monopoly as being characterized by scale economies, which, for any profitable price-output vector, allow a single firm to provide the output at less cost than any multifirm producer configuration could. The issue that these authors investigate is whether there exists a price-output vector that is profitable for the monopolist and at which no new entrant would be able to capture profitably a suitable subset of the total output at a lower price. If such an entry-resistant, price-output vector exists, the natural monopoly is said to be sustainable. As it turns out, rather strong conditions appear to be required to assure sustainability of a natural monopoly, at least at prices that have any claim to social efficiency. Thus the study of regulation of natural monopolies has to be extended to include the question of when entry barriers should be provided to prevent inefficient cream skimming (new entrants' skimming off the profitable portion of demand while increasing the total social costs of providing goods and services originally provided by a monopoly). Research on this question will certainly be a major influence on the study of public enterprises in the future.

The development of the theory of peak-load pricing and the interest in its application to utilities is another force affecting regulation. Wellisz (1963) and Bailey (1972, 1973) pioneered the study of the implications of peak-load pricing for regulation. Starting with the Steiner framework, these authors investigate how a rate-of-return regulated monopolist would set peak and off-peak prices. Among other results, they emphasize how regulation benefited the peak consumers. Recently the study of peak loads and regulation has come to include the effects of stochastic demand and the effects on reliability of supply of regulation (Crew and Kleindorfer, 1976, 1978a; Sherman and Visscher, 1978a).

III. A Review of the Contributions

We have categorized the chapters in this book under three headings, although it will soon become apparent that our assignment is, in some cases, arbitrary.

Public Utility Regulation

The chapters by Arzac and Edwards, Bailey, and Sudit deal with one or more of the important current problems in regulation. They all raise fundamental issues and could prove instrumental in affecting not only future research in regulation but also actual policy.

Elizabeth E. Bailey's chapter is interesting from several points of view. As a member of the Civil Aeronautics Board and as a professional economist who has made important contributions in the field of public utility economics, her views on the problem of regulatory reform are of immediate interest to all public utility economists because she is uniquely placed to relate some of the problems of applying theories to actual problems. Her chapter is additionally of considerable interest in view of the problem it addresses and the apparent success of its solution. She deals with introducing deregulation, a considerable achievement in view of the various arguments, notably of Stigler (1971) and Posner (1974), to the effect that the motivation for regulation may not, in fact, be the public interest or the public good of all; instead motivation may be supplied by producer groups who attempt to use regulation to promote their own interests such as the erection of entry barriers, that are well worth the costs that regulation imposes. Another important message of Bailey's contribution is how successful the reforms (deregulation) have been. This success is very important and should make economists and government take a much more skeptical view of regulation. Perhaps the main message to them when faced with a regulatory environment is to answer the question of whether regulation is necessary.

Enrique Arzac and Frank Edwards, in line with the earlier discussion of the broadening view of efficiency, examine some of the features of X-inefficiency under regulation. Their chapter is noteworthy for its extension of the earlier work of Williamson (1964), Edwards (1977), and Crew and Kleindorfer (1979a) on managerial discretion to regulation. Their analysis indicates that rate-of-return regulation, contrary to the expectations of the A-J thesis, may actually reduce X-inefficiency. They call for a closer look at the objective function of regulated firms because this exercise seems to offer the prospect of above-normal returns to research effort.

Fred Sudit's chapter is important in at least two main respects. First, it provides an alternative to the present system of regulation. Second, it is related to the work of Williamson (1975) on markets and hierarchies and transactions costs. Sudit proposes a system of regulation based upon automatic adjustment utilizing the Divisia index of total factor productivity. Unlike existing automatic fuel adjustments, Sudit's proposal is intended to promote efficiency in a number of ways. For example, the companies will have a productivity target, which will penalize them if they fail to achieve it but benefit them if they beat it. This system opens up a number of possibilities for a regulatory system with explicit incentives and with possibilities of sharing productivity gains between companies and consumers. There seems to be every prospect that such schemes would be preferable to the incentives apparently provided by regulatory lag under the current system.

Sudit's proposal offers not only the prospect of improved productivity and incentives toward efficiency but may be attractive compared to the current system in terms of its possibilities for reduction in transaction costs. One effect of his automatic adjustments might be that reduction in the frequency of rate hearings could lead to substantially reduced transaction costs. At the very least, this opens up an attractive prospect for future research.

Applications of Peak-Load Pricing

The chapters by John T. Wenders and R. Ashley Lyman and by Colin Blaydon, Wesley A. Magat, and Celia Thomas are important applications of peak load on marginal cost pricing to, respectively, the electricity and gas industries. Wenders and Lyman throw some light on the extent to which economists' beliefs hold about the applicability of peak-load pricing in electricity supply. The Blaydon-Magat-Thomas chapter applies marginal cost and peak-load pricing principles to the problem of gas supply. With the eventual decontrol of natural gas and the importance of energy conservation, both of these chapters are likely to have an important part to play in illuminating the problems that are likely to follow.

Wenders and Lyman's chapter is probably one of the first of a series of publications that will follow on the application of peak-load pricing to electric utilities. The benefit-costs framework that they develop arises out of some of the analysis of peak loads and marginal costs in the Electric Utility Rate Design Study. They provide case studies of two utilities to derive the net benefits of seasonal and seasonal-time-of-day rates when compared with uniform rates. They show the importance of metering costs in their analysis. Their estimates of the potential benefit of seasonal-time-of-day rates makes it possible to decide which customers should have the rate based upon consumption levels.

The Blaydon-Magat-Thomas chapter was in part motivated by the severe gas shortages of 1976-1977 winter, which made it apparent that efficient pricing of gas was not solely an academic issue. Their work is based upon two supply models—a single period and a multiperiod model—and a demand model. They discuss the use of an iterative process to solve for optimal (marginal-cost-based) prices. Their estimated solution employs a summer-winter price differential and takes into account such practical considerations of rate making as revenue requirements and pipeline tracking increases. The chapter should be of interest not only to economists wishing to apply marginal cost pricing and peak-load principles but also to utility and regulatory professionals interested in rate making.

Peak Loads and Regulation

The chapters by Sherman and Visscher, by Faulhaber, and by Crew and Kleindorfer all deal in varying degrees with the interaction between peak loads and regulation. Sherman and Visscher are concerned with the distortions to various pricing schemes that arise from rate-of-return regulation. Faulhaber deals with a somewhat similar point but takes as his example some rules of cost allocation of the Federal Communications Commission. We further our earlier ideas on reliability (Crew and Kleindorfer 1978) to explore the effects of regulation, peak-load pricing, and stochastic demand.

Sherman and Visscher are concerned with the effect of rate-of-return regulation on various monopoly-pricing policies. They show the distortion from the actual prices derived from the inverse elasticity rule when a profit-maximizing monopolist is subject to rate-of-return regulation. They also discuss the peak-load case under regulation. Their exploration of the effects of rate-of-return regulation on two-part tariffs or nonlinear pricing schedules deals with an apparent omission in the literature. In view of the popularity of two-part and block rates with utilities, this lack of interest in the interaction of rate-of-return regulation and such tariffs is surprising. Sherman and Visscher's analysis is indicative of the possible returns from further examination of this area and offers another explanation beyond just a simple monopoly exploitation of the popularity and durability of two-part and declining block rates.

Although the motivation for Gerald Faulhaber's work arises out of some of the effects of the accounting rules for allocating capacity cost as applied by the FCC to, principally, AT&T, the importance of the chapter for the practical application of peak-load pricing to other utlitities must not be underestimated. His general point is that the cost allocation rules imposed by the FCC cause deviations from the optimal Steiner peak-load prices. This effect creates a number of problems, aside from the distortion of the welfare optimal prices, including the possibility of entry by rivals with higher costs in a situation where the natural monopoly was sustainable with Steiner prices. The net effect could be higher social costs through duplication of facilities and the presence of higher cost rivals, where entry had been induced solely by the regulatory rules. In short, Faulhaber adds a further dimension to the current revival of interest in natural monopoly and its sustainability.

Finally, we examine the effect of rate-of-return regulation in peak-load situations where demand is random. We discuss some of the implications for welfare of various rationing schemes when demand exceeds capacity, as well as determination of optimal capacity. However, we view examination of the relationship between reliability and regulation as having more effect on the scope of future research. Although our analysis and results must be regarded as preliminary, the hypothesis that rate-of-return regulation lead to excessive reliability is worth considering. If this conclusion is substantiated, then many further questions are raised not just about regulation but also about the methods used to plan for reliability.

Notes

1. The first part of this section is based upon Crew and Kleindorfer (1979b), chaps. 2-3.

2. See, especially, the recent book by Mitchell et al. (1978) reviewing the experience of European utilities with peak-load pricing.

3. See the summary document "Rate Design and Load Control: Issues and Directions," Electric Utility Rate Design Study (Palo Alto, Calif.: EPRI, November 1977).

4. The examples in this section are based upon Crew and Kleindorfer (1979b).

5. See Crew and Kleindorfer (1975b, 1979b) for a discussion of peak-load pricing with multiple plant types.

6. See Wenders and Taylor (1976, p. 535) for a clear statement of the traditional approach.

7. See Electric Utility Rate Design Study, "Ratemaking: Topic 5 and Illustrative Rates for Five Utilities" (Palo Alto, Calif.: EPRI, June 6, 1977).

8. We are grateful to Ingo Vogelsang of the University of Bonn for bringing this idea to our attention.

9. Some attention has already been given to related issues. See, for example, Dansby (1978) and Panzar and Sibley (1978).

10. Indeed, in this volume the issue of sustainability and regulation is raised by Faulhaber. See chapter 8.

2 Reform from Within: Civil Aeronautics Board Policy, 1977–1978

Elizabeth E. Bailey

On October 24, 1978, the Airline Deregulation Act of 1978 became law (PL 95–504). It terminates the Civil Aeronautics Board's authority over domestic routes on December 31, 1981. Fare and charter regulations and merger authority expire a year later. The act is an extraordinary document, which goes far beyond the proposed reforms of its parent bill, S. 689 (the Cannon–Kennedy bill) as reported by the Senate Commerce Committee on October 27, 1977.

The CAB's administration of regulatory reform during the 1977–1978 period contributed substantially to the shaping of this legislation. During this period, it gave structure to a program to liberalize entry, especially by devising and authorizing a multiple and permissive entry concept on a case-by-case basis. It put in place a zone of fare flexibility, which institutionalized liberal discount fare policies and made a start at permitting at least some unrestricted low fares to be offered. It has been effective internationally in proposing that new route rights into the United States be offered to countries willing to permit low scheduled fares and liberal charter regimes. The Deregulation Act affirmed the CAB's advocated policy of deregulation and entrusted it with supervising the transition.

This chapter describes the major policy thrusts undertaken by the Civil Aeronautics Board during the chairmanship of Alfred E. Kahn, June 10, 1977 to October 26, 1978.

Pricing Policy

Perhaps the best-known example of former CAB pricing policy is the World Airways application for low-fare, coast-to-coast service filed on April 26, 1967, which was dismissed as stale on November 21, 1973, because a majority of the board did not believe it was important enough to be heard. This lack of interest in price competition was codified between 1970 and 1974 in the Domestic Passenger Fare Investigation (DPFI), which set minimum prices based on an industry-wide load factor standard of 55 percent, a distance taper, and a 12 percent industry rate-of-return on investment. Under the DPFI, standard fares are set nationwide rather than determined competitively. Coach fares can go up only if industry costs go up, and, similarly, they can go down only when industry costs go down. Any flexibility in fares is limited to nondiscriminatory discount fares that can be offered only after the carrier has given advance public notice of the new fare and obtained CAB approval. It is well known that these impediments to price competition have led to scheduling and other forms of service competition and to a different price/service outcome than might have been expected in the absence of regulatory intervention[1]

In particular, a rather different equilibrium occurred in the intrastate California and Texas markets where the CAB had no jurisdiction over purely local transportation. Here, fares are substantially lower and load factors are substantially higher than are the normal CAB levels. For example, Southwest Airlines in Texas adopted a peak-off-peak price policy with intrastate fares that are lower for both high-density markets such as Dallas-Houston (39.5 percent peak and 63.7 percent off-peak) and for lower-density markets such as Harlingen-Houston (47.5 percent peak and 68.5 percent off-peak). Not only are the prices lower, but there is evidence that these low fares stimulate substantial new traffic. Figure 2-1 shows the traffic stimulation in the Dallas-Houston market as a result of Southwest Airlines's entry and contrasts it with a number of similar high-density markets served under the DPFI pricing policy.

The low-fare policy has been highly profitable for the carriers offering it. Southwest Airlines, for example, earned rates of return between 18 and 24 percent during the four years 1974-1977, more than double the average earned by certificated trunk and local service carriers. The low-fare service is also difficult to predate against, as was discovered when the new entrants offering these fares survived stiff competitive responses by the incumbent carriers.[2]

These experiences suggested that the time was ripe for the CAB to encourage low fares in markets within its jurisdiction. The difficulty that the board faced during the chairmanship of Alfred E. Kahn, however, was that the DPFI rules were in place, and it would take at least a year for any new rule making to take effect. The strategy we adopted was to make it known to the carriers that we would follow a liberal policy toward discount fares, approving any brought before us in a pro forma fashion. We also began giving route cases entailing low-fare services expedited treatment and used low fares as a decisional variable in seeking carriers to serve markets. These policies resulted in the institution of new low fares and in decisions, such as that in the Transcontinental low fare case, to award authority to World Airways and other low-fare applicants.[3] The policies also were a factor in a plethora of low-fare proposals brought before the board during 1977 and 1978. These are summarized in appendix 2A, where they are grouped in part by effective date of fare and in part by type of discount.

Many of the fares entailed off-peak pricing principles; that is, they

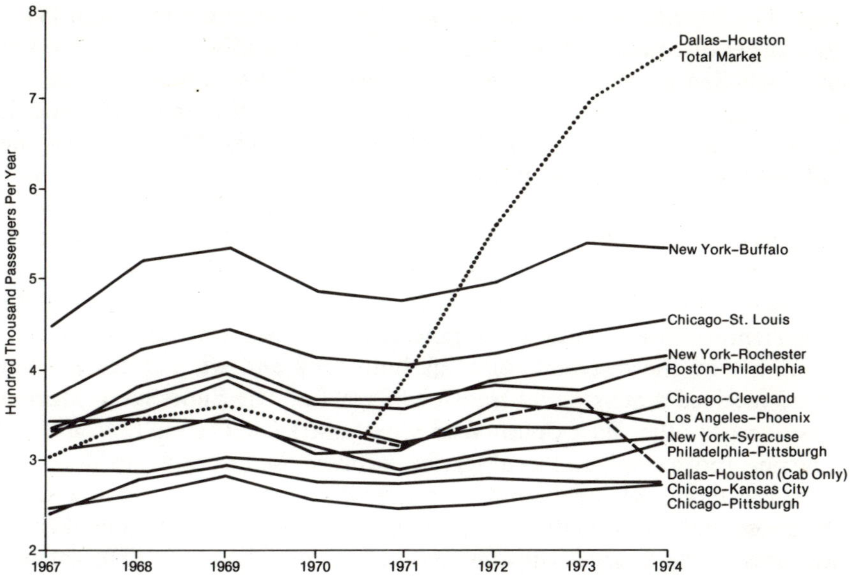

Figure 2-1. Comparative Traffic Growth of Dallas-Houston Market with the Average of the Ten Most Similar Markets under 500 Miles Served by CAB Carriers Exclusively

were designed primarily to increase the load factors of low load factor flights. Off-peak principles in the form of night coach fares had been well established in aviation, but with the exception of Southwest Airlines, there had been little use of these principles other than during the evening period. Even before Kahn's arrival at the board, the Peanuts fare was introduced by Texas International, in part as a competitive response to Southwest's two-tier price structure. The fare provided for 50 percent discounts on any flight determined by the carrier to be off-peak. The fare spread first to another Texas carrier, Braniff, and later to Allegheny. Another fare concept introduced by Allegheny that was aimed at increasing load factors on specific flights was the SimpleSaver fare, which offered a price reduction to passengers willing to take multistop flights rather than the more attractive nonstop flights offered by competitors. Tag-end fares offered discounts on flight segments that had a disproportionate number of empty seats.

A second major type of discount fare that spread widely during 1977–1978 was the SuperSaver fare. It had been introduced before Kahn's arrival and continued a long tradition of excursion fares. Traditionally such fares had discounts of from 20 to 30 percent and were offered primarily to vacation travelers going to Florida, Las Vegas, on ski trips, or to the West

Coast. The SuperSaver, as introduced by American Airlines in March 1977, had a larger discount than usual (35 to 45 percent) and was confined to the New York–San Francisco/Los Angeles market. The fare had a number of restrictions: a thirty-day advance purchase, a stay requirement of seven to forty-five days, and a capacity limitation that at most 35 percent of the available seats could be sold at this fare.

Table 2–1 indicates that the lower fares led to a substantial increase in passengers carried (30 percent or more). It also shows a substantial conversion in the Los Angeles market of scheduled carrier charter seats to SuperSaver seats. The demand for charter seats was transferred to the supplemental carriers. Thus, the supplemental carriers were not driven from the market by the discount fares, as both they and we had feared, but instead received a substantial transfer of traffic. The SuperSaver concept spread first to other East Coast–West Coast markets. Then in March 1978, all carriers (both trunk and local service) adopted the fare systemwide.

A third type of significant fare reduction occurred after the CAB announced that it was willing to alter its formerly rigid ratio that held first-class fares of trunk carriers at some 160 percent of coach fares. The carriers responded by reducing first-class fares to 130 percent of coach and then a few months later reduced the fares again to 120 percent of coach.

A fourth type of fare reduction is that involving unrestricted low fares. TWA's Supercoach was originally such a fare, which attempted to lower prices to passengers willing to fly on planes configured for charter traffic. The fare was later matched by United on a capacity-controlled basis. The Miami–Los Angeles unrestricted low fare was a direct result of CAB intervention, for we in essence threatened that Western Airlines might be replaced in this market unless it were a low-fare carrier. The fare has proven successful for Western, which has received larger load factors and which was excused by the board from the usual joint fare provisions of the

Table 2–1
April–December Passengers

	New York–Los Angeles			*New York–San Francisco*		
	1976	*1977*	*% Change*	*1976*	*1977*	*% Change*
Scheduled	1,012,289	1,322,120	+30.6	720,197	950,580	+32.0
Charter scheduled	49,359	18,759	−62.0	28,794	35,400	+22.9
Supplemental	1,188	30,612	25.8 times	644	2,248	3.5 times

DPFI. When Delta offered a round-trip low fare in its Midway market, its load factors climbed from 18 to 60 percent.

Not all low-fare concepts have worked. The Chickenfeed fare caused a lot of consumer complaints and has been replaced. The NoStrings fares to Florida had uneconomically high no-show rates and were withdrawn.

The CAB first tried to revise the DPFI rate making during 1977-1978 and created a zone of downward fare flexibility. The zone was formed with the presumption that any fare in it is lawful unless there is clear and convincing evidence to the contrary. The rule limited upward fare flexibility, with more flexibility given to workably competitive markets than to monopoly markets, thus preventing an abuse of monopoly power during the period when there are still substantial barriers to entry. The new rule still contains restrictions, such as the point-beyond rule, which provides that a joint fare to a point cannot be higher than a joint fare to a point more distant via the same routing. Such restrictions have made the adoption of unrestricted low fares potentially very costly to carriers operating systems, and it is our intention to review them. Ideally our policy should be to modify our rules so that complete fare deregulation is accomplished before the fare provisions of the new act go into force.

Entry Policy

The Federal Aviation Act of 1958 requires notice and hearing before granting new route authority. Under the Administrative Procedures Act, this has traditionally meant a full evidentiary hearing with opportunity for cross-examination. As a result, even the simplest route cases typically take one to two years to complete, and more complicated cases take even longer. This entry barrier caused by CAB procedures is supplemented by another barrier in how these procedures have been administered. Typically new competitive route authority has been granted to only a single carrier on any route (carrier selection), and there have been times in CAB history where virtually no awards have been made. One such period occurred in the early 1960s and another in the period from 1969 through 1974, when overcapacity plagued the industry.

In recent years, the board has conducted a step-by-step program to change its procedural requirements to speed the process of entry and to increase the number of carriers authorized to operate in particular markets. It recognized that the number of carriers that can profitably operate in a particular market is limited by such economic factors as local traffic demand, the availability of connecting traffic, and so on, but a more open entry regime is thought to create a pool of entrants able to enter if and when existing service fails to match consumers' needs or if price in a market becomes too high. The 1977–1978 program relied on the idea that the forces of the marketplace are more likely to result in an economically rational initial and continuing carrier selection process than the board could hope to achieve with its traditional regulatory mechanism.

One of the highlights of board policy is route realignment, an idea that was well underway at the time Kahn arrived at the board. The purpose of a route realignment is to remove restrictions, such as the requirement that a carrier must make one or more intermediate stops between two particular cities or that it must go to a beyond point, thus preventing turnaround service. Many of these restrictions were imposed to protect carriers that no longer exist or for procedural reasons that are no longer relevant. In the Allegheny realignment, for example, the board removed or modified restrictions in some five thousand markets, each of which was individually relatively minor, but the sum total of which contributed substantially to increased operating efficiency and flexibility for the carrier.[4] We have been systematically realigning the carriers, starting with the local service carriers and proceeding to the trunks. The procedure used is a show-cause or tentative order based on written pleadings, which asks concerned persons to explain in detail why they would want to cross-examine on any of the issues concerned. The new act continues this process of restriction removal, directing the CAB to go well beyond the guidelines developed under the old act.

Show-cause procedures have also been used in 1978 in granting fill-up authority for U.S. carriers serving international routes. This authority permits carriers to accept additional passengers on the within-U.S. portions of international trips—for example, Pan American could accept Detroit-Boston passengers on that segment of a Detroit-Boston-London flight. The fill-up concept is clearly economically efficient, for the planes are flying anyway, and at least some travelers will be made better off (as will the carrier) if they are permitted to fill the empty seats. The fill-up concept has also been put into law in the new act.

Other situations where nonoral hearing procedures seem appropriate were also sought out. One of the first uses was in the *service-to-richmond case*, where the board decided in 1976 to reconsider a decision made in 1974.[5] Since new data were needed, the board employed procedures that called for the submission of direct and rebuttal exhibits with written testimony only.

In the Piedmont case involving entry into Boston, the board used show-cause procedures even where an incumbent carrier (Eastern) objected and alleged that Piedmont's services would divert up to $3 million in revenues from it and that the new service would be unprofitable.[6] We put Eastern on notice that unless it was prepared to show that diversion by Piedmont's new Boston services would threaten its solvency or impair its ability to provide essential air transportation, the different calculations of diversion would not be considered to create an issue of material fact or the need for an oral hearing. Similarly profitability would no longer be required to be demonstrated; instead the applicant would only have to show a plausible operating plan. It was our hope that dispensing with these traditional issues for litigation would permit us more easily and quickly to allot additional entry in cases where a single applicant puts forward a relatively conventional proposal for new and/or improved services in small or medium-sized markets.

Another step in our program of easing entry barriers was to adopt the policy of multiple permissive entry on a case-by-case basis. Two of the most significant uses of the policy were in the Chicago-Midway case and the Oakland case.[7] Both involve the opening up of underutilized airports. In the former case, two new carriers—Midway and Midway Southeast Airlines—proposed to use idle airport capacity at the Midway Airport in Chicago to provide low-fare, round-trip service between Chicago and a number of other midwestern cities, such as St. Louis, Kansas City, Detroit, and the Twin Cities. To expedite the decision following a public hearing, the record was certified directly to the board rather than having an initial decision by a judge. The board instructed the staff to grant all the authority that had been requested—service to all six cities at issue by the two new entrants and by North Central—and the new authority requested by Northwest and Delta. In addition, we instructed the staff not to impose any restrictions on incumbent carriers that would prevent them from either matching fares out of O'Hare or from instituting low-fare service at Midway in these markets. Thus we adopted an innovative policy based on a traditional record. The policy was selected because it seemed the most likely to serve the public interest and to ensure the reactivation of the airport.

The Oakland case combines the new multiple permissive entry policy with new procedures. We recognized that the single issue that complicates and prolongs route proceedings the most is that of comparative carrier selection, and we decided to eliminate the issue in this case. As we stated in our order:

> No applicant will be required to submit exhibits designed to show that its service proposal will produce greater public benefits than any other applicant's, or that its service will be more profitable or will provide a greater reduction in subsidy need or will otherwise result in a greater or more needed degree of route strengthening, or that it will divert less revenue from an incumbent—or, in general, that it outranks all other applicants in any of the numerous factors which the Board has historically employed in choosing among competing applicants for the same authority. [P.55]

This policy was declared at the outset. We intend to grant permissive authority to every fit applicant with a plausible service proposal in each of the Oakland markcts at issue in which a need for additional authority is found in this proceeding.

We continued throughout 1978 to seek broad classes of cases in which we could separate need-for-service questions from carrier-selection questions, and were contemplating more liberal uses of rule making, such as authorizing unlimited entry into a limited group of very large markets, for applicants already certificated or found to be fit, willing, and able. However, the Airline Deregulation Act of 1978 has rendered at least some of these plans moot. Because free entry will be in effect, it seems more sensible to establish procedures that permit a carrier to enter any market it wishes with minimum effort.

Another issue in route policy is that of service to small and medium-sized communities, many of which are concerned that they might lose service under a more permissive environment for both entry and exit. There does appear to be a problem in this area in the short run, particularly because of the capacity shortage that became evident as 1978 progressed. New route authority is often sufficiently attractive that carriers reroute planes and reduce service to small communities. In other instances, local service and trunk carriers ground their Convair fleets, again with negative effects on service to these communities. Fortunately, the new act recognizes these problems and directs the CAB to develop a program for small communities with new possibilities for subsidized service tailored to community needs rather than to carrier needs. Moreover, in the interim, both the board and the new act have increased the size limit applicable to commuter carrier aircraft so that the unregulated commuter carriers can enter and fill part of the need.

Experience has shown that the commuter industry has been able to attract capable entrepreneurs willing to provide high-frequency, high-quality service attuned to the demands of small and medium-sized communities. Experience also indicates that the commuters rapidly enter service voids created by the discontinuance of certificated service. Take, for example, the case of Allegheny Airlines's elimination of its two round trips from Ithaca, New York, to Washington, D.C., in April 1978. This decision was a matter of some concern to CAB chairman Alfred E. Kahn, who has a home in Ithaca. But he found that although Allegheny was grounding its Convair fleet, Commuter Airlines planed to introduce its own refurbished Convair fleet into this and other New York markets in early July 1978, and to offer, among other services, three round trips per week in the Ithaca-Washington market. Thus the disruption was short-lived.

It is our belief that the new act will alleviate rather than aggravate the long-run problem of service to these communities. The procompetitive policy coupled with less complicated procedures that reduce legal costs associated with gaining entry should encourage new applicants to serve such communities. The CAB has never found a way to force an unwilling carrier to provide attractive and convenient service. Our hope is that new subsidy provisions combined with lower barriers to entry will make competition easier for willing carriers.

International Aviation Policy

About a month after Kahn's arrival at the board, the United States and the United Kingdom signed a bilateral air agreement (Bermuda II of July 23, 1977) that was a significant regressive departure for U.S. policy. The United States agreed to capacity controls that restricted U.S. carriers' opportunities to increase their market share. The United States gave up multiple designation of the U.S. carriers in six city pairs, leaving only two cities with two U.S. carrier service, and also gave up significant traffic rights for U.S. carriers beyond London and Glasgow. The positive features of the aggreement included opening new gateways from the interior United States and the start of the Laker Skytrain. Two major international decisions followed almost immediately involving CAB disposition of the competitive response to Laker fares and designation of carriers to serve the interior U.S. points.

The competitive response of the transatlantic carriers such as Pan Am and TWA to the Laker fare of $236 round trip was to propose new standby and budget fares at $256 and to lower the price of their advance purchase excursion (Apex) fare tickets from $350 to $290. Charter services ran between $260 and $310. Our decision at the CAB was initially conservative, and I now consider it to have been a mistake. We disapproved the reduction in the Apex fare and raised the proposed levels of the budget and standby fares. We reasoned that it had taken Laker seven years to get the Skytrain authority, and we feared this service needed a protective corridor to be viable financially. Also, we were aware that 82 percent of the supplementals' business was in the U.S.-Europe market and felt that the charter services could not compete at the proposed price levels, at least not without substantial liberalization (which would take months) of the terms under which they were entitled to fly. Furthermore, we realized that if either Laker or the supplemental carriers were driven from the market, we had no authority to prevent the scheduled carriers from rescinding their low fares. If the competitive spurs to low fares were thus removed, we feared that the end of the competitors would mark the end of competition because of the difficulties in certificating new carriers internationally and in negotiating liberal charter agreements with foreign governments. Thus we were in the paradoxical position of voting to hold fares up so that low-fare options for travel to Europe would continue. The problem with our reasoning was that it was based on fears, not on facts. And as experience has proven, the fears turned out to be unfounded for the most part.

Presidential review was extremely useful here. President Carter used his review powers to overturn the CAB and permit the lowest possible fares for the consuming public. He was responsive to board fears that Laker and/or the supplemental carriers might go out of business and directed the State Department to negotiate agreements with foreign governments to give the CAB permission to suspend the fares on six weeks' notice if they were proving extremely destructive. This turned out to be an excellent strategy. It permitted us to observe from experience whether the fares were destructive to Laker and/or the supplementals and to offer the public new low-fare options in the interim.

The second decision of the CAB entailed carrier selection from interior U.S. points to London. Again, the board made what was in my opinion an error of policy, and this time I wrote a nineteen-page dissent. Since there could be little outright competition on routes with only a single U.S. carrier, it seemed to me to be important to encourage competition by having parallel awards, as when one carrier is given Dallas/Forth Worth-London authority, another carrier is granted Atlanta-London authority, and still a third is granted the Miami-London route. However, the board was unwilling to support this policy completely. It permitted National Airlines to stay in the Miami-London route that it had so successfully pioneered, and it awarded Delta Airlines Atlanta authority. However, Texas authority was given to Pan American, in spite of the obvious incentives Pan Am had to operate one stop through New York rather than to exercise the nonstop authority it was being given and in spite of Pan Am's record in Chicago and elsewhere of not implementing authority once it had obtained the exclusive right to it. Again, fortunately as it has turned out, President Carter overturned the board and awarded the Dallas/Fort Worth route to Braniff.

An examination of the operating results since late 1977 reveals that Laker has done very well indeed, achieving profits of several million dollars while running high load factors. The sunbelt carriers (Delta, Braniff, and National), despite start-up costs for two of them and despite the restriction that their planes land at Gatwick where there are virtually no connecting opportunities, also did very well. Their rates of return on total investment were over 20 percent, substantially higher than those of Pan American and TWA. The yields of the sunbelt carriers (where yield is a price surrogate) were under six cents a mile compared with yields of Pan Am and TWA services of about seven cents a mile. Thus, we had a fine example of the sort of gains that can be achieved when there is entry of carriers that are efficient and eager to compete.[8]

The supplemental carriers were only moderately profitable during 1978, and one of them, ONA, went out of business. However, the demise was not a bankruptcy but a selling of planes that resulted in the achievement of a substantial profit for the shareholders. Indeed, for the twelve months ended

September 30, 1978, the corporate rate of return for the large charter carriers was 7.73 as opposed to 6.51 the year before.

Thus, for all four groups—Laker, the supplementals, the traditional scheduled carriers, and the new scheduled carriers—the low-fare policies have proven to be viable. The biggest winner of all has been the traveling public.

The real CAB initiative on low-fare international policies began in the first quarter of 1978, when we began to trade route rights for low-fare articles. I was part of the negotiating team with the Dutch in the spring of 1978 where we obtained for the first time a country-of-origin fare article, under which a foreign country can no longer take unilateral action suspending fares on rates proposed by a U.S. air carrier for flights originating in U.S. territory. This provision has recently been liberalized even further to a mutual-suspension article under which neither country can reject low-fare offerings by carriers without mutual agreement. One or the other of these articles has now been incorporated into bilaterals with Belgium, Germany, Peru, Israel, and Poland.

We are continuing to try to remove international restrictions on aircraft types, schedule approval, and frequency restrictions. At times we have been tough, as we were when Great Britain was reluctant to approve the Braniff low-fare proposal from Dallas-Fort Worth to London, and we started action against a British carrier wanting to serve London from Houston. At other times, we offer greater access to U.S. markets. We are not always successful. Pan Am was unable to operate a Los Angeles to Paris service because of a change of gauge dispute with the French government, but the liberal policies are spreading.

Other actions we are taking are also aimed at removing restrictions. We have disapproved IATA agreements that permit the fixing of commission rates paid by carriers to retail travel agents and cargo agents.[9] Another important step was the new public charter rule, which gives substantial flexibility to tour organizers and supplemental carriers to provide charter service. Also we have tentatively decided to disapprove the IATA rate-setting mechanism, thus ensuring a continuation of the current open rate situation in the transatlantic market. These recent changes, along with our active bilateral negotiation efforts, should provide us with a good opportunity to observe international operations in a much less restrictive environment. The year 1979 will be important not only because of the number of additional carriers in the market and the new charter rules but also because the carriers will have had this year of experience and experimentation with different types of service options as a basis for planning the summer's service.

Finally, we are moving to increase further the benefits to be had from linking domestic and international authority. The addition of Delta, Braniff, and Northwest to the transatlantic was one step. Another step is the exemption authority we granted Pan Am in August 1978 to put new interstate legs on some of its international flights between Houston and Los Angeles, San Francisco, and Miami. We also encouraged the carrier to come forward with a plan for a domestic system linked to its international routes for us to consider. Thus, no matter how the board might ultimately rule on the Pan American–National merger, if Pan Am wants a domestic system, it can probably have one soon. A third is our proposal to end the distinction between domestic and international air freight forwarders.

We are prepared to test in international service many of the multiple permissive entry issues recently discussed in the Oakland and Midway cases. The board pointed out in both proceedings that regulatory approaches that may have seemed correct in an age when all carriers were subsidized and aviation technology was very new hardly look rational now when almost the entire population flies.

We recently opened up the Benelux countries to new scheduled service by a number of carriers.[10] For two of them, World and Capital International, it is their first opportunity to provide scheduled service. Similarly, we applied the multiple permissive entry approach in the Philadelphia–Bermuda market. We have also used our exemption powers to grant immediate route rights to carriers willing to institute low-fare services to France, Switzerland, Israel, Belgium, the Netherlands, Guam, Hong Kong, and Taiwan.

Financial and Market Structure Issues

The investment community can contribute to the stable growth of the air transportation industry during its transition into a competitive environment. The year 1978 was marked by high profitability in the industry. From June 1977 to June 1978, corporate rates of return increased by 5.1 points to 13.1 percent for the trunks and by 4.6 points to 15.9 percent for the locals. The highest rate of return in the industry, some 29.3 percent, was achieved by Texas International, a relatively small, local-service carrier, which has been able to grow rapidly in recent years through a combination of creative low-fare policies and an able management. The five next highest earners were Allegheny at 20.7 percent, Western at 19.1 percent, Southwest at 18.29 percent, Delta at 16.9 percent, and United at 16.6 percent. There are two local service carriers, one intrastate carrier, and three trunks in the six highest profit makers. Moreover, many of the largest trunk carriers—such as American, TWA, Pan American, and Eastern—are not on the list. Thus, at the present time, it is clear that biggest is not synonymous with most profitable. Moreover, biggest has not been synonymous with most profitable in the past. History shows that some of the largest trunks have been the carriers most consistently plagued by mismanagement. I believe that in the future as well, biggest will not necessarily mean most profitable in terms of investment opportunities in aviation.

We should not lose sight of the fact that some of the smaller carriers and new entrants represent important investment opportunities that the financial community might overlook because of preconceived notions that only another big carrier can compete against United or American either for passengers or, more importantly, for the money necessary to purchase new aircraft. A new entrant can make a lot of money for investors if it is successful. But even if it fails, losses could be relatively small.

A new entrant can succeed because, at least during the first few years, operating costs tend to be somewhat lower than for incumbents because aircraft are such a flexible asset. The latter point is often overlooked by investors who are used to viewing capital-intensive industries as having high fixed costs. (It was this misconception about the industry's cost structure that in large part led to the enactment of the Civil Aeronautics Act in 1938.) Thus a new carrier that has authority to operate in a number of markets can test different city pairs. The entrant's ability to pick from a group of markets and enter on relatively short notice makes it extremely difficult for incumbents to pick it off. If the competition is too strong in one market, the new entrant can easily shift to another. The concept of total flexibility was an important element in the board's Midway decision and in our decision to institute a proceeding to grant authority in twenty-four additional markets. I believe that awarding Midway Airlines or Midway (Southwest) authority in a few particular markets—even if we excluded incumbents from those markets for a short time—would have set them up for a much more serious competitive fight than they are likely to face when they have thirty markets to choose from in instituting their service.

The odds that a new entrant with an experienced management team can be successful are good. But even if the airline fails, losses could be mitigated. The only significant capital cost a new airline has is its equipment. Thus Midway Airlines projected in the Midway proceeding that of an initial investment base of $50 million, about $40 million was the value of the aircraft it planned to lease.

There is now—and has been for several years—a very good market for used aircraft. CAB records indicate that worldwide sales of used commercial jets have averaged about 100 aircraft per year for the last eight years. In fiscal 1978, 116 used aircraft were sold. The important fact is that taking depreciation into account, this equipment is sold at a profit, not a loss. In 1978, aircraft sales resulted in a book gain of over $158 million. Of equal interest is the fact that the local service carriers as a group sold 15 DC-9 aircraft over the last fiscal year for almost $10 million more than the original cost and had a book gain of $19 million. Used aircraft sales is now a sellers' market, and, barring a recession, this trend should continue for at least a couple of more years as traffic growth forces carriers not to carry out all of their scheduled fleet retirements. So even in this sellers' market, if a new entrant goes bankrupt after a year and the corporation must sell off its five or six aircraft, the investors probably have not suffered a big loss. Of course, no one can predict accurately what the used-aircraft market will be like in two or three years, but it is possible that the selling price after depreciation could cover a year's operating losses. It seems to me that given this possibility of recoupment, that supporting a knowledgeable new entrant could be a very wise decision.

The same is true for many of the local service carriers. Most of them have fairly well integrated regional route systems that feed into medium and large hubs. They operate efficiently and profitably. The board discussed in the Midway opinion that although North Central ranked as the lowest of all certificated carriers in system characteristics, such as hop, haul, traffic per station, and revenue per departure that contribute to profitable and efficient operations, it ranked first among certificated carriers in departures per employee and second in passengers enplaned per employee.[11] Incidentally North Central's corporate rate of return for the year ending June 1978 was 15.4 percent.

Given the composition of its fleet, North Central or any of the locals could not be expected to attempt to break into long-haul markets immediately. But these carriers are in a good position to make logical extensions of their systems while paring back service in unprofitable markets. Whether the merger with Southern represents such a logical extension will be an issue that will soon come before the CAB. I am certainly not ruling out a priori the possibility that a merger by two local service carriers might have a procompetitive impact on the industry. Although both North Central and Southern currently have typical local service fleets, they might, by purchasing some larger jets, be able to interconnect some of their major hubs, thus creating a corporation that would in effect be a new trunk and one perhaps able to compete effectively with sister trunks. The CAB will certainly examine this possibility in the North Central–Southern merger proceeding.

As they currently exist, these two carriers, as well as the other locals, have the incentive and ability to compete as long as they have access to financing, and this incentive and ability exists whether there are mergers. But the potential for many of these carriers to continue as competitive forces depends in large part upon the willingness of the investment community to recognize that being a relatively small carrier is consistent with profitable operations. By external financing of aircraft acquisition programs for such carriers, the investment community can make a major contribution to the balanced growth of the industry.

Summary

The traditional airline regulatory framework was designed in the 1930s for an infant industry whose revenues came largely from mail pay. In 1937, the Senate chose regulation as the appropriate approach in air transport since it feared "future disorderly development" caused by "destructive competition" and because of "the recognized and accepted principles of regulation of public utilities, particularly as applied to other forms of transportation."[12] The statute was written, however, to encourage competition wherever it was found to be in accordance with the public convenience and necessity. Much has been learned since 1938. Air transport does not have the cost structure characteristics of other public utilities; it is capital intensive, but its capital is mobile and not fixed in place. Competition has not been destructive in aviation. Unsubsidized air taxis can effectively compete, even in markets where local service carriers receive subsidy; intrastate airlines can and have entered successfully in competition with trunk carriers; and numerous markets are certificated for service by many carriers without ill effect. Laker has shown that he can operate a very successful service between New York and London without any system at all. And, finally, we have learned that a carrier does not have to be big or be regulated to be profitable. One of the most financially successful carriers over the past five years has been Southwest Airlines, an intrastate Texas carrier whose estimated rate of return on investment has exceeded 18 percent every year since 1974.

The recent experience under the reform CAB has not damaged the industry—as some predicted it would—but instead has contributed to its financial health and greater efficiency. The period 1977–1978 was one of unsurpassed profitability for the airlines and of substantially lowered prices for consumers. While the recently increased rates of return are in part due to an economic upswing, they are also clearly in part due to the newly discovered elasticity from lower prices and to the ability to design price options to fill empty seats and thus substantially increase load factors. Under such circumstances, it became much easier for Congress to deregulate—rather than merely reform—for the CAB made it clear that both consumers and carriers were better off with less regulation.

Notes

1. See, for example, Levine (1965).

2. The competition in Texas was so fierce that a federal grand jury has indicted Braniff and Texas International, in two counts, with participation in a combination and conspiracy in restraint of trade. U.S. v. Braniff Air-

ways, Inc., 453 F. Supp. 724 (1978). An excellent description of the competitive responses in the California market appears in Levine (1965).

3. Instituted by order 77-1-94, January 14, 1977.

4. Order 73-10-24, October 4, 1973.

5. Order 76-11-131, November 24, 1976.

6. Order 78-4-69, April 14, 1978.

7. Chicago-Midway Low-Fare Route Proceeding, orders 78-7-40, 78-8-203; Oakland Service Case, order 78-4-121.

8. For a discussion of how much room for efficiency gain there is, see Pustay (1978).

9. Order 78-8-87, adopted August 17, 1978.

10. Order 78-9-2.

11. Order 78-7-40, no. 112.

12. U.S. Senate, report no. 686, 75th Cong., 1st sess. 1937, p. 2.

Appendix 2A:

Table 2A-1
Significant Domestic Service on Low-Fare Filings, 1977-1978

Name of Fare	*Proponent Carrier*	*Board Order*	*Effective Date of Fare*	*Discount*	*Markets*	*Restrictions*
Peanuts and related rates	Texas Int'l	77-2-133	2-1-77	50%	Albuquerque-Los Angeles, Denver-Salt Lake City, Houston-New Orleans, Dallas-Austin, Dallas-Midland	Limited to certain flights operated at off-peak (night/very early A.M.) times
	Texas Int'l	78-2-11	3-15-78	30%	Dallas-Little Rock	Limited to one flight in each direction
	Texas Int'l	78-2-11	3-15-78	31%	Baton Rouge-Houston, Hot Springs-Memphis, Houston-Lake Charles, Memphis-Shreveport	Limited number of flights
	Braniff	None	6-15-78	35%	Austin-Kansas City, Brownsville-Kansas City, Corpus Christi-Kansas City, Dallas/Ft. Worth-Kansas City, Denver-Houston, Houston-Las Vegas, Kansas City-New Orleans, San Antonio, Shreveport	Applies on flights designated as shoulder coach
	Allegheny	None	7-1-78	30%	All markets	Applicable 9:30 A.M.-2 P.M. and 8:30 P.M.-7 A.M. and capacity controlled
SuperSaver and related fares	American, United TWA	77-3-80	4-25-77 3-23-78	45% Tues, Wed, & Thur, 40% Mon. & Fri 35% Sat. & Sun.	New York-LA/SFO[a]	30-day advance reservation & purchase, 7-day minimum stay, 45-day maximum, limited to 35% of aircraft capacity
Super Coach	American	None	9-1-77	30%	Buffalo-LA, Indianapolis-LA	Capacity controlled
	Northwest			30%	LA-Madison, Milwaukee, Portland-Seattle, Seattle-Spokane	Capacity controlled
	CO, AA, UA	None	9-1-77	37%	Chicago-LA	Limit on number of seats available at this fare
	TWA	77-7-29	9-8-77	37%	Chicago-LA, Denver-NY, Baltimore-Chicago	Available on round trips, has tighter seating.
	United	None	10-7-77	37%	Chicago-San Diego, Milwaukee-Los Angeles	Limit on number of seats available at this fare

Table 2-1 (cont'd)

Name of Fare	*Proponent Carrier*	*Board Order*	*Effective Date of Fare*	*Discount*	*Markets*	*Restrictions*
Super Coach Cont'd.	United	78-1-7	1-5-78	30%	Chicago-LA, Pittsburgh, San Diego, Denver-NY/Newark, Des Moines-Omaha, Kansas City-LA, LA-Milwaukee, Pittsburg, NY/Newark-Pittsburgh, Portland-Reno, Seattle, Reno-Seattle	Capacity control
	TWA	77-12-89	1-5-78	36%, 29% Fri.-Sun, 42% Mon.-Thur.	Baltimore-Chicago, New York-Denver	Limited number of flights with aircraft having high density seating
	United	78-7-21	7-28-78	30% weekend, 10% midweek	Chicago-Pittsburgh, NY-Pittsburgh, Des Moines-Omaha, Eugene-Portland, Portland-Reno, Reno-Seattle	Capacity control
Night Super	Eastern	78-4-71	5-15-78	40% Fri.-Sun., 50% Mon-Thur.	All EA domestic markets	Night coach flights only, 30-day advance purchase, 7-day minimum stay
Unlimited mileage	Eastern	77-8-110	9-11-77	$299 per adult, $199 per child for unlimited mileage trips	Whole EA system	2 people must travel together and stop-over at at least 3 cities, must be gone at least 7 days but no longer than 21 days
SimpleSaver & related fares	Allegheny	77-8-108	8-1-77	30%	Boston-Chicago/St. Louis, Chicago-Detroit/Albany/NY/Providence/Hartford, NY-Detroit, NY-Louisville	Multistop flights, capacity controlled
	Allegheny	77-11-92	11-20-77	25%	Boston-Detroit/Minneapolis, Chicago-Philadelphia, NY-Nashville/St. Louis/Toledo	Multistop flights, capacity controlled
	Ozark	78-1-44	1-15-78	30%	14 Ozark markets	Multistop flights
	Southern		3-11-78	30%	Atlanta-Detroit, Tallahassee, Chicago Fort-Lauderdale, Jacksonville, N. Orleans, Orlando, Ft. Lauderdale- N. Orleans, St. Louis, Orlando-St. Louis.	Carrier-determined capacity range of 20 passengers
	Delta		3-13-78	30%	Atlanta-Detroit, Chicago-Ft. Lauderdale, Jacksonville, New Orleans, Orlando, Columbus, Washington, Detroit, Jacksonville, Nashville-Orlando, Ft. Lauderdale-N. Orleans, St. Louis	Multistop flights, capacity controlled

	Eastern[b]		4-78-78	30%	Atlanta-Detroit, Charlotte-Washington, Chicago, Ft. Lauderdale, Jacksonville, Orlando and 10 other Eastern markets.	Multistop flights, capacity controlled
	Piedmont	77-12-118	1-4-78	30%	NY-Atlanta/Charlotte/Nashville/Memphis/Greensboro/Louisville/Washington-Memphis	Multistop flights, 35% capacity limited
	American	78-6-99	7-1-78	50%	18 markets (tag end or entry)	Capacity controlled
	Texas Int'l	78-2-111	3-15-78	30%	LA-Austin/Houston/Little Rock/Memphis/San Antonio/Shreveport, Houston-Little Rock/Memphis, Memphis-Dallas, Denver-N. Orleans	Multistop flights
Super No-Frills[b]	Eastern	77-11-124	12-1-77	50% Mon.-Wed., 31% Thur., Fri., Sat.	New York-Memphis/Ft. Lauderdale	Limited number of seats at fare
	National	None	6-15-78	30% Fri.-Sun. (day), 40% Mon-Thur. (day), 50% Mon.-Thur.(night) 40% Fri.-Sun (night) 40% Fri.-Sun. (day), 50% Mon-Thur. (day)	All markets except major 22 All markets except major 22 All markets except major 22 All markets except major 22 All markets except major 22 All markets except major 22	Capacity controlled Capacity controlled Capacity controlled Capacity controlled Capacity controlled Capacity controlled
Group-50	United	77-12-260	1-1-78	25-38%	U.S. Mainland-Hawaii	Groups of 50 or more, 6-day minimum stay, 30-day advance reservations
Home Free	Braniff	78-1-48 78-1-133	2-1-78	50%	Chicago-Kansas City, Dallas-Amarillo/Brownsville/Chicago, Denver/Miami/Minneapolis/New Orleans, Denver-Atlanta/Miami	6-night minimum stay, 14-day advance purchase, 20% capacity limited, 50% cancellation penalty
First Class Freedom Fares	Braniff	78-1-115	2-17-78	15% summer, 20% rest of year	All Braniff continental U.S. markets	7-day advance purchase, return no earlier than Sunday following day of departure, 50% capacity controlled
Reduced first class fares	Continental[c]	78-4-149	5-15-78	First class fares reduced to 140% of coach	Continental U.S.	None
Reduced first class and coach fares	Delta	78-5-152	6-15-78			None

Table 2-1 (cont'd)

Name of Fare	*Proponent Carrier*	*Board Order*	*Effective Date of Fare*	*Discount*	*Markets*	*Restrictions*
New low fares	TWA	78-2-59	3-1-78	40%	Atlanta-St. Louis/Kansas City	No meals, limited number of flights
	Northwest	78-5-115	6-8-78	14-48%	Chicago-Minneapolis/St. Paul, Detroit, Cleveland.	None except applies only to or from Chicago's Midway Airport
No Strings	Western	78-3-106	3-23-78	35%	Miami-Los Angeles	None
	TWA	78-6-98	7-1-78	31-51%	7 markets (tag end or entry)	None
Super Jackpot	TWA	78-3-70	4-1-78	43% Tue.,Wed., & Sat., 37% Mon. & Fri., 20% Thur. & Sun.	To Las Vegas from Chicago, Detroit, Pittsburgh, Philadelphia, NY, and Boston.	14-day advance purchase, 2-night minimum stay, $25 tour add-on
Money Saver	Frontier	None	4-15-78	30-40%	Numerous	Capacity controlled and some hour-of-day or day-of-week blackouts
Fair Fare	Pan Am	78-3-147	4-17-78	25%	Boston-Detroit, LA-SFO, NY-Washington, Miami-Tampa/Portland-Seattle	None
Apex Fare	Pan Am	78-3-147	4-17-78	42% Mon.-Thur., 35% Fri.-Sun.	Same as Fair Fare	30-day advance purchase, 7-day minimum stay
Fill-up Fare	Pan Am	78-3-147	4-17-78	50% all times	Same as Fair Fare	Standby, limited to 50 seats per flight
Commuter	Airwest	78-146	4-17-78	30%, 30-50%	25 interstate markets served by Airwest intra-Calif. markets	Limited number of flights
	United	None	5-1-78	30%	LA-Reno, Oakland-Reno, SFO-Reno, San Diego-Reno.	None
Systemwide restructuring	Airwest	78-3-146	4-19-78	30%	Short-haul markets	Selected flights
Senior Saver	TWA	78-4-102	5-15-78	33⅓%	TWA domestic system	65 or older, no reservations taken until 24 hours before flight time
Chickenfeed	Continental	78-4-149	5-15-78	30% Fri.-Sun, 40% Mon.-Thur.	Continental U.S.[d]	Capacity limited to no more than 40% and no less then 15%

Small Potatoes	Braniff	None	6-15-78	25-50%	Amarillo-Dallas/Ft. Worth, Austin-Dallas/Ft. Worth, Corpus Christi-Dallas/Ft. Worth, Dallas/Ft. Worth-Houston, Las Vegas, Lubbock, Reno, Houston-Las Vegas, Lubbock, Reno, Las Vegas-Reno, NY/Newark-Washington.	Capacity contolled
American Standby	American	STP 4827	6-16-78	40% (free if not accomodated on a flight within 24 hours)	All markets	7-day advance purchase, applicable only through 9-5-78
Tag end	Allegheny	None	7-22-78	50%	Boston-Hartford, Buffalo-Detroit, Cincinnati-Hartford, Cleveland-Rochester, Columbus-Dayton, Hartford, Indianapolis, Detroit-Rochester, Syracuse, Hartford-Indianapolis, Louisville, NY/Newark, St. Louis, Indianapolis-St. Louis, NY/Newark-Pittsburgh	Capacity limitation carrier determined
	Eastern	78-9-113	10-16-78	50%	14 markets, incl. & intra-Florida	Capacity controlled
Low-fare between Dal/Ft. Worth-Las Vegas	Braniff	Info Memo F0066	7-30-78	35%	Dallas/Ft. Worth-Las Vegas	Off-peak flights, capacity controlled
Proposition 13 Fare	Western	None	9-23-78	50%	Los Angeles-San Francisco	Round trip only, capacity controlled
Intra-California fare modifications	Western	Info Memo F0072	9-23-78	Revision of Fares	LA-Ontario, Palm Springs, Sacramento, San Diego, San Francisco, Ontario-Palm Springs, Sacramento, San Diego, San Francisco, Sacramento, Sacramento-San Diego, San Francisco, San Diego-San Francisco	None
Special round trip	Western	None	9-23-78	50%	Los Angeles-San Diego	Round trip only, capacity controlled
Short-haul segment	Delta	None	10-29-78	50%	Baltimore-Philadelphia, Boston-Hartford, Ft. Lauderdale-Orlando, Tampa, Miami-Orlando, Tampa, NY/Newark-Philadelphia	Applies for transportation in day coach or night coach compartment of combination compartment aircraft, Capacity limitation carrier determined

Table 2–1 (cont'd)

Name of Fare	*Proponent Carrier*	*Board Order*	*Effective Date of Fare*	*Discount*	*Markets*	*Restrictions*
Short-haul-segment (cont'd)	Easter	78-9-133	10-16-78	50%	Baltimore-Philadelphy, Boston-Hartford, Corpus Christi-Houston, Daytona Beach-Miami, Ft. Lauderdale-W. Palm Beach, Gainesville-Miami, Hartford-NY/Newark, Houston-San Antonio, Miami-Orlando, Sarasota, Tampa, NY/Newark-Philadelphia	Same as Delta's

[a] Boston/Philadelphia-Los Angeles/San Francisco added in May; fifteen other transcontinental markets added in September. Expanded systemwide in March 1978 by all U.S. trunk and local service carriers.

[b] These fares were withdrawn in September 1978 (no order).

[c] First-class fares were 150–163% of coach. In May and June 1978, all trunk carriers further reduced first-class fares to 130% of coach (order 78-5-41), and in November 1978 the fares were reduced to the present level of 120% of coach (no order).

[d] Continental cancelled the fares in most markets in August 1978.

Note: No very short-term, one-shot, introductory type fares have been included.

3 Efficiency in Regulated and Unregulated Firms: An Iconoclastic View of the Averch–Johnson Thesis

Enrique R. Arzac and
Franklin R. Edwards

During the past two decades, economists have published numerous articles condemning regulation. Beginning perhaps with the controversial study of electric utility regulation by Stigler and Friedland (1962), which concluded that rate regulation by states has had no effect on the level of electricity prices, economists have subjected regulation to close scrutiny and have concluded that many regulations are either ineffective in achieving their stated social objectives or have such widespread and unanticipated perverse effects as to make them of questionable social value.

An important dimension of the skepticism about regulation is the belief that regulated firms are not efficient. There is increasing concern that regulation will make firms less efficient internally, even though it may enhance allocative efficiency. Internal inefficiency is clearly important. Indeed it may be more important than monopoly pricing or allocative inefficiency. For example, assuming a relatively inelastic demand, the welfare loss that would be associated with an increase of only 1 percent in a firm's costs is equivalent to the welfare loss that would result from a 20 percent increase in the price of the good produced by the firm (Williamson, 1968, pp. 22-23). Thus, if internal inefficiency is generated by regulation, this must be viewed as a serious adverse effect of regulation.

The view that regulation causes internal inefficiency has gained credence by the theoretical work of Averch and Johnson (1962), which shows that rate-of-return regulation induces firms to adopt suboptimal factor input combinations (specifically, to overcapitalize). The Averch–Johnson (A–J) view is especially damning because it concludes that even managers with the best of intentions—those who are profit maximizers—will operate inefficiently under regulation. The subsequent stream of empirical work

We wish to thank Michael Crew, Linda Edwards, and Harvey Leibenstein for their comments on an earlier draft of this chapter.

generated by this thesis is now well known to economists. However, a little-recognized effect of this literature has been to divert attention away from other, and perhaps more important, aspects of internal efficiency. The A–J studies focus on what may be only the tip of the efficiency iceberg and ignore the dark mass just beneath the surface. Other reasons for internal inefficiency exist that are common to both unregulated and regulated firms and about which we know little.

The purpose of this chapter is to counterbalance the previous literature by providing a more general perspective on the issue of internal inefficiency in regulated and unregulated firms. To some degree, the chapter can be viewed as an antidote to the implications of the A–J theory. An important aspect of our approach is that we explicitly analyze the implications that spring from recognizing that neither unregulated nor regulated firms may be profit-maximizing enterprises. More specifically, if managers of regulated and unregulated firms can be characterized as having managerial discretion, we show that rate-of-return regulation may improve rather than worsen internal efficiency. In addition, we argue that the empirical work associated with the A–J thesis, as well as other empirical studies, provide considerable support for the notion that firms are not in fact profit-maximizing entities. Our chief conclusion, therefore, is that neither theory nor fact provides strong support for the claim that regulated firms are less efficient than unregulated, monopolistic firms.

Sources of Internal Inefficiency in the Unregulated Firm

In recent years, three distinct streams of economic research have analyzed internal efficiency in unregulated firms. The first of these is concerned with determining the market environment (or structure) most conducive to technological progress. Technological innovation has clearly been of great importance in increasing the amount that can be produced by a given set of resources. Unfortunately, neither the theoretical nor the empirical literature dealing with this issue has reached a clear consensus. At present, the evidence shows no clear relationship between technological progressiveness and any particular type of market structure (Kamien and Schwartz, 1975).

The second stream of literature has come to be known as the X-efficiency theory of the firm and is largely associated with the work of Leibenstein. This theory is a major departure from the conventional microtheory of the firm. It views the basic microunit as being the individual rather than the firm, and it argues that firms do not minimize costs (or maximize profits, or anything else). It is, therefore, a nonmaximization theory of the firm, unlike neoclassical theories of the firm. The postulation is that different degrees of X-inefficiency emerge under different circumstances, where, according to Leibenstein (1975, p. 582), the degree of X-inefficiency is measured by the difference between maximal effectiveness of utilization and actual utilization. An important conclusion of Leibenstein's theory (1975, p. 604) is that a greater degree of X-inefficiency will arise in monopolistic industries than in competitive industries because monopolies can pass higher costs on to consumers.

The third strand of literature that may be construed as dealing with internal efficiency is the managerial discretion view of the firm. This is perhaps the oldest and the most developed of the three streams and stems from the concern that economists have had about the divorce of management from ownership common to the large modern corporation. In this view, managers have considerable discretion to pursue goals other than (or in addition to) profits: security, pleasant surroundings, congenial colleagues, high salaries, empire building, and so forth. Thus, while managers are still maximizers, they have maximands other than profits.

Underlying the various theories of managerial discretion is the view that managers gain freedom because of the monitoring costs that arise from the organizational structure of the modern corporation. In particular, with a large and diffuse ownership structure, stockholders must enter into principal-agent contracts with managers, which are usually complex, difficult to structure, and require extensive policing. Evaluating and monitoring managerial behavior is difficult and costly. Consequently it is usually not optimal for stockholders to eliminate all managerial perquisites. Hence, some managerial discretion is a concomitant of the modern corporation.

One might ask why the modern corporation's ownership structure arose, if its effect is to divest owners of some of their profits. The answer, obviously, is that there are benefits as well. The multifaceted demands on the modern corporation may require a management team consisting of many diversified professional skills. There may also be capital-raising advantages. (Jensen and Meckling, 1976). On balance, it is presumably advantageous to adopt the modern corporate organization structure over the single proprietorship so that the loss that the modern owners (stockholders) suffer because of managerial discretion may be more than offset by what they gain from such an ownership structure.[1]

Given this perspective, what constitutes internal inefficiency in the context of a managerial discretion firm? Managerial discretion may result in two kinds of inefficiency: the use of incorrect factor proportions and the "consumption" by managers of suboptimal combinations of salary and perquisites. The first of these is characterized by the firm that is operating at the wrong place on its production efficiency frontier and will occur if managers derive utility from the use of some productive input over and above that which the input contributors to the firm's output and/or profits. For example, if managers have a preference for a large supporting staff, they will employ excessive labor.[2] Both stockholders and managers may be happy with an arrangement that produces social inefficiencies. The traditional monopoly firm with its high profits is an obvious example.

The second type of inefficiency concerns managerial pecuniary and nonpecuniary compensation. A frequent assertion is that managerial salaries are excessive and thus constitute a source of inefficiency because the higher salaries mean higher costs to the firm. But is there an inefficiency simply because the firm's costs have increased? Has the firm consumed any resources unnecessarily? No. Excessive salaries are not a form of inefficiency but rather a transfer of wealth from stockholders to managers. Although we may care about such a transfer (as may stockholders and regulators), it is neither a private nor a social inefficiency.

Suppose, however, that stockholders are quick to view high managerial salaries as excessive, just as society has historically viewed high interest rates as usurious. In such a case managers may retreat to a second-best alternative: they may take less salary but consume nonpecuniary benefits on the job by furnishing their offices lavishly, hiring a large supporting staff to ease their work load, engaging in extensive travel and entertainment, and so forth. In this case, there may be a social inefficiency: there may be a difference between the utility managers derive from these perquisites and the utility they could attain if they were free to spend the same amount on items (or resources) they might prefer to consume. In other words, an inefficiency occurs if there is a difference between the dollar value of the total compensation paid by the firm to the managers and what it would cost managers to purchase an equivalent amount of utility if they were free to consume any basket of goods that they desired. This is a form of consumption inefficiency and should be distinguished from the inefficiency that arises because of the use of incorrect factor combinations.

Consumption inefficiency need not be a necessary concomitant of managerial discretion. If the perquisites managers enjoy are part of a superior joint consumption good for them, there need be no inefficiency at all. Managers may conceivably derive more utility from consuming an on-the-job bundle of goods than from consuming any other bundle of goods that they could buy with an equivalent amount of dollars. A manager who works long hours may find it more pleasurable to have a Picasso in the office than one at home. Thus, managerial perquisites have a wealth distribution dimension, as well as an efficiency dimension.[3]

It is also commonly believed that the inefficiencies associated with managerial discretion increase with the firm's degree of monopoly power (just as in the case of X-inefficiency). In his study of managerial discretion, for example, Williamson (1963, p. 1040–1044) says that discretionary expenditures should be positively correlated with concentration ratios and entry barriers.

In summary, internal inefficiency may exist in unregulated firms because of the failure to optimize the rate and direction of technological change, because of X-inefficiency, and because of the existence of managerial discretion. Further, both X-inefficiency and the inefficiency associated with managerial discretion are thought to increase as the firm's monopoly power increases. Unregulated firms, therefore, may not in reality be the profit-maximizing, cost-minimizing ideal firms that have become the standard against which the efficiency of regulated firms is judged.

II. Efficiency in The Regulated Firm

Aside from the Averch–Johnson type of inefficiency, economic theory tells very little about how regulation affects a firm's internal efficiency. Research on the impact of regulation on the rate and direction of technical change is in its infancy, and results to date are inconclusive. In a recent theoretical article, Magat (1976) examines the effect of three forms of regulation (rate of return, ceiling price, and mark-up) upon the rate and direction of technical advance in the profit-maximizing firm. He shows that both ceiling price and mark-up regulation lead to a faster rate of technical progress than would occur in the absence of regulation, while rate-of-return regulation may in some cases stimulate and in other cases retard the rate of technical advance. In addition, Magat concludes that neither ceiling-price regulation nor mark-up regulation affects the direction of technical advance; and while rate-of-return regulation does alter the direction of technical change, it does not necessarily distort input usage.[4] Thus, while the implications of economic theory are mixed, if they suggest anything it is that regulation is unlikely to have an adverse effect on the rate and direction of technical change.[5]

The effect of regulation on internal efficiency is also ambiguous in the context of Leibenstein's X-inefficiency theory of the firm. Leibenstein (1975, p. 604) argues that various degrees of X-inefficiency can emerge as a result of differentials in pressure from the environment on managers and employees or because of impediments related to the transmission of motivation or pressure within the firm. With respect to the latter, we see little difference between regulated and unregulated firms. The internal organizational structures of these firms do not differ in any clear and systematic way; and, with respect to pressure from the environment, it is not clear which exerts more pressure on monopoly firms—regulators or the threat of a future potential competitor. Leibenstein, nevertheless, suggests that the degree of X-inefficiency may be greater in regulated industries since these firms may be sheltered by such devices as price regulation (which guarantees a fair return) and the use of cost-plus contracts. Our interpretation of this argument is that it is simply a matter of where the firm's insulation is greatest. We can see an argument either way. Whether the degree of X-inefficiency is greater in regulated than unregulated monopolies is an empirical issue.

The impact of managerial discretion on internal efficiency in regulated versus unregulated firms has received little attention. In an early article, however, Williamson (1963, pp. 1053–1054) suggested that in regulated firms subject to a profit constraint, managers will engage in more utility-enhancing expenditures. He argues that such expenditures will be increased once the regulatory constraint on profits is encountered. Even so, it is not clear that the result will be an increase in internal inefficiency. Discretionary expenditures may largely constitute a wealth transfer from stockholders to managers, in which case there need be no resource misallocation or social waste. Williamson also does not explore other possible reactions of the firm to regulation, which change the way the firm utilizes its resources. These may reinforce or mitigate the inefficiencies associated with managerial discretion. Thus, the interrelationships among regulation, managerial discretion, and internal efficiency remain unclear.

Some research along these lines has already been done by Bailey and Malone (1970). They explore the effects of profit regulation on firms that maximize sales or output and find that its effect depends importantly on what assumption is made about the firm's objective function. For example, under a rate-of-return constraint, profit-maximizing firms will tend to overcapitalize, and sales or output-maximizing firms will tend to undercapitalize.

Crew and Kleindorfer (1970a) also analyzed the effect of rate-of-return regulation on the expense-preference firm and concluded that A–J overcapitalization effects will persist for these firms as well. However, they do not focus directly on internal inefficiency and, consequently, do not distinguish between wealth-transfering and wasteful discretionary expenditures. In addition, their results depend crucially upon the kind of expense-preference firm they presume to exist.

To summarize, except for the Averch–Johnson thesis, economic theory is quite vague about whether regulated firms are more or less inefficient than unregulated monopolies. Thus, the poor rating that economic theory gives to regulated firms in terms of their efficiency stems primarily from the Averch–Johnson literature.

III. The Expense-Preference Firm, Regulation, and Efficiency

The managerial-discretion firm—one with expense preference—may be a more realistic characterization of large corporations than is the profit-maximizing paradigm, and the impact of rate-of-return regulation on it has received little attention. A fundamental conclusion of our analysis is that rate-of-return regulation may make the managerial-discretion firm more rather than less internally efficient.

To demonstrate why this may be true, we utilize a model of the expense-preference firm that encompasses what we believe to be the two prevailing views of expense-preference behavior. The first view hypothesizes managers as first making all of the usual choices necessary to maximize profits and then simply appropriating part of the firm's profits in the form of utility-enhancing perquisites. (Alchian and Kessel 1962). In this view the firm's output, prices, and input proportions are all independent of the level of managerial perquisites. The second view envisions managers as deriving utility from the excessive use of productive inputs (such as staff). Here the firm hires more labor than necessary and expands output beyond the profit-maximizing point (Rees 1974).

Both of these views are incorporated in the following managerial utility function:

$$u = u(\pi,\ell,m) \tag{3.1}$$

where π is total profits, ℓ is labor expense, and m is (nonproductive) managerial perquisites.[6] In addition, consistent with the Averch-Johnson framework, the firm is assumed to produce only one output (q) with two inputs, capital (K) and labor (L):

$$q = f(K,L), f_K = \frac{dq}{dK} > 0, \quad f_L = \frac{dq}{dL} > 0, \quad f(0,L) = f(K,0) = 0. \tag{3.2}$$

Profits are

$$\pi = pq - rK - wL - m \tag{3.3}$$

where $p = p(q)$ and $dp/dq < 0$, r and w are the competitively determined factor prices, and $\ell = wL$.

We also assume that the firm is subject to the following (A-J type of) rate-of-return profit constraint:

$$\frac{\pi + rK}{K} \leq s \qquad \text{or } \pi \leq (s - r)K, \tag{3.4}$$

where s is the allowed rate of return and $s > r$.

Efficiency and Input Choice

The first-order conditions for a maximum of 3.1, subject to equations 3.2-3.4, are

$$K\colon (u_\pi - \lambda)(MRf_K - r) + \lambda(s - r) = 0, \qquad K > 0, \tag{3.5}$$

$$L\colon (u_\pi - \lambda)(MRf_L - w) + u_\ell w = 0, \qquad L > 0, \tag{3.6}$$

$$m\colon -(u_\pi - \lambda) + u_m \leq 0, \quad m(-u_\pi + \lambda + u_m) = 0, \quad m \geq 0, \text{ and} \tag{3.7}$$

$$\lambda\colon -\pi + (s - r)K \geq 0, \quad \lambda[\pi - (s - r)K] = 0, \quad \lambda \geq 0, \tag{3.8}$$

where $u_\pi = \partial u/\partial_\pi$, $u_\ell = \partial u/\partial \ell$, $u_m = \partial u/\partial m$, $MR = p + qdp/dq$, and λ is the Lagrange multiplier associated with the regulatory constraint. These conditions are applicable to profit-maximizing as well as expense-preference firms and to unregulated as well as regulated firms. If the firm is unregulated, $\lambda = 0$ in equations 3.5–3.7, and 3.8 is ignored. If the firm is a traditional profit-maximizing entity, $u_\ell = 0$ and $u_m = 0$ in equations 3.6 and 3.7. In addition equations 3.5 and 3.6 yield the marginal rate of substitution of capital for labor for the general case:[7]

$$\frac{f_K}{f_L} = \Omega_{KL} \frac{r}{w}, \tag{3.9}$$

where

$$\Omega_{KL} = \frac{u_\pi - \lambda s/r}{u_\pi - \lambda - u_\ell}. \tag{3.10}$$

Thus,

$$\Omega_{KL} \gtreqless 1 \text{ as } u_\ell \gtreqless \lambda(s/r - 1) \tag{3.11}$$

It follows from 3.9 and 3.10 that, if $u_\ell = 0$ and regulation is effective, $\Omega_{KL} < 1$.[8] This occurs even if $u_m > 0$. Under diminishing marginal rate of substitution, $\Omega_{KL} < 1$ implies that the firm is overcapitalized. This is the standard A–J effect. Alternatively, if $u_\ell > 0$, and either there is no regulation ($\lambda = 0$) or regulation is ineffective, $\Omega_{KL} > 1$ and the firm uses too little capital. This is the standard expense-preference case. Finally, if $u_\ell > 0$ and regulation is effective, the tendency of the unregulated expense-preference firm to use too little capital must be balanced against the tendency for rate-of-return regulation to cause firms to use too much capital. Indeed, these two forces may totally offset one another, so that there is no internal inefficiency at all. In particular, fixing the allowed rate of return such that $u_\ell = \lambda(s/r - 1)$ would entirely eliminate internal inefficiency ($\Omega_{KL} = 1$ in 3.9).[9] (It should be recognized that all of these results are independent of managerial perquisites, or whether $u_m \geq 0$.) Thus, regulation may actually make firms more efficient internally.

Although the elimination or reduction of internal inefficiency is clearly a benefit, it does not necessarily follow that regulation will on net be socially beneficial. To make this judgment, many other factors must be considered. For example, if rate-of-return regulation were to decrease the output of the unregulated, monopolistic, expense-preference firm, there could conceivably be a net welfare loss. While the response of the output to regulation has been discussed extensively in the literature dealing with regulation profit-maximizing entities, with the conclusion that rate-of-return regulation should increase (not decrease) firm output (Bailey, 1973, p. 92), the issue is less clear in the case of the general expense-preference firm ($u_\ell > 0$ and $u_m > 0$). In the latter case, the response of firm output to regulation depends on the relative values of the second derivatives of the managerial utility function, which are unobservable. However, for the two cases where either $u_\ell = 0$ or $u_m = 0$, it can be shown that (under diminishing returns and input complementarity in the production of a variable output) some amount of regulation also should increase output in the expense-preference firm.[10] It is important to recognize, nevertheless, that since our focus here is internal inefficiency, we do not attempt to deal with other important dimensions of regulation.

In sum, if firms are not profit-maximizing entities but are better characterized by an expense-preference model of the firm, rate-of-return regulation may reduce or even eliminate internal inefficiency.[11]

The Effect of Regulation on Perquisites

It is commonly assumed that rate-of-return regulation has the effect of increasing managerial perquisites. Although this phenomenon may be more of an income distribution than an efficiency issue, it nevertheless seems worthwhile to point out that for the general case of the expense-preference firm (where $u_\ell > 0$ and $u_m > 0$), even this effect is ambigous. Regulation may conceivably increase, decrease, or leave unaffected the level of managerial perquisites, depending upon the specific characteristics of the managerial utility function and on the firm's market circumstances.[12] However, for the special case where $u_m > 0$ but $u_\ell \equiv 0$, perquisites will definitely increase as the rate-of-return constraint is tightened.[13] Thus, it is not obvious that the imposition of rate-of-return regulation will increase managerial nonpecuniary compensation (or perquisites). It depends upon exactly what type of expense-preference firm is under discussion. In any case, even if perquisites were to rise with regulation, the appropriate policy response is not entirely clear. Distinguishing managerial perquisites induced by rate-of-return regulation from those induced by other distorting laws and regulations, such as the imposition of a personal income tax on pecuniary but not on nonpecuniary income, would obviously be quite difficult.[14]

IV. Evidence of Managerial Discretion

The power of the A–J criticism of regulation rests squarely on the assumption that firms behave as classical maximizers. An important empirical issue, therefore, is whether firms actually behave in this manner. Evidence suggests that neither unregulated nor regulated monopolistic firms may in fact be profit maximizers. This evidence comes from three sources: a reexamination and reinterpretation of the empirical work on the Averch-Johnson hypothesis; analysis of relative firm performance when firms are managerial controlled as opposed to owner controlled; and direct tests of firms' objective functions.

A close look at empirical studies that seek to test for the presence of the A–J effect reveals that their results do not rule out the possibility that firms are not profit maximizers. The conclusions of these studies largely rest on the finding that regulated firms have excessive capital-to-fuel ratios. This is not, however, inconsistent with expense-preference behavior. For example, if a third productive input, fuel, is introduced into our model of expense-preference firm, it is easy to show that this firm will have an excessive capital-to-fuel ratio as well under rate-of-return regulation. However, the expense-preference firm will also have an excessive labor-to-fuel ratio, and its capital-to-labor ratio may be either too high or too low. In principle, therefore, a complete test of factor usage in regulated firms could distinguish whether such firms were profit maximizers. For instance, if the firm were to employ an excessive labor-to-fuel ratio or an excessive labor-to-capital ratio, it clearly would not be a profit maximizing A–J type of firm.[15] To date none of the A–J studies have estimated a complete enough system of factor demand functions to enable us to distinguish the A–J hypothesis from the managerial discretion hypothesis. It is also noteworthy that the findings of these studies with respect to the capital-to-labor ratio are particularly weak (most do not investigate the labor-to-fuel ratio).[16] Finally, a study by Vinod (1972), who estimates a production function for the entire Bell System, suggests that Bell is undercapitalized with respect to labor, a result consistent only with the expense-preference hypothesis.

More direct evidence of managerial discretion perhaps is the extensive empirical literature investigating the performance of owner-controlled versus management-controlled firms. These studies examine the relationship between ownership structure and various aspects of firm performance, such as the firm's profit rate on its equity (book value) or its assets and its stock return.[17] While the findings of these studies are mixed, on balance they suggest that the performance of owner-controlled firms is superior, which implies the existence of managerial discretion in management controlled firms.[18]

It may be perilous to infer too much from these studies, however. They are clearly subject to alternative interpretation. In particular, it is not obvious why we should observe a lower (or higher) profitability in management-controlled firms. Presumably firms evolved from owner controlled to management controlled because there were advantages in doing so. Further, both types of firms exist side by side, competing directly with one another. If one form of ownership structure were clearly superior to another, we would expect to see a movement toward the dominant form. If anything, the trend has been toward management-controlled firms.[19] Thus, while the results of performance studies of owner- versus management-controlled firms may suggest the presence of managerial discretion in unregulated monopolistic firms, they are, like most empirical studies, hardly conclusive.

A preferable approach to investigating managerial discretion is to formulate alternative models of discretionary behavior and compare them directly to the profit-maximizing model of the firm. Specifically, it may be possible to compare the responses of firms to a given regulatory change (such as a change in the allowed rate of return or a tax change) to see which model better predicts behavior. A promising source of data for this purpose may be differences in state regulation.

A recent study that utilizes this approach is Edwards (1977). Using cross-section data to analyze the demand of commercial banks for labor, he concludes that the behavior of banks is better explained by an expense-preference model of the firm than by a profit-maximizing model. More specifically, he finds that banks with monopoly power employ relatively more labor than do banks operating in competitive markets, a result that is inconsistent with a profit-maximizing model of the firm and consistent with an expense-preference model.

In sum, there is certainly some evidence to support the notion that neither regulated nor unregulated (monopolistic) firms behave as profit maximizers. Consequently the Averch-Johnson paradigm may not be the best framework within which to appraise the internal efficiency of regulated versus unregulated firms. A fruitful area for future research, therefore, may be to investigate alternative objective functions for firms and to explore their implications for regulatory policy.

Notes

1. Once this is recognized, it also reveals why the takeover bid does not constitute a market discipline capable of eliminating all managerial discretion. Such a takeover may simply replace one kind of managerial discretion with another.

2. See also Rees (1974), who examines the unregulated expense-preference firm.

3. Even viewed as simply a wealth transfer, of course, we may still have

a keen interest in managerial perquisites. One reason often cited for breaking up or regulating monopolies is that they earn "excessive" profits and that these profits should be distributed to consumers. From a regulatory perspective, one may feel the same way about managerial perquisites. Regulation may be able to reduce the transaction costs of monitoring managers and thereby redress the distributive consequences of the modern corporate structure.

4. But see also Smith (1974 and Okuguchi (1975).

5. These results hold only for the profit-maximizing firm. It remains to be explored whether they hold for a firm where managerial discretion exists.

6. Preference for labor expense could be limited in this model to only certain types of labor (such as staff), but no additional insights would be derived from such a procedure. Formally, a model incorporating preferences for some but not all types of productive labor is equivalent to the three-input model we employ.

7. Note that Ω_{KL} is well defined and positive. In fact, equation 3.7 implies that $u_\pi > \lambda$. In turn, equation 3.5 implies $u_\pi - \lambda s/r = (u_\pi - \lambda) MRf_K/r > 0$ under the assumption that $MR \neq 0$ ($MR = 0$ cannot be ruled out in the present model). Finally, $u_\pi > \lambda$ and equation 3.7 imply $u_\pi - \lambda - u_\ell > 0$.

8. Regulation is effective if $s < s^*$, where s^* is the rate of return that would be attained by the unregulated, utility-maximizing, monopoly firm.

9. Such a policy may not be feasible if $u_\ell > u_\pi$, since $u_\ell > \lambda(s/r - 1)$ for all $s < 2r$.

10. For example, let $u = u(\pi,\ell)$, $f_{KK} < 0$, $f_{LL} < 0$, and $f_{KL} > 0$. Applying standard comparative statistics techniques to the maximum conditions, one obtains:

$$\frac{dq}{ds} = \frac{Ku_\pi MR}{|H|}[(w - MRf_L)(f_L f_{KK} - f_K f_{KL}) + (s^* - r)(f_K f_{LL} - f_L f_{KL})]$$

at $s = s^*$ which is the rate of return attained by the unregulated monopoly. $|H|$ is the bordered Hessian determinant of the maximum problem. Since $|H| > 0$, $s^* - r > 0$ and $w - MRf_L > 0$ (see equation 3.6 above), it follows that $dq/ds < 0$.

11. Of course, the optimal rate-of-return constraint (or that which maximizes social welfare) need not be a level that eliminates all internal inefficiency. The optimal rate will depend upon a number of additional factors, such as the elasticity of demand, the degree of factor substitution, the extent of increasing returns to scale, and the rate of substitution at which managers trade between profits and output-enhancing labor expenditures. It is also obvious that there may be different optimal rate-of-

return constraints for expense-preference firms than for profit-maximizing firms.

12. When $u = u(\pi,\ell,m)$

$$\frac{dm}{ds} = \frac{K}{|H|} [(u_{KK}u_{LL} - u_{KL}{}^{2}) - u_{Lm}(w - MRf_L - u_{KL}(s^* - r)]$$

at $s = s^*$, where s^* is the maximum rate of return that can be obtained by the unregulated monopolist. Further, $u_{Lm} = (u_{\pi\pi} - u_{\pi m})(w - MRf_L) + ru_{\ell m}$ and $u_{KL} = u_{\pi}(MR'f_L f_K + MRf_{LK})$. The sign of these two expressions cannot be determined without making additional assumptions about u and MR, so that $dm/ds \gtreqless 0$.

13. When $u = u(\pi,m)$ one can show that $dm/ds = k/|H|(u_{KK}u_{LL}u_{KL}{}^{2})$ at $s = s^*$, where the $|H|$ is the Hessian of the constrained problem and is negative and $u_{KK} - u_{LL} - u_{KL}{}^{2} > 0$. The latter is the second-order condition of the maximum of the unconstrained problem which ought to be satisfied at $s = s^*$. This result is consistent with the result obtained by Crew and Kleindorfer (1979a) using numerical simulation. They analyzed large, discrete reduction in s but must assume specific functional forms. In contrast, our result does not require any restrictions on functional forms but is limited to changes in s close to s^*.

14. Although we do not rigorously analyze X-inefficiency within the firm, it seems worth noting that this kind of inefficiency might also be separated into internal as opposed to consumption inefficiency. Further, in the context of X-inefficiency, it is possible that regulation (especially of large corporations) may chiefly affect income distribution rather than internal efficiency.

15. These conclusions implicitly assume a decreasing marginal rate of substitution between factors. In addition, to test these conclusions, it would have to be assumed that firms operate on their production efficiency frontiers (as assumed in the A–J theory).

16. See, for example, Courville (1974) and Spann (1974). In Courville's study, a further issue arises because of his finding that there is no substitution between labor and other inputs at the plant level. One such case is where labor is a function of output alone. In this case, the kind of plant data Courville used can also be used to test the expense-preference hypotheses. In fact, when $L = g(q)$, the firm's profit and production functions in three inputs become $\pi = pq - wg(q) - rk - cF$ and $q = f(K,F)$, where c and F denote the price and quantity of fuel, respectively. Thus, using similar procedures to those applied in this chapter, one can verify that profit maximization requires $f_F = c/(MR - Wg')$, while a preference for labor expense requires $f_F < c/(MR - Wg')$. Even if labor is not a substitute input, therefore, the value of the marginal product of fuel can be used to

discriminate between the profit-maximization and expense-preference hypotheses.

17. See Williamson (1964), Monsen, Chiu, and Cooley (1968), Kamerschen (1968), Larner (1970), Elliot (1972), Palmer (1973), Sorenson (1974), and Stano (1976).

18. Further, consistent with our model of managerial discretion, Palmer (1973) found that ownership structure is important only for firms with a high degree of monopoly power.

19. See Jensen and Meckling (1976), who analyze the reason for this movement.

4 Automatic Rate Adjustments Based on Total Factor Productivity Performance in Public Utility Regulation

E. Fred Sudit

Although the concept and use of two-way automatic rate adjustments in U.S. regulated sectors is not new, its actual implementation has been infrequent. Regulatory systems in general and rate-of-return regulation in particular are designed on the basis of an implicit assumption of a stable price level. Periods of high inflation, when they occur, are presumed to be transitory by nature, resulting in a built-in reluctance to resort to full-scale monetary correction systems. Sweeping price indexation is often portrayed as tacit capitulation in the struggle against inflation. The idea of indexation in regulated industries is treated with even greater suspicion. Automatic rate corrections are politically vulnerable, being easily associated with abandonment of regulatory control and responsibility and excessive rate increases and profits for regulated firms, resulting from abdication of effective public scrutiny.

The relatively high rates of inflation prevailing in the U.S. economy since the mid-1960s have reexposed familiar strains in regulatory systems in general and in public utility rate-of-return regulation in particular. Moreover, the current twelve-year-old inflationary surge does not give any indications of being a transitory phenomenon. To make matters worse, rates of productivity growth have been generally declining throughout the past decade. Consequently, the question of automatic rate corrections may assume a new dimension of urgency.

The purpose of this chapter is to propose automatic rate adjustment formulas based on the relationships between changes in input prices and changes in total factor productivity, to assess their relative merits and potential performance, and to compare them with alternative adjustment formulas recently proposed in regulatory literature and testimony.

A public interest oriented model of public utility rate of return regulation is formulated in section I. Section II outlines the traditional regulatory process based on periodic rate hearings as it relates to the model in section I. The cost-productivity relationships are derived in section III. Automatic rate adjustment formulas based on cost absorption effects of total factor productivity growth, as measured by Divisia index specifications, are developed in section IV. Section V reviews the efficiency and purchasing incentives built in the proposed automatic adjustment formulas. These corrective adjustments are compared in section VI with approaches of similar intent either currently in existence or proposed and occasionally implemented in the past. Section VII examines some empirical observations of hypothetical effects of the suggested automatic rate adjustment formulas on rates of selected regulated industries. Finally, section VIII examines some of the implications of the analysis for future research and policy.

A Public-Interest-Oriented Model of Rate-of-Return Regulation

A general model of rate-of-return regulation can be established to reflect the public interest in meeting a set of objectives subject to socioeconomic constraints. The movement equation constraint forms the base for the automatic adjustment formulae proposed below.

From a public interest viewpoint, public utility rate-of-return regulation can be modeled as follows:

$$\text{Min } (\dot{\mathbf{P}} - \bar{\dot{\mathbf{P}}})^2 \mathbf{U} \tag{4.1}$$

$$\text{Subject to } T\dot{C} = \dot{\mathbf{W}}\mathbf{X} + \dot{\mathbf{X}}\mathbf{W} = T\dot{R} = \dot{\mathbf{P}}\mathbf{Y} + \dot{\mathbf{Y}}\mathbf{P} \tag{4.2}$$

$$\bar{w}_K \leq w_K \leq s \tag{4.3}$$

$$\hat{w} \leq \hat{w}^M \qquad \hat{w} \subset w \tag{4.4}$$

$$\hat{\mathbf{P}} \leq \hat{\mathbf{P}}^R \qquad \hat{\mathbf{P}} \subset \hat{\mathbf{P}} \tag{4.5}$$

$$F(\mathbf{X},\mathbf{Y}) \leq 0 \qquad \text{(a)} \quad f(\mathbf{X}^u,\mathbf{Y}) = 0 \qquad \text{(b)} \quad \mathbf{X} - \mathbf{X}^u \leq \gamma \tag{4.6}$$

$$\frac{f_i}{w_i} - \frac{f_i}{w_i} \leq \delta_{ij} \qquad i \neq j \tag{4.7}$$

$$\mathbf{Q} \geq \bar{\mathbf{Q}} \tag{4.8}$$

where $\mathbf{X} = \{x_1, x_2, \ldots, x \ , \ldots, x \ \}$ is a physical input vector; $\mathbf{Y} = \{y_1, y_2, \ldots, y_j\, y_m\}$ is a vector of physical output; $\mathbf{W} = \{w_1, w_2, \ldots, w_i, \ldots, w_m\}$ is an input unit price vector; and $\mathbf{P} = \{p_1, p_2, \ldots, p_j, \ldots, p_m\}$ is an output prices (rates) vector. The "dot" signs are first derivatives with respect to time indicating change of the respective variable over time: $\mathbf{P}$ is a vector of regulatory targets for prices (rate) changes; $\overline{w}_K$ is the rate of return on the capital input; and w_K and s are, respectively, minimum and maximum limits for the rate of return on capital.[1] $\hat{\mathbf{W}} = \{w_1, \ldots, w_i, \ldots, w_{n-1}\}$, $i \neq K$ is a vector of the firm's input unit prices excluding w_K. $\hat{\mathbf{W}}^M = \{w_1^M, \ldots, w_i^M \ldots, w_{n-1}^M\}$. $i \neq K$ is a vector of competitive market reference or target input prices excluding the rate of return on capital. $\hat{\mathbf{P}}$ is a vector of certain output prices (a subset of $\mathbf{P}$), which cannot exceed certain commission-specified ceiling rates $\hat{\mathbf{P}}^R$ for the corresponding services. $F(\mathbf{X},\mathbf{Y})$ is and n-input, m-output production function of the regulated firm.

The expression in equation 4.1 is an objective function of the regulatory agency and reflects the desire of regulators to hold rate changes $\dot{\mathbf{P}}$ as close as possible to certain target $\dot{\mathbf{P}}$, of desirable levels of price changes. The price changes can be either negative or positive, indicating increase or reductions in rates. $\mathbf{U}$ is and m component vertical vector of subjective political utility weights assigned by the commission to deviations of actual rate changes from targets. Since $\dot{\mathbf{P}}$ are rate change standards set by the commission, they presumably reflect public interests either as they are understood by the commission or as they are brought to bear through relative political pressures of the principal parties to the regulatory process. It is in this sense that the framework in equations 4.1–4.8 is viewed as a public-interest-oriented model. The same model can be reformulated as an economic normative model by specifying that the desired rate level $\overline{p}$ is set to maximize some measure of social benefit—for example, the sum of producer's and consumers' surplus.

Expression 4.2 reflects the identity between the change in total cost of the firm $\dot{TC}$ and the change in total revenuew $\dot{TR}$. This identity holds since the capital input and its unit price, the rate of return on capital or the user cost of capital, are accounted among the inputs. The constraint in 4.3 is representative of the rationale behind rate-of-return regulation. The actual rate of return w_K should not exceed s, the rate-of-return ceiling allowed by the commission, so as to prevent realization of excessive monopoly profits. $\overline{w}_K$ is a floor below which the rate of return should not be allowed to fall, since it is normally judged to be the minimum rate required for fund raising in capital markets without eroding book values of equity.

Regulatory commissions often have specific price subsidy objectives, which are reflected in constraint 4.5. Prices of certain services $\hat{\mathbf{P}}$ may be required not to exceed prespecified levels $\mathbf{P}^R$ in order to guarantee rate levels for specific groups of customers. Finally, the whole process is constrained by the underlying production possibilities, the state of technology, and capacity planning as expressed by the production function in 4.6. Expression 4.6a represents the requirement that production be technically efficient by stipulating that the firm operate on the frontier production function when the inputs **X** are adjusted for their respective degrees of utilization (specified as $\mathbf{X}^u$). Expression 4.6b sets minimum standards for excess capacity. Constraint 4.7 limits the extent of departure from cost-efficient production where f_i denotes the marginal product of the ith input. Expression 4.8 is a quality constraint where **Q** is an m-component vector of output quality index (corresponding to the m-component output vector **Y**), and $\bar{\mathbf{Q}}$ is a vector of minimum acceptable quality standards set by the commission.

II. The Traditional Regulatory Process

In the absence of automatic rate-adjustment clauses, the minimization procedure outlined in expressions 4.1–4.6 is discrete rather than continuous. The regulated firm will normally request hearings for the purpose of rate increases if it perceives its actual rate of return to be falling below its cost of capital (the lower limit of the constraint in expression 4.3 is violated) or if it perceives the range $\bar{w}_K - s$ to be too low relative to market conditions. Regulatory agencies will normally order rate reductions if they perceive the actual rate of return rising beyond the s ceiling. A regulatory review can be initiated by the commissions if firms pay for labor services and materials significantly more than justified by their competitive market prices (a violation of expression 4.4). Review of pricing methods, rate structure, and overall rate levels may also be induced if the prices of certain services exceeds sociopolitically acceptable levels (a violation of expression 4.5). Finally, a variety of questions with respect to efficiency in production may come up. Is the production process F, which reflects the most efficient technology utilized efficiently (that is, expression 4.6 hold). Such reviews with respect to methods of production may give rise to a series of important subsidiary questions relating to the rate of technological innovation and capacity planning, Averch–Johnson effects, and gold plating. All such questions, when deemed sufficiently important, may and should activate regulatory hearings.

If commissions are sensitive to changes in quality of service, mainly as a response to pressure from consumer groups, the quality monitoring can take the form

$$\mathbf{Q} > \bar{\mathbf{Q}}^C \tag{4.9}$$

where $\mathbf{Q} = \{q_1, q_2, \ldots, q_i, \ldots, q_m\}$ is a vector of measurable quality of service levels corresponding to the m services. $\mathbf{Q}^C$ is a vector of minimum acceptable quality levels for these services as perceived by customers (rather than be the commission).

The sequential process of a comprehensive regulatory procedure normally starts with the determination of the quantity demanded of the various services $\widetilde{\mathbf{Y}} = f(\mathbf{p} + \dot{\mathbf{p}})$. The input requirements to satisfy $\widetilde{Y}$, given technology F, are determined by the production function $F(\widetilde{\mathbf{X}},\widetilde{\mathbf{Y}}) = 0$. The unit prices of the inputs are determined with reference to competitive levels to satisfy expression 4.3 and 4.4. Determination of total costs leads to the determination of revenue requirements $(\mathbf{p} + \dot{\mathbf{p}})\widetilde{\mathbf{Y}} = TR(\widetilde{\mathbf{Y}})$ and the required change in revenue $\boldsymbol{TR}$, which in turns leads to the ultimate decision of the required change in rates $\dot{P}$. The vector of changes in rates $\dot{P}$ is set to minimize 4.1, subject to 4.4 and 4.5.

To conclude, conventional rate procedures are activated by violations in one or more of the constraints 4.2 through 4.7. Consequently regulatory reviews are discrete and periodic. The optimization process as envisaged by the regulatory proceedings is sequential and iterative in nature. The target levels of the constraints $\overline{w}_K$, $s, \hat{w}^M, \hat{P}^R$ and the rate increase targets $\dot{\mathbf{P}}$ are determined through bargaining among the commission, the regulated firms, consumers, and other interested parties mitigated by the facts of market conditions.

III. Productivity and Cost Absorption

Here we use constraint 4.2 as a basis for deriving the basic well-known relationships among changes in total factor productivity, unit costs, and prices over time. The movement or state equation 4.2 equating changes in total revenues to changes in total costs could be partitioned to physical input-output changes and unit price changes. Rewriting 4.2 in summation form we obtain:

$$\sum_i \dot{w}_i x_i + \sum_i \dot{x}_i w_i = \sum_j \dot{p}_j y_j = \sum_j \dot{y}_j p_j \qquad (4.10)$$

$$i = 1, \ldots, n \qquad j = 1, \ldots, m.$$

Dividing and multiplying each of the increment terms by its level variable, we get:

$$\sum_i \frac{\dot{w}_i}{w_i} x_i w_i + \sum_i \frac{\dot{x}_i}{x_i} x_i w_i = \sum_j \frac{\dot{p}_j}{p_j} y_j p_j + \sum_j \frac{\dot{y}_j}{y_j} y_j p_j. \qquad (4.11)$$

Since $\Sigma_i w_i x_i = \Sigma_j y_j p_j$ we can divide the left-hand terms in 4.11 by $\Sigma_i w_i x_i$ and the right-hand terms of 4.11 by $\Sigma_j p_j y_j$. Rearranging we obtain:

$$\frac{\dot{TFP}}{TFP} = \sum_j \frac{\dot{y}_j}{y_j}\beta_j - \sum_i \frac{\dot{x}_i}{x_i}\alpha_i = \sum_i \frac{\dot{w}_i}{w_i} di - \sum_j \frac{\dot{p}_j}{p_j}\beta_j \tag{4.12}$$

where $\alpha_i = w_i x_i / \sum_i w_i x_i$ and $\beta_j = p_j y_j / \sum_j p_j y_j$.

The expression in 4.12 is known as a Divisia index total factor productivity change $\dot{TFP}$ (the difference between the sum of the percentage change in physical outputs weighted by their respective shares in total revenue and the sum of the percentage change in physical inputs weighted by their respective share in total costs). A more detailed discussion of the Divisia index and its discrete approximations is presented in appendix 4A. Rewriting 4.1 we obtain:

$$\sum_j \frac{\dot{p}_j}{p_j}\beta_j = \sum_i \frac{\dot{w}_i}{w_i}\alpha_i - \frac{\dot{TFP}}{TFP}. \tag{4.13}$$

This expression clearly demonstrates the extent to which advances in total factor productivity $\dot{TFP}/TFP$ can absorb or offset increases in input prices $\dot{w}_i/w_i$ thereby, modifying rate increases $\dot{p}_j/p_j$. Thus, to maintain rates unchanged $\dot{p}_j/p_j = 0$ without deviation from normal profits ($\sum_j p_j y_j = \sum_i w_i x_i$), weighted changes in unit input prices have to be offset by advances in productivity:

$$\frac{\dot{TFP}}{TFP} = \sum_i \frac{\dot{w}_i}{w_i}\alpha_i . \tag{4.14}$$

Any significant deviation from this will indicate deviation from normal profits, giving grounds for regulatory correction in rates.

IV. Automatic Rate-Adjustment Formulas

Expression 4.13 clearly demonstrates that protracted periods of inflation in input prices, which are significantly higher or lower than industry productivity trends, will call for rate adjustments. The more pronounced the business cycle, the more frequent the need for rate adjustments. The speedier the adjustment, the less severe are the effects of regulatory lags. Consequently, quasi-continuous, automatic rate-adjustment processes could serve to reduce the frequency of rate hearings and, at the same time minimize the distortive effects of regulatory lags.

Consider the following automatic rate-adjustment formula:

$$\sum_i \left[\left(\frac{\dot{p}_j}{p_j} \right)^4 \beta_j \right] = \sum_i \left[\left(\frac{\dot{w}_i}{w_i} \right)^M \alpha_i \right] - \left(\frac{\dot{TFP}}{TFP} \right)^{\min} \tag{4.15}$$

subject to

$$(\dot{p} - \bar{\dot{p}})^2 \leq \epsilon \tag{4.16}$$

$$\overline{w}_K \leq w_K \leq s. \tag{4.17}$$

The adjustment formula in 4.15 is based on the relationship in 4.13, substituting competitive market references changes in input prices $(w_i/w_i)^M$ for changes in actual market input prices $\dot{w}_i/w_i$ and substituting certain minimum required productivity advances $(\dot{TFP}/TFP)^{\min}$ for actual productivity advance $\dot{TFP}/TFP$. The resulting $(p_j/p_j)^A$ indicate the automatic allowed adjustments in rates. The adjustment formula in 4.15 is subject to the constraints in 4.16 and 4.17 where ϵ is a vector of tolerable deviations of rate increase $\dot{P}$ from commission objectives $\bar{\dot{P}}$. A subset of ϵ may for example reflect the sociopolitical importance of not raising certain rates (such as public telephone charges) beyond a certain magnitude.

Violation of constraints 4.16 and 4.17 on a continuing basis would be likely to invoke regular rate hearings and rate proceedings. The hearings usually will be initiated by the regulated firm when the rate of return on capital falls below the lower limit in spite of automatic adjustment. The commission will normally initiate action when the rate of return rises beyond the s ceiling or when rate increases for certain services deviate from commission targets by more than the tolerable level ϵ.

Apart from, and in addition to, outright violation of constraints 4.16 and 4.17, the commission will normally reserve its traditional discretionary powers to monitor periodically its standards for s, w^M and $\bar{\dot{P}}$ relative to changing economic conditions, and it will initiate regulatory review proceedings on its own behalf or in response to petitions on behalf of other parties. The purpose of such proceedings is to review and possibly vary the upper and lower limits in 4.16 and 4.17 in response to the socioeconomic environment.

The concept and measurement of $(\dot{TFP}/TFP)^{\min}$ needs some elaboration. It is the minimal advance in productivity that can be reasonably expected on the part of the regulated firm. Productivity performance below that level would be viewed as erosion in efficiency of operations, which the firm, in turn, would be required to absorb. Its determination could therefore be based on a composite of the following factors: past trend and cyclical patterns of the firm's productivity record; relationships between the productivity performance of the regulated firm and that of the industry it operates in, and related industries; and international comparisons with productivity records of related foreign industries.

A possible procedure for computing $(\dot{TFP}/TFP)^{\min}$ can be outlined in this way:

$$\left(\frac{\dot{TFP}}{TFP}\right)^{\min} - \left(\frac{\dot{TFP}}{TFP}\right)^{F} \cdot C_t^F \leq \delta \tag{4.18}$$

Subject to

$$\left(\frac{\dot{TFP}}{TFP}\right)^{I} \cdot C_t^I - \left(\frac{\dot{TFP}}{TFP}\right)^{\min} \leq \psi \tag{4.19}$$

$$\left(\frac{\dot{TFP}}{TFP}\right)^{RI} \cdot C_t^{RI} - \left(\frac{\dot{TFP}}{TFP}\right)^{\min} \leq \eta, \tag{4.20}$$

where $(\dot{TFP}/TFP)^F$, $(\dot{TFP}/TFP)^I$, and $(\dot{TFP}/TFP)^{RI}$ are, respectively, the total factor productivity trends of the regulated firm, its industry, and a composite of related industries. C_t^F, C_t^I and C_t^{RI} are the respective cyclical adjustment factors. ψ and η are certain commission-imposed limits to deviations from industry reference trends.

The cyclical adjustment to total factor productivity is important because of pronounced cyclical patterns exhibited by productivity trends. For instance, in periods of stagflation, increases in unit prices of inputs may be relatively high, but productivity advances should be anticipated to be below trend. This has to be taken into account in the adjustment formula if the frequency of rate hearings is to be reduced. Additionally, the commission could always use its discretionary powers of monitoring, reviewing, and changing productivity standards in 4.15 relative to changes in structure and trends of the economic environment.

It is also noteworthy that although total factor productivity can be interpreted as an overall measure of efficiency, a subset of variables that affect productivity performance may be beyond the firm's internal control. Consequently, deviations in productivity should not be fully blamed on or credited to internal company performance. Nevertheless, internal control over productivity performance is normally significant enough to justify the use of total factor productivity in the adjustment formula as an incentive for increased company efficiency. If the regulatory firm, in fact, confronts a set of circumstances under which much of the change in total factor productivity is beyond its internal control, the burden of proof in terms of substantiating the case should be upon the management in the framework of regulatory hearings.

Finally, the adjustment formula in 4.15 does not rely on actual unit cost and productivity data of the regulated company. Rather, it requires publicly available data of market reference unit costs and industry productivity trends. The availability of this information reduces the extent of controversy over the accuracy and reliability of internally generated, company-specific data, thereby reducing the scope of audit and verification efforts and inducing further savings in transaction costs.

V. Efficiency Incentives, Purchasing Incentives, and Applicative Efficiency

The automatic rate-adjustment formula in 4.15 incorporates two important sets of incentives. There is a clear incentive for the firm to outperform the productivity advance guideline $(\dot{TFP}/TFP)^{\min}$. The higher the edge of actual productivity performance over the minimum $(\dot{TFP}/TFP) - (\dot{TFP}/TFP)^{\min}$, the higher (other things being equal) the allowed automatic increase in rates $\Sigma_j(\dot{p}_j/p_j)\beta_j$, which enables the firm to stay near the upper bound of the allowed rate of return. Thus, the $(\dot{TFP}/TFP)^{\min}$ term in 4.15 safeguards incentives for improving operational efficiency. The second set of incentives relates to prices negotiated and paid for input services. The regulated firm is induced to obtain lower-than-average market prices for the factors of production it purchases, since any savings relative to market reference prices $(\dot{\mathbf{w}}/\mathbf{w})^M - (\dot{\mathbf{w}}/\mathbf{w})$ will allow higher automatic rate increases (other things being equal), resulting in higher rates of return within the allowed range.

A word of caution is appropriate in this context. Efficiency and purchasing gains can be obtained at the expense of quality of service. It is therefore assumed that as the automatic adjustment formula in 4.15 is implemented, the regulatory agency will monitor quality-of-service levels subject to the quality constraints in 4.9. From the viewpoint of efficiency in application, it should be emphasized again that the formula in 4.15 enables the commission to rely almost exclusively on externally available data since $(\dot{\mathbf{w}}/\mathbf{w})^M$ and $(\dot{TFP}/TFP)^{\min}$ are based on information sources outside the regulatory firms. The only company data required relate to the α_j and β_j weights. This minimum reliance on company-furnished data is likely to provide for a more reliable corrective regulatory mechanism.

VI. Comparison with Existing Automatic Rate-Adjustment Processes

Overall automatic rate adjustments are still the exception rather than the rule in U.S. public utility regulation. In the wake of the OPEC cartelization and the abrupt increases in the price of fuel, numerous commissions have approved two-way automatic rate adjustments for changes in the average cost of fuel (in the case of electric utilities) and in the average cost of purchased gas (in the case of gas distribution utilities). These clauses, by their nature, are limited to only one input, taking this simple form:

$$\left[\left(\frac{\dot{p}_j}{p_j}\right)^{Ae} \beta_j\right] = \frac{\dot{\mathbf{w}}_e}{\mathbf{w}_e}\alpha_e, \tag{4.21}$$

where $(\dot{p}_j/p_j)^{Ae}$ is the automatic energy-related adjustment in rates, $\dot{\mathbf{w}}_e/\mathbf{w}_e$ is the percentage increase in the price of the energy input (fuel or gas), and α_e is the share of the factor cost of the energy input in total costs. Such exclusive fuel-adjustment clauses are of dubious benefit. They may be preferable to the absence of any adjustment formula in the sense that they are likely to reduce to a certain limited extent the frequency of rate proceedings in times of pronounced fluctuations in energy prices by mitigating the regulatory lag, but they will not respond to cycles in prices of other inputs. However, the main problem with energy-adjustment clauses in that they fail to provide efficiency incentives and may induce wasteful behavior on the part of the firm. From 4.21, it is fairly obvious that the firm has no built-in incentive to economize on energy inputs. Moreover, with automatic adjustments applying only to energy, the regulated firm may be provided with a built-in incentive to become energy intensive (by increasing α_e), thereby moving to a nonoptimal input ratio in order to stay close to the upper bound of the allowed rate-of-return range by benefiting from the liquidity advantage of larger immediate adjustment in rates. Thus, automatic fuel-adjustment costs accomplish little and are potentially wasteful.

On April 22, 1975 the New Mexico regulatory commission approved a comprehensive automatic rate-adjustment clause for electric utilities which was modified in January 1979. The original formula was essentially a cost-plus scheme following this form:

$$\sum_j \left[\left(\frac{\dot{p}_j}{p_j}\right)^{AC} \beta_j\right] = \sum \frac{\dot{w}_i}{w_i}\alpha_i \tag{4.22}$$

subject to (4.3). The problem with a cost-plus adjustment is that it does not provide the firm with any built-in incentives for efficiency and economy or penalties for inefficiency and waste.

The adjustment formulas proposed for New Jersey Bell and Bell Canada contain productivity incentives with respect to labor only, with cost-plus adjustments of other nonlabor aggregate input categories (depreciation on fixed capital, property taxes, and other expenses). Broadly, these adjustments take the following form:

$$\sum_j \left[\left(\frac{\dot{p}_j}{p_j}\right)^{AL} \beta_j \right] = \sum_i \left(\frac{\dot{w}_i}{w_i}\right)_i - \left(\frac{\dot{LP}}{LP}\right)^{\min} \tag{4.23}$$

subject to (4.3) where the percentage change in labor productivity $\dot{LP}/LP$ is defined as

$$\frac{\dot{LP}}{LP} = \sum_i \frac{\dot{y}_j}{y_j} \beta_j - \sum_{\ell}^{L} \frac{\dot{x}_\ell}{x} \alpha_\ell \tag{4.24}$$

subject to (4.3), x_ℓ is the physical input level of the ith labor input, assuming there are L labor input categories involved in production.

The $(\dot{LP}/LP)^{\min}$ in 4.23 is a minimum productivity reference change (five-year period output per man-hour increase in the U.S. telephone communication industry in the case of N.J. Bell, and ten-year average of labor productivity for all Canadian manufacturing in the case of Bell Canada).

The major problems with the New Jersey and Canadian formulas lie in their use of a partial productivity measure—output per man-hour. It is therefore easy to see that because of a partial coverage of the productivity index, a straightforward application of the formula in 4.2 is too generous for the regulated firm when compared to 4.24. This is so since

$$\sum_i \frac{\dot{x}_i}{x_i} \alpha_i > \sum_{\ell}^{L} \left(\frac{\dot{x}_\ell}{x_\ell}\right)^{L} \alpha_\ell,$$

owing to the fact that $X = \{x_1, \ldots, x_n\} \supset \{x^L = x_j, \ldots, x_L\}$. Stated alternatively, the nonlabor input in 4.21 is adjusted on a cost-plus basis, while the total factor productivity change in 4.13 incorporates productivity of all inputs. This overcompensation effect may be partially offset in an industry that is undergoing a technological change involving pronounced substitution of capital for labor to the extent that $(\dot{LP}/LP)^{\min} > (\dot{TFP}/TFP)^{\min}$. In addition, the cost of capital w_K on a replacement-cost basis in 4.1 is a user-cost of capital $w_K = v_K(\delta + r - \dot{v}_K/v_K)$, where v_K is the unit price of capital services, δ is the depreciation rate, and r is the opportunity cost of the firm. On a historical-cost basis, $w_K = B_K(\delta + r)$, where B_K is the book value of the capital base. Since δB_K is included as expense, w_K in the N.J. Bell and Canada Bell formulas reduces to $w_K = B_K r$, which is inconsistent with the underlying economic structure of a productivity-based adjustment as outlined in 4.10 through 4.14.

The most comprehensive adjustment formula proposed to date is the Illinois Bell proposal, which resembles the formula suggested in 4.15. The clause takes essentially the following form:

$$\sum_j \left[\left(\frac{\dot{p}_j}{p_j} \right) \beta_j \right] = a \sum_i \frac{\dot{w}_i}{w_i} \alpha_i + b \frac{T\dot{F}P}{TFP}, \tag{4.25}$$

where a and b are weights arbitrarily set at $a = 0.5$ and $b = 1.5$ respectively. Thus, according to 4.25, the regulated company has to absorb half of its unit cost increases ($a = 0.5$) but is rewarded by a factor of 1.5 ($b = 1.5$) for every 1 percent actual improvement in its total factor productivity performance. However, 4.25 differs from 4.15 in the following important aspects:

1. Actual current advances in total factor productivity $T\dot{F}P/TFP$ are employed rather than the reference minimum advances $(T\dot{F}P/TFP)^{min}$, making it more difficult to compute for continuous application without time lags.
2. The Illinois TFP measure is based on Laspeyres indexation rather than Divisia indexation in 4.15, which is theoretically superior and also is better suited for a straightforward derivation of 4.15 based on the general relationship in 4.10.
3. Assigning values to the cost and productivity component weights is purely subjective, providing a potential source of conflict among the parties. By contrast, the adjustment formula 4.15 does not require subjective weights.
4. The Illinois formula requires company internal productivity and cost data, while the formula in 4.15 relies mostly on externally available market data.
5. Finally, and perhaps most importantly, the adjustment mechanism proposed in 4.15 is the only one of the existing formulas that is theoretically traceable to generalized cost production relationships in 4.13. The Illinois formula in 4.25 can be reduced to 4.13 only if $a = 1$, $b = 1$, and productivity change is subtracted from rather than added to the unit cost term.

Regarding the implementation record of these formulas, the New Mexico adjustment formula is currently in effect. The New Jersey formula was in effect for a while to allow New Jersey Bell to improve its earnings position and then was terminated by the commission. The Bell Canada proposal was initially supported by the Canadian Transportation Commission but was allowed to expire in view of political opposition. The Illinois Bell proposal was rejected by the commission after extensive hearings.

VII. Some Empirical Observations

A retrospective examination as to how the automatic rate-adjustment formula proposed above would have worked if implemented in key regulated industries seems in order. Five regulated industries, with the two major public utility sectors among them, were selected. Total factor productivity estimates based on Laspeyres indexes for these industries were available for the 1948–1966 period. Those productivity growth rates are presented in table 4–1 (column 1). Rough estimates of changes in weighted input costs (labor and capital) associated with the chosen industries were computed for the corresponding periods based on national income statistics. This was done by making rough estimates of average capital, labor, and materials shares in total cost over the period and applying these shares as weights to changes in overall labor, capital, and materials costs in the manufacturing sector. The formula in 4.15 was applied to the rates of

Table 4–1
Automatic Rate Adjustments versus Actual Price Changes, 1948–1966
(estimates of average annual percentage change)

Industry	*Total Factor Productivity Growth*	*Hypothetical Change in Rates (Formula)*	*Change in Rates (Actual)*
Air transportation	8.0	−2.0	−0.3
Railroad and related services	5.0	0	+1.0
Electric and gas utilities	4.0	0	+1.1
Telephone and Telegraph	4.0	0	+1.8
Intercity bus lines	2.0	+4.0	+3.5

Sources: *National Income and Product Account of the U.S.: Statistical Tables 1929–1974.* Washington, D.C.: U.S. Department of Commerce.

Survey of Current Business issues 1974–1976. Washington, D.C.: U.S. Department of Commerce.

John W. Kendrick, *Postwar Productivity Trends in the U.S., 1948–1969.* New York: National Bureau of Economic Research, November 1973.

growth in productivity and unit input costs to compute the automatic rate change required by this adjustment technique. These formula-required rate changes are presented in column 2 of table 4–1. They reflect the changes in rates that hypothetically would have occurred had the adjustment formula in 4.15 been applied throughout the period. Finally, the formula-based rate adjustments are compared (in column 3) with approximate estimates of the actual rate changes (as reflected in available price indexes for the respective industries) that did in fact take place during the period.

The estimates in the table suggest that if automatic rate adjustments had been implemented, they would have either fallen short of or stayed relatively close to commission-approved rate increases. Although these numbers represent rough approximations of national averages, they could be interpreted as suggestive of the efficiency potential inherent in appropriate automatic adjustment clauses. The findings in table 4–1 provide at least tentative empirical support to theoretical expectations that automatic rate adjustments are likely to reduce the frequency of hearings and the magnitude of regulatory lags. Also, the numbers suggest that public concerns to the effect that automatic adjustment could result in excessive growth in rates and profits of regulated firms may be too great.

Table 4–2 presents the same analysis for the 1966–1976 period, with the estimates generally compiled in a way similar to the computations for table 4–1. Since total factor productivity estimates for the period were not available, reductions in productivity growth proportional to the reduction in national productivity performance relative to the previous decade were imputed. Also, the dramatic fuel price increases of the 1970s were taken into account in computing roughly estimated overall growth rates in weighted input prices. For all industries, except for telephone and telegraph, formula adjustments fell short of actual commission-approved rate increases.

The comparisons in the two tables may provide some conjectural insights as to the efficiency of regulations. They seem to indicate that commissions, on the average, have shown propensities to approve higher rates than may be justified by cost and productivity changes. In so doing, they have generally resorted to more cumbersome and costly procedures to accomplish a taks that could have been attained more efficiently by more frequent resort to automatic corrections.

VIII. Some Implications for Future Research and Pricing

The automatic rate-adjustment formula we propose has the potential for reducing the costs of the regulatory process and providing incentives toward X-efficiency. Its direct benefits should result from probable reduction in

Table 4-2
Automatic Rate Adjustments versus Actual Price Changes, 1966–1976
(estimates of average annual percentage change)

Industry	*Total Factor Productivity Growth*	*Hypothetical Change in Rates (Formula)*	*Change in Rates (Actual)*
Air transportation	4.0	+7.0	+6.6
Railroad and related services	3.0	+7.0	+5.8
Electric and gas utilities	3.0	+6.0	+8.8
Telephone and telegraph	3.0	+5.0	+3.0
Intercity bus lines	1.0	+9.0	+9.2

regulatory transaction costs, as well as probable contractions in the magnitudes of regulatory lags. Savings in regulatory transaction costs will be realized through reductions in the frequency of full-fledged hearings, with regulated firms, commissions, and third parties being able to divert the freed resources to more efficient uses. The decrease in the magnitude of regulatory lags afforded by the quasi-continuous corrective mechanism is likely to benefit customers by facilitating less abrupt changes in rates. At the same time, the reduction in lag-induced uncertainties faced by the regulated firms could reduce their costs of capital, thereby potentially benefiting shareholders and customers. Finally, diminished regulatory lags could alleviate long-term planning uncertainties, particularly with regard to capacity planning, thus potentially improving managerial performance and the quality of planning.

In addition to the direct benefits, the purchasing and efficiency incentives built into the two-way automatic-adjustment mechanism in 4.15 could generate important spillover effects to the extent that managerial responses to these stimuli do in fact induce a more efficient and economical production of services.

The rate indexation formula is also related to the important issue of reliability in regulation. (See chapter 9 of this book.) Continuous rate adjustment without lags may facilitate low plant capacity margins with the same degrees of system reliability. The built-in total factor productivity incentive, with a capital input not adjusted for utilization, could introduce earning penalties for excessive reliability. Thus, regulated firms may be motivated to plan more carefully for plant capacity margins.

It is important to note, however, that the actual effectiveness of the efficiency incentives built into the indexation process in 4.15 strongly depends on several implicit behavioral assumptions. It is tacitly assumed that the primary objective of managers is to maximize profits subject to regulatory constraints and that an important objective of commissioners is to maximize the efficiency of the regulatory process within the framework of social welfare maximization. On the other hand, if managements actually exhibit mainly expense-preference behavior—as suggested by Williamson (1963), Edwards (1977), Crew and Kleindorfer (1979a), and Arzac and Edwards (chapter 3 of this book)—and commissioners are motivated to maximize political influence and public exposure, the automatic-adjustment mechanism proposed may either lose its attractiveness to the parties involved or fail to provide the desired incentives. It therefore seems desirable for future research in this area to explore automatic-adjustment clauses based on alternative behavioral assumptions and subject the formulas and their underlying hypotheses to empirical testing.

Our preliminary conclusions thus suggest the need for further extensive research in the area of rate indexation. The adjustment mechanism in 4.15 is just one new alternative in a whole set of potential approaches. Rigorous modeling and empirical experimentation should either refute or confirm our claims for the potential advantage of indexation. Furthermore, little is known about the pattern and magnitude of transaction costs under existing regulatory systems. More systematic research in this area should provide a base of comparison, opening the way for estimation of transaction cost savings induced by the implementation of alternative rate indexation schemes.

Notes

1. The rate-of-return concept in 4.3 does not follow the traditional rates-of-return measurements employed in regulatory proceedings. Rather, they are user cost of capital equivalents, computed on a replacement cost basis.

Appendix 4A:

The total factor productivity Divisia index can be computed by the application of the continuous expression in 4.12. For relatively large input and/or output changes, the Tornquist formula for a discrete approximation is:

$$\frac{TFP_1}{TFP_0} = \frac{\prod_{j=1}^{m} \left(\frac{y_{j1}}{y_{j0}}\right)^{½(\beta_{j0} + \beta_{j1})}}{\prod_{i=1}^{n} \left(\frac{x_{i1}}{x_{i0}}\right)^{½(\alpha_{j0} + \alpha_{j1})}},$$

where subscripts 0 and 1 denote periods 0 and 1, respectively. Accordingly 4.13 can be rewritten in discrete approximative form:

$$\prod_{j=1}^{m} \left(\frac{P_{j1}}{P_{j0}}\right)^{½(\alpha_{j0} + \alpha_{j1})} = \prod_{i=1} \left(\frac{w_{i1}}{w_{i0}}\right)^{½(\beta_{i0} + \beta_{i1})} - \frac{TFP_1}{TFP_0}.$$

Divisia indexes are less restrictive in their underlying assumptions than either Laspeyres or Paasche indexes. They do not depend on the assumption of fixed contributory weights over time, and their underlying aggregator functions are of a more general nature. It can be shown that the functions underlaying the Divisia aggregators are of the homogeneous translog type, which could be shown to provide a second-order local approximation to any arbitrary functional form. See Christensen et al. (1973). Divisia indexes also possess the attractive theoretical property of correspondence to Fisher's ideal index, which is the geometric mean of the Laspeyres and Paasche indexes and, unlike the latter two, is unbiased in its measurement of quantity and price change. For a detailed discussion of the properties of Divisia indexes relative to other prevalent indexes, see Fisher (1922), Diewert (1976), Hulten (1973), and Sudit (1977).

5 An Analysis of the Benefits and Costs of Seasonal–Time–of–Day Electricity Rates

John T. Wenders and
R. Ashley Lyman

In a recent article evaluating research on the economics of regulation, Paul Joskow and Roger Noll conclude that "the one great practical triumph of theory is the literature on peak-load or variable pricing."[1] Although their conclusion may be overstated, one can seriously argue that the peak-load pricing question has been the foremost area of debate in the electric power industry since the late 1960s. The primary focus in this literature is the specification of the optimal set of prices to be charged over the daily, weekly, and annual cycles that electricity consumption displays. What has been largely ignored is the fact that the proper application of peak-load pricing depends on more than just a specification of the optimal prices; it also depends on an empirical analysis of the benefits and costs of going from one set of prices to some other set, both of which may be nonoptimal from the standpoint of economic welfare.

The purpose of this chapter is to look at the peak-load pricing problem from this benefit-cost perspective. Two aspects of the problem will be analyzed. First is the traditional question of the incremental metering cost of adopting a pricing scheme that distinguishes consumption by time of day (TOD). A second consideration is the possible nonoptimality of both present electricity prices, from which we must start, and the kind of seasonal or seasonal-time-of-day (STD) prices that are likely to be implemented in a regulatory proceeding. As we have argued in the past, the theoretically correct procedure for measuring the benefits to full STD pricing is to compute the gain in welfare in going from a set of optimal seasonal prices to a set of optimal STD prices.[2] This is the gain that can be achieved solely by the installation of the TOD meter. However, in a regulatory environment, we

A portion of the analysis presented in this chapter was developed under a research contract from the Power Plant Siting Program of the Department of Natural Resources of the State of Maryland to Data Resources, Inc. Additional financial support came from the University of Arizona and the University of Idaho. Finally, we would like to thank Michael C. Slota for his help in obtaining some of the data necessary for the completion of this chapter.

are not so sure that optimal STD prices are possible or that the real alternative to STD prices is a set of optimal seasonal prices. Perhaps the relevant measure of the benefits of STD prices is the welfare gain that can be achieved by going from a set of feasible non-STD prices to a set of feasible STD prices without any assumption that either of these is optimal in the sense that economists use the term.

If this is the framework for making a decision on the desirability of full STD pricing, then some counterintuitive results become possible. For example, it is quite possible for STD pricing to fail the benefit-cost analysis going from optimal seasonal to optimal STD prices and yet pass the test when going between the feasible set of prices, and conversely.

We shall proceed in the following manner. First, we shall lay out the benefit/cost framework for judging whether or not full STD pricing is desirable. Second, we shall apply this framework to the average sized customer in each customer class for Baltimore Gas and Electric Company (BGE). This analysis will spell out the benefits and costs of going from present prices to optimal seasonal prices, and then from optimal seasonal prices to marginal cost prices. Our conclusion is that full STD meters and pricing can be justified for all but the smallest half of the residential customer class (below 7342 kwh/year). The next section applies the same methodology to data from Public Service Company of New Mexico (PNM), a utility with a different load pattern and therefore a different set of pricing periods and prices. The major difference between PNM and BGE is that PNM is not such a pronounced summer peaking utility—it has only been summer peaking for a half dozen years—and has a much higher annual load factor. Taking account of the size differences between the average customers of PNM and BGE, the results regarding the desirability of full STD pricing are strikingly similar between the two utilities. On the other hand, due to the stronger summer peak of BGE, purely seasonal pricing yields relatively greater gains for BGE's customers, and purely time-of-day pricing yields relatively greater gains for PNM's customers. Looking at the gain in welfare going from proposed seasonal prices to proposed STD prices does not change these overall results.

While the methodology used is certainly subject to error and modification, we believe that it is unlikely that further research would upset our general conclusion that full STD pricing is certainly beneficial for all customers in the industrial and large commercial classifications. In the small commercial and residential classes, widespread applicability of STD pricing is dependent on a more detailed analysis of the utility in question. For some utilities, as many as 60 percent of the customers in these classes may have the benefits of full STD pricing exceed the costs.

I. The Theoretical Framework

Benefit Cost Analysis

The framework used in judging the desirability of seasonal-time-of-day electricity pricing is a reasonably straightforward application of standard welfare theory.[3] Let us assume that there are two pricing seasons (summer and winter), each with day (peak) and night (off-peak) pricing periods. For simplicity, assume all four pricing periods are of equal length, the demands in each of the four periods are independent, and we know the relevant marginal costs and demand functions. Thus, there are four independent markets for electricity.

It is important to understand that not all of the present welfare losses existing in these four markets are due to the failure to set proper time-of-day prices. At any given set of present nonoptimal prices, the resulting welfare losses can be divided into two parts: losses that are due to the failure to set the proper seasonal prices and additional losses that result from the failure to employ TOD prices. Presumably the first of these can be eliminated by setting the optimal seasonal prices, which requires no additional metering costs. It is only those welfare losses remaining after optimal seasonal prices have been set that are solely due to the failure to employ TOD prices, and it is only these remaining welfare losses that should be thought of as the potential benefits available from TOD metering and pricing. Put another way, before computing the benefits to strictly TOD pricing, which involves a new metering technology, we should exhaust all of the welfare gains possible from the meters that are already in place.

These results are easily interpreted graphically. Consider figure 5-1, which shows the summer market for electricity. If prices were set equal to marginal cost, they would be set at p_1 during summer days and p_2 during summer nights. However, without special meters, only one price, p_s , can be charged. The problem, therefore, is to choose the p_s that minimizes the welfare losses of departing from p_1 and p_2. Suppose p_s is initially set equal to p_2. Then there will be a welfare loss of *abc* in the summer-day market but no welfare loss in the summer-night market. Now suppose that the common price in the two markets is raised to p_s . This results in a gain in welfare equal to *c′b′bc* in the summer-day market but produces a welfare loss equal to *def* in the summer-night market. If the former is greater than the latter, then there will be an improvement in overall welfare as a result of this move, and p_s should be raised incrementally as long as the incremental gains exceed the incremental losses in welfare. The welfare-maximizing summer price will be closer to p_1 the flatter is D_1 and the steeper is D_2. In the

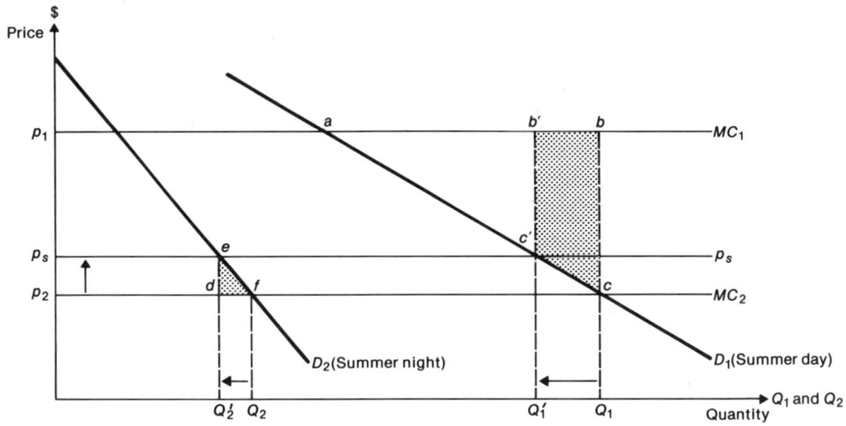

Figure 5–1. Optimal Seasonal Pricing

extreme, if D_2 is perfectly inelastic, then no welfare losses result in the summer-night market due to raising p_s above p_2, and p_s should be set equal to p_1. Similarly, p_s should be set equal to p_2 if D_1 is perfectly inelastic. Thus, the general rule is similar to the more familiar quasi-optimal pricing principle: price should depart from marginal cost most in the market with the most inelastic demand. A similar procedure should be used to find the welfare-maximizing winter price for electricity.

Once seasonal prices have been optimized, the next step is to assess the further welfare gains that are possible by TOD pricing. These are merely the welfare losses that remain in each of the four markets after optimal seasonal prices have been set. In figure 5–1, if p_s is the optimal seasonal price, areas *def* plus $ab'c'$ are the additional gains in welfare that are possible in the summer season with TOD metering and pricing. There are two similar welfare triangles in the winter markets. It is the sum of the welfare gains in these four markets that must be weighed against the increased metering cost of TOD pricing.

Adjustments to this basic model to account for the complications imposed by pricing periods of unequal length, interdependent demand, and nonlinear demand functions are straightforward but messy. The computer program used to perform the calculations presented later in this chapter takes all of these complications into account.

The Markets Analyzed

The above framework is applied by using the average customer in each customer class, in terms of annual kwh consumption, as the unit of analysis.

This means that we shall weigh the annual benefits of full STD pricing against the annual cost of additional metering for an average customer in each class. This use of the average customer as the unit of analysis is only a first approximation to what we would like to do if we had more specific data for different customers in each class. Ideally, we would like to have consumption patterns and demand elasticities for a range of customer sizes to allow us to be more discriminating within customer classes as to which customers should be looked upon as candidates for full STD pricing. Since the benefits to STD pricing are strongly related to customer size, ceteris paribus, if the average customer passes the benefit-cost test for full STD pricing, probably all customers of greater than average size would also pass the test. And depending on the strength of the results, the average customer may pass the test, but some of the smaller-than-average customers may not.

Demand Functions and Elasticities

In all cases, we used demand functions of the constant elasticity form. We feel confident that the use of demand functions of some other form would not materially change our overall conclusions. Very little is known about demand elasticities by time of day, and still less is known about cross-elasticities between STD pricing periods. And there is still a good deal of controversy about what simple, non-STD, price elasticities are. The first column of table 5-1 gives the range of long-run elasticities found by Taylor in his survey of the demand for electricity.

We have used non-STD elasticities estimates and assumed that these would be applicable to the STD pricing periods. Thus, for example, it was found that the long-run summer elasticity of demand for the residential users fo Baltimore Gas and Electric was −0.90. We assumed that this same

Table 5-1
Price Elasticities Used for Welfare Analysis

		BGE		*PNM*
Class	*Taylor*	*Summer*	*Winter*	*All Seasons*
Residential	−1.02 to −1.89	−0.90	−0.82	−0.93
Commercial	−1.36	−0.79	−0.25	−0.56
General power				−0.63
Industrial	−1.25 to 1.82	−1.00	−1.00	−0.63

Sources: Taylor (1975, p. 101); Data Resources (1978) for BGE; Mount and Chapman (1976) for BGE industrial. The elasticities for PNM were used by a consultant, Kent Anderson of National Economic Associates, in a load forecast.

value applied to both summer day and night elasticity. These elasticities are shown in table 5-1 also. On the whole, the elasticities used are on the low side of the range found by Taylor. Since the size of the benefits to STD pricing increases with the elasticity of demand, it might be argued that our use of rather low elasticities biases the results against the desirability of full STD pricing. On the other hand, there is no way to assess the possible bias from using the same elasticity for both peak and off-peak pricing periods.

The calculations carried out below assume that the cross-elasticities of demand among all pricing periods are zero. In most cases, we tend to think that day and night electricity are substitutes, implying that a rise in the price of day electricity would cause the demand for night electricity to increase. On the other hand, consider the situation where much of the demand for electricity in both day and night periods results from use of the same appliance—perhaps an air conditioner in Arizona. In this case, a rise in the price of day electricity might, in the long run, cause an energy-saving adjustment in the stock of air-conditioning appliances, which in turn might result in a decrease in the demand for night electricity. In short, it is not inconceivable that day and night electricity are complements. The substitution relationship seems more likely in northern utilities where electricity consumption is less likely to be dominated by a single appliance. But even there, electric space heating might be sufficiently dominant to produce a complementary relationship between day and night electricity. If, indeed, the true cross-elasticities are of substitutes, then our assumption of no cross-elasticities would understate the benefits to full STD pricing.

As a somewhat weak defense of our assumptions about demand elasticities, we would point out that the United States has never had STD pricing of smaller customers and very little STD pricing of even larger customers. This means that no amount of econometric manipulation of existing data can ever reveal what these STD direct and cross-elasticities are. Of course, there have been recent actual and experimental implementations of STD pricing, but these are not likely to yield long-run elasticities for many years, and even then, the revealed elasticities may not be long run because of the failure of the appliance- or capital-producing industries to adjust to STD opportunities. Our point is that real, long-run elasticities are not likely to be available in the near future. In the meantime, some assumptions about such elasticities are going to have to be made if any benefit-cost analysis is to be carried out.

Marginal Costs

The marginal cost used as the basis for our analysis were calculated by the utilities in question according to the methodology put forth in the

NARUC Rate Design Study.[4] We believe that the results are reasonable and the best available.

Measuring the Quantity of Electricity

The marginal cost of serving an electricity customer can be thought of as having three components: a customer component, a capacity (kw) component, and an energy (kwh) component.[5] In costing, it is relatively easy to distinguish between these various components, even though marginal costs are frequently quoted on a purely energy basis by appropriately computing the capacity cost on a kwh basis. This latter convention is further encouraged by the fact that probably most electricity customers are metered and priced solely on a kwh basis. On the demand for electricity side, almost all elasticity studies have been done on a kwh basis; few have attempted to compute the demand for capacity as distinguished from the demand for energy.

For these reasons, we have carried out our analysis by measuring the quantity of electricity solely on a kwh basis, although, of course, the use of electricity clearly has both capacity and energy dimensions (we have been unable to determine what bias our measurement imparts to our analysis). This problem is greatly complicated by the fact that there may be strong cross-elastic effects between the demand for capacity and the demand for energy. Further, the question of whether to price on both a capacity and energy basis or on only an energy basis is similar to the problem of whether to employ time-of-day pricing. By pricing on only a kwh basis, the implicit price of capacity (kw) to the consumer is zero, ceteris paribus, and capacity is thus underpriced and energy overpriced. The question then becomes whether it is worth the extra price of a capacity (demand) and energy meter, over the price of kwh-only meter, to eliminate the welfare losses caused by pricing kwh only. Formally, this problem is identical to the one we are addressing here. Finally, it is quite possible that "demand" meters might not be justified under non-STD pricing but justified under full STD pricing. In fact, it is possible that full STD pricing might not pass our benefit-cost test assuming kwh-only meters but might pass the test if a "demand" and energy meter were assumed. This question of the relationship between "demand" and energy pricing needs to be explored in more detail.

Metering Costs

It is clear that metering technology is unfolding rapidly, and therefore it is difficult to predict the cost difference between standard, non-TOD meters and TOD meters. Table 5-2 shows the annual difference in metering costs computed by Baltimore Gas and Electric Company. We believe that these estimates are reasonable.

Calculating the Benefits to STD Pricing

Welfare losses that can be eliminated by full STD pricing are the benefits to that form of pricing. In performing our calculations of these benefits, we have used estimates of the long-run elasticities of demand, which presume that consumers adjust instantaneously to the STD prices. This assumption is clearly wrong. In order to take account of the fact that consumers will need time to adjust to STD prices, we have computed the present value of the calculated stream of benefits under two assumed adjustment paths. The first, and more conservative, assumes that consumers fully adjust to STD prices smoothly over a twenty-year period. The second assumes that this adjustment takes place over a ten-year period. We do not believe that these assumptions bias our welfare estimates upward.

II. The Theory Applied to Baltimore Gas and Electric Company

Selecting the STD Pricing Periods

Baltimore Gas and Electric (BGE) is a medium-sized utility (1977 peak: 3588 Mw) operating in a predominantly urban area.[6] The utility became summer peaking in the late 1950s, and the summer-winter differential has widened continually since then. The annual peak almost always occurs in July or August. Although there is a short, but clear, secondary peak in either December or January, it was judged that there was little danger of this secondary peak's pressing against system capacity, even after allowing for maintenance, so the winter season was judged to be off-peak. June through September were designated as the peak months; the other months were classified as off-peak.

The BGE system daily load is characterized by a broad daytime peak, especially in the winter. Defining the daily peak period as falling between 8 A.M. and 11 P.M., the daily peak-trough ratio in the winter is 1.62:1 on the average, while in the summer this same ratio is 1.82:1. Similarly, in the winter over 88 percent of the hours during the peak period have load in excess of 90 percent of the peak, while in the summer this same percentage is about 69 percent. Generally, the daily peak hours fall in the afternoon in the summer and early evening in the winter, but the hours on either side of the peak are usually very close to the peak.

This definition of the daily peak period might seem unduly broad; how-

Table 5-2
Annual STD Metering Costs

Customer Class	*Annual STD Metering Cost*	*Present Value*[a]
Residential	$ 29.88	$ 298.80
Commercial		
Under 60 kw	32.28	322.80
Over 60 kw	110.76	1107.60

Source: Baltimore Gas and Electric Company, *Response to Maryland Public Service Commission order 62586,* exhibit C-1.
[a]At 10 percent per year

ever, it seems to be justified by the observed load pattern. Another possibility is to define a high peak period within the peak period where prices would be somewhat higher. However, unless the price during this high peak period was very close to the price during the hours on either side, there is a real danger that the peak would eventually shift out of the high peak period. Another alternative is to put two short shoulder periods at the end of the defined peak period where prices would be somewhat lower during the peak. This approach would soften the sharp drop in price from the peak to off-peak periods. On the other hand, the addition of more daily pricing periods would complicate the tariff and might have relatively little payoff in terms of incentives. In any event, it is difficult to argue that the definition of the pricing periods unduly biases the results in one direction or another.

The same arguments can be made with respect to the weekends, which have been considered as off-peak. But this treatment raises the possibility that a heavy movement of load to the weekends would cause the peak hours to move too. In a sense, this possibility would be rather easy to handle by changing the peak hours of the weekends to a kind of intermediate or shoulder price treatment.

In summary, BGE has defined its summer peak season as the months from June through September, with all other months designated as seasonal off-peak. The daily peak period is from 8 A.M. to 11 P.M. in both summer and winter, and all weekends are designated as off-peak and receive the same price treatment as the daily off-peak period.

STD Marginal Costs for BGE

The marginal costs for each of the selected pricing periods were determined by the methodology developed in the NERA Report. Some alterations were made, but they were relatively minor. Table 5-3 shows these marginal costs on a synthesized kwh basis.

The energy portion of the marginal costs in table 3-5 are similar across classes of users for the same pricing period. The difference between these is attributed to the fact that these classes take their power at different voltages, thus producing more transformation losses for the lower voltage customers. However, the difference in the capacity portion of the marginal costs shown in the table is much wider across user classes during the same pricing period, for two reasons. First, as with the energy portion of the tariff, there are more transformation losses for the low voltage customers. For example, the marginal cost per kw for the residential, commercial, and industrial classes in the summer peak period was $84.82, $84.67, and $75.60, respectively. However, when computed on a kwh basis, these differences become much more pronounced because of the differing load factors of these three classes. For example, the industrial class was responsible for 712 Mw of demand during the system peak in 1977 and used 849,568,647 kwh during the summer daily peak period. Put another way, the industrial class used each of its coincident peak kw's for 1,193 hours during the summer peak period. On the other hand, the residential class contributed 1,504 Mw to the system peak but used only 1,018,770,695 kwh during the summer daily peak period. This class then used each of its coincident kw's

Table 5-3
BGE Synthesized Marginal Costs
(¢/kwh)

	Summer Marginal Costs					
	Summer Peak			*Summer Off-Peak*		
Class	*Capacity*	*Energy*	*Total*	*Capacity*	*Energy*	*Total*
Residential	12.522	2.938	15.46	0	1.846	1.846
Commercial	7.870	2.920	10.79	0	1.835	1.835
Industrial	6.336	2.827	9.163	0	1.777	1.777
	Winter Marginal Costs					
	Winter Peak			*Winter Off-Peak*		
Residential	1.233	2.892	4.125	0	2.01	2.01
Commercial	0.795	2.874	3.669	0	1.996	1.996
Industrial	0.639	2.783	3.422	0	1.933	1.933

Source: Data Resources Inc. (1978)

for 677 hours during the summer peak period—only about 57 percent of the use that the industrial class made of its coincident peak kilowatts. Thus, when marginal costs are quoted on a kwh basis, the cost per kwh is much higher for the residential class than for the industrial class. The commercial class falls between these two but is closer in marginal capacity cost to the residential class.

Comparison of Present Prices with Marginal Costs

Table 5-4 shows the marginal costs for each pricing period and the present marginal prices during these same periods for the average customer in each class. For purposes of comparison, present marginal "demand" prices for the commercial and industrial classes have been converted to a kwh basis. This table also shows the consumption characteristics for the average customer in each class. The consumption was determined by dividing the appropriate class consumption (kwh) in each pricing period for each month of 1977 by the average number of customers during that month. These were then appropriately aggregated over the season. The marginal prices for each average customer were found by observing their marginal block of consumption in the appropriate rate schedule and then converting the results to a kwh basis where appropriate. Table 5-4 shows that both the average residential and average industrial customers are underpriced during the peak

Table 5-4
Characteristics of Average Customer in Each BGE Class

Class	*Summer Peak*	*Summer Off-Peak*	*Winter Peak*	*Winter Off-Peak*
Residential				
kwh	1,423.4	1,347.9	2,254.6	2,316.0
Marginal price	3.26¢	3.26¢	2.26¢	2.26¢
Marginal cost	15.460¢	1.846¢	4.125	2.01¢
Commercial				
Billing kw	15.65/mo.		13.36/mo.	
kwh	13.223	9,113	22,724	16,685
Marginal price	4.18¢	4.18¢	4.18¢	4.18¢
Marginal cost	10.790¢	1.835¢	3.669¢	1.996¢
Industrial				
Billing kw	2,052.69/mo.		1,868.23/mo.	
kwh	1,924,278	1,606,156	3,475,528	3,005,264
Marginal price	2.0050¢	2.0050¢	2.0910¢	2.0910¢
Marginal cost	9.163¢	1.777¢	3.422¢	1.933¢

periods and overpriced during the off-peak periods. On the other hand, the average commercial customer is overpriced in all but the summer peak periods.

Optimal Seasonal Prices and Welfare Gains

The purpose of optimal seasonal pricing is to exhaust the welfare gains that can be achieved with present metering. It is admittedly a second-best solution, but it has the advantage of being costless. Table 5-5 shows the optimal seasonal prices and the long-run annual gain in welfare for the average customer achieved by going from present to optimal seasonal prices. Multiplying the average welfare gain by the total number of customers in each class reveals that the total long-run annual welfare gain from optimal seasonal pricing for all classes amounts to $85,142,223. Of course, these welfare gains have been computed by using long-run elasticities of demand in each instance, and we would expect the realization of these elasticities, and the associated welfare gains, to take several years. Thus, it would be optimistic to expect these full gains to be realized soon after the implementation of seasonal pricing. Nevertheless, any gains to seasonal pricing are costless, and thus there is no economic reason for delaying the implementation of optimal seasonal pricing.

Welfare Gains from Optimal STD Pricing

Table 5-6 shows the additional annual welfare benefits that are available in moving from optimal seasonal to full marginal cost, STD prices. For the residential and industrial classes, these additional gains are less than the initial gains from implementing seasonal pricing, implying that most of the gains from more efficient pricing can be achieved in these classes by optimal seasonal pricing. On the other hand, the gains from full, marginal-cost, STD pricing are relatively greater for the commercial class. The total long-run annual gain for all customers in all classes amounts to $62,789,680, which is considerably less than the total gain from optimal seasonal pricing.

The question still remains of whether it is worth the additional costs to move from optimal seasonal pricing to optimal STD pricing. Our earlier discussion (see table 5-2) showed that the present value of the additional costs incurred by going to STD pricing is $298.80 for a residential customer, $322.80 for a small commercial customer (under 60 kw), and $1,107.60 for a large commercial customer (over 60 kw). Since industrial customers already have meters capable of recording by time of day, there are no additional costs for them of going to STD pricing. Table 5-7 presents the

Table 5-5
Optimal Seasonal Prices and Annual Welfare Gains from Optimal Seasonal Pricing for Average BGE Customer

Class	*Optimal Seasonal Prices*		*Annual Welfare Gain Present Prices to Optimal Seasonal Prices*
	Summer	*Winter*	
Residential	8.84¢/kwh	3.05¢/kwh	$64.16
Commercial	7.14¢	2.96¢	151.89
Industrial	5.80¢	2.73¢	64,154.46
Industrial: kw	$13.12 per kw per mo.	$6.29 per kw per mo.	
kwh	2.745¢	2.035¢	

Table 5-6
Annual Welfare Gains for Average BGE Customer from TOD Pricing

Class	*Annual Welfare Gain Seasonal Prices to STD Prices*
Residential average customer	$46.52
Commercial average customer	$249.67
Industrial average customer	$25,835.34

present value of the annual welfare gains shown in table 5-6 under two different assumptions. The first number shown presumes that the customer adjusts to the STD prices, as indicated by their long-run elasticity of demand, over a twenty-year period; the second number assumes that this adjustment takes ten years.

We interpret these results to imply that full STD pricing is certainly beneficial for all customers in the industrial class, and this conclusion would hold even if these customers were not already metered by time of day. For the commercial class, full STD metering and pricing can probably be justified for all but the smallest users in this class—say, those below 8,000 to 10,000 kwh consumption per year. For the residential class, the average customer passes the benefit-cost test only if it is assumed that these customers adjust to their long-run elasticity of demand in fewer than approximately twelve years. On the basis of this analysis, we would be reluctant to apply full STD pricing to any smaller-than-average residential customers of BGE.

III. The Theory Applied to Public Service Company of New Mexico

STD Pricing Periods

Public Service of New Mexico (PNM) is a medium-sized utility (the 1977 summer peak was about 740 Mw). Its service territory is dominated by the Albuquerque metropolitan area; it also serves several smaller towns and cities, as well as an extensive, low-density, geographical area. PNM has become clearly summer peaking only since the early 1970s, and there still remains the possibility that an increase in the winter space-heating load might make the utility become winter peaking again. On the other hand, PNM has interconnections with other utilities that are strongly summer peaking so that the overall generation capacity of PNM's system might not be seriously affected by an increase in winter load. Three seasonal pricing periods were found to be appropriate by PNM's marginal cost study: summer (June–August), winter (December–February), and shoulder (March–May, and September–November).[7]

An analysis of daily load curves and loss-of-load probabilities resulted in the selection of the following daily peak pricing periods: summer weekdays, 11 A.M.–7 P.M.; winter and shoulder, 8 A.M.–10 P.M. All other hours, including weekends, were designated as off-peak.

STD Marginal Costs and Prices for PNM

Table 5–8 presents the size characteristics of the average customer in each class, synthesized marginal cost, and present and proposed marginal prices for the average customer in each class. Since PNM is not as strongly summer peaking as is BGE, more capacity costs are attributed to the peak periods of the off-peak seasons (winter and shoulder). Nevertheless, there still are more than two to one differences between the peak marginal costs of the summer and other seasons, compared with BGE's differences of more than three to one in some cases.

Three sets of marginal prices are presented for each class. The marginal price shown is the non-STD price offered by the utility during the test year. The proposed STD price is the seasonal-time-of-day price, which was proposed by PNM in a rate case no. 1419. The proposed marginal price is the non-STD price proposed by PNM in the same case. The presence of proposed STD and non-STD prices allows us to compute the welfare gains of going to proposed STD prices where the real alternative is not optimal seasonal pricing but a set of proposed alternative prices that are not optimal.

Comparing the proposed STD prices with marginal costs reveals that

Table 5-7
Present Value of Welfare Gains and Costs to STD Pricing for Average BGE Customer

Average Customer	*Present Value of Welfare Gains*[a]	*Present Value of Costs*[b]
Residential	$217.82-314.43	$298.80
Commercial	$1,169.10-1,687.50	322.80
Industrial	$120,972.96-175,549.69	0

[a] Assumes a twenty- and ten-year adjustment period to STD prices, respectively, and a 10 percent discount rate.

[b] See table 5-2.

Table 5-8
Synthesized Marginal Costs and Prices for Average PNM Customers

	Summer		*Winter*		*Shoulder*	
Class	*Peak*	*Off-Peak*	*Peak*	*Off-Peak*	*Peak*	*Off-Peak*
Residential[a]						
kwh	416	953	728	830	1,189	1,397
Marginal cost	10.81¢	1.99¢	5.55¢	1.86¢	5.23¢	2.19¢
Marginal price	3.54¢	3.54¢	3.74¢	3.74¢	3.68¢	3.68¢
Proposed STD price	6.7 ¢	2.0 ¢	4.6 ¢	1.9 ¢	3.9 ¢	2.2 ¢
Proposed price	4.5 ¢	4.5 ¢	4.1 ¢	4.1 ¢	4.0 ¢	4.0 ¢
Commercial[b]						
kwh	1,792	3,228	2,427	2,156	4,864	3,966
Marginal cost	11.06¢	1.99¢	4.60¢	1.86¢	5.09¢	2.19¢
Marginal price	4.84¢	4.84¢	4.04¢	4.04¢	4.98¢	4.98¢
Proposed STD price	7.6 ¢	2.0 ¢	4.0 ¢	1.9 ¢	2.2 ¢	2.2 ¢
Proposed price	5.2 ¢	5.2 ¢	4.5 ¢	4.5 ¢	4.5 ¢	4.5 ¢
General power[c]						
kwh	40,591	92,502	51,618	58,086	111,702	113,327
Marginal cost	11.96¢	1.99¢	5.27¢	1.86¢	5.22¢	2.19¢
Marginal price	2.92¢	2.92¢	3.20¢	3.20¢	3.19¢	3.19¢
Proposed STD price	10.21¢	2.0 ¢	6.15¢	2.1 ¢	6.12¢	2.1 ¢
Proposed price	4.46¢	4.46¢	4.03¢	4.03¢	4.12¢	4.12¢
Industrial[d]						
kwh	543,789	1,383,287	914,611	958,348	1,868,001	2,026,521
Marginal cost	10.38¢	1.85¢	4.43¢	1.74¢	4.64¢	2.06¢
Marginal price	2.59¢	2.59¢	2.79¢	2.79¢	2.73¢	2.73¢
Proposed STD price	9.02¢	1.9 ¢	5.13¢	2.0 ¢	5.29¢	2.0 ¢
Proposed price	3.88¢	3.88¢	3.54¢	3.54¢	3.55¢	3.55¢

[a] Residential overhead class.

[b] Small power overhead class.

[c] General power overhead class.

[d] Large power class.

for the residential and commercial classes, the proposed off-peak prices are very close to marginal cost, with the peak-period prices set somewhat less than marginal cost, especially in the summer. For the general power and industrial classes, the proposed STD prices are closer to marginal cost, but with prices at or above marginal cost in the winter and shoulder seasons. Summer peak period prices are actually rather close to marginal cost for the general power and industrial classes.

Optimal Seasonal Prices and Welfare Gains

Table 5-9 shows the optimal seasonal prices for PNM and the long-run annual gain in welfare for the average customer achieved by going from present to optimal seasonal prices. The results given in this table are comparable to those presented in table 5-5 for BGE. The striking feature that emerges from a comparison of the results for these two utilities is the comparatively larger gains to be had from seasonal pricing for BGE's customers. For example, the average residential customer for BGE consumes about 1.33 times as much electricity as PNM's average residential customer (7,342 versus 5,513); yet the gains to seasonal pricing are some thirty-two times greater ($64.16 versus $1.99). For the commercial classes, the results are similar. BGE's average customer is 3.35 times larger than PNM's, but the gains to seasonal pricing are almost fifteen times larger. PNM's general power class undoubtedly includes many of the larger commercial customers in BGE's commercial class. If PNM's general power class is compared with BGE's commercial class, the difference in gains to seasonal pricing is relatively larger for BGE's commercial customers. Similar conclusions hold for the industrial classes. All of these results are largely due to the fact that seasonal load differences are generally much larger for BGE's customers. This same fact makes the gains to time-of-day pricing (compared to seasonal pricing) relatively greater for PNM's customers.

Table 5-9
Optimal Seasonal Prices and Annual Welfare Gains from Optimal Seasonal Pricing for Average PNM Customer

	Optimal Seasonal Prices			*Annual Welfare Gain Present Prices to Optimal Seasonal Prices*
Class	*Summer*	*Winter*	*Shoulder*	
Residential	4.67¢	3.58¢	3.59¢	$1.99
Commercial	5.23	3.31	3.79	10.39
General power	5.03	3.46	3.69	523.63
Industrial	4.26	3.05	3.30	6,303.18

Welfare Gains from Optimal STD Pricing

Table 5–10 shows the possible welfare gains of going from optimal seasonal prices to optimal STD prices. The results are comparable to the BGE results given in tables 5–6 and 5–7. Taking into account the size differentials between the comparable average customers for these two utilities, the results are strikingly similar. The average residential customer for PNM is about 75 percent as large as BGE's average customer, and the annual welfare gain from STD pricing is about 68 percent as large. Similarly, PNM's average commercial customer is only about 30 percent as large as BGE's average commercial customer, and the welfare gain is about 30 percent as large too. PNM's average general power customer is 7.58 times larger than BGE's average commercial customer, and the welfare gain is about 7.3 times larger.

Thus, although full STD pricing cannot be justified for the average residential customer for PNM, certainly those residential customers with usage greater than, say, 140 percent of average would be reasonable candidates for it. Similarly, about the largest 60 to 70 percent of PNM's commercial class probably would find full STD pricing beneficial. On the other hand, all of PNM's general power and industrial customers would find full STD pricing beneficial.

Finally, relative to optimal seasonal pricing, there are larger welfare gains to be had from full STD pricing for PNM's customers as compared to BGE's customers. This conclusion is not surprising. PNM is not as strong a summer peaking utility as BGE is, so there are relatively more gains to be had from the time-of-day feature of full STD pricing.

Welfare Gains from Feasible STD Pricing

Comparisons of optimal seasonal pricing with optimal STD pricing may be somewhat academic. One can reasonably argue that neither of these alternatives is realistic under present institutional arrangements. Thus, we argue that regulatory practices should be adapted so that these alternatives become feasible. On the other hand, it is useful to see if full STD pricing can be justified where we consider the possible gains going from feasible seasonal prices to feasible STD prices.

Our example of PNM allows us to make this comparison because the company has actually proposed a set of seasonal and STD prices. (See the prices in the last two lines of the data for each class given in table 5–8.) The question to be asked then becomes, What will be the improvement in welfare for the average customer in each class going from the proposed non–STD, seasonal prices to the proposed full STD prices? Table 5–11 gives the results. It shows that the gain in welfare is slightly greater for the aver-

Table 5-10
Welfare Gains and Costs STD Pricing for Average PNM Customer

Class	*Annual*	*Present Value of Welfare Gains* [a]	*Present Value of Cost* [b]
Residential	$31.52	$147.59-213.04	$298.80
Commercial	73.84	345.76-99.08	322.80
General power	1.822.55	8.534.26-12,318.51	1,107.60
Industrial	22,114.88	103,552.05-149,474.48	1,107.60

[a] Assumes a twenty- and ten-year adjustment period to STD prices, respectively, and a 10 percent discount.
[b] See table 5-2.

Table 5-11
Feasible Annual Welfare Gains, PNM

Class	*Annual*	*Present Value of Welfare Gains* [a]	*Present Value of Costs* [b]
Residential	$28.12	$131.68-190.06	$298.80
Commercial	72.67	340.28-491.17	322.80
General power	794.27	3,719.13-5,368.49	1,107.60
Industrial	22,000.38	103,015.90-148,700.57	1,107.60

[a] Assumes a twenty- and ten-year adjustment period to STD prices, respectively, and a 10 percent discount rate.
[b] See table 5-2.

age customer in the general power class but slightly smaller for the other classes. None of these differences is significant, indicating that at least in the present case, the desirability of full STD pricing is not altered by considering the gains between proposed seasonal and STD prices.

Conclusions

Although our methodology and analysis are certainly not the final work on the subject of the desirability of STD pricing, we hope that we have focused the discussion on the scientific question by which the desirability of STD pricing can be judged. Based on our analysis, we offer the following conclusions.

1. Full STD pricing is beneficial for all customers in the industrial and large commercial classes. We do not believe that any reasonable alteration of our assumptions and methodology would overturn this conclusion.

2. The residential and small commercial classes of each utility need to be investigated before much can be said about the desirability of full STD prices for these users. Nevertheless, our analysis points out that up to 60 percent of these users are likely to be candidates for full STD pricing.

3. Although we should always try to implement optimal seasonal and STD prices, it is possible that such optimal prices are not politically feasible. In this case, the welfare analysis must be applied to determine the welfare improvement between feasible sets of prices. It is possible that the welfare improvement may justify full STD pricing, whereas that between optimal prices may not justify it.

4. There are potentially large improvements in economic welfare to be had from optimal seasonal pricing for utilities with strong seasonal peaks. Such pricing should be especially attractive for smaller users where the additional metering expense required for STD pricing is likely to appear relatively large.

Notes

1. Joskow and Noll (1978, p. 26).
2. See Wenders and Taylor (1976) and Wenders and Lyman (1977).
3. See Wenders and Taylor (1976) and Ramu Ramanathan (1977).
4. See National Economic Research Associates (1977).
5. In the electric utility industry, the capacity components of costs and prices are usually called *demand* costs and *demand* prices. This use of the term demand is different from economists' use of it. When this term is used as a substitute for capacity, we have placed it in quotes. Otherwise, we have used it in the usual economic sense.
6. The results presented in this section are discussed in more detail in Data Resources Inc. (1978).
7. See Public Service Company of New Mexico (1977).

6 Marginal Cost and Rate Structure Design for Retail Sales of Natural Gas

Colin C. Blaydon,
Wesley A. Magat and
Celia Thomas

The severe gas shortage of the 1976–1977 winter intensified interest in a problem that had begun to command attention as a result of the curtailment of interstate gas supplies in this country beginning in the early 1970s. The problem is one of allocation, and viewed from the perspective of a state utility or regulatory commission, it has two aspects. The first involves determining what possible sources of gas should be utilized in supplementing supplies to consumers whose primary source has been curtailed. These supplemental sources might include emergency purchases of unregulated gas (EP), which the Federal Energy Regulatory Commission (FERC) has been allowing gas distribution companies to make for several years, synthetic natural gas (SNG), and imported liquefied natural gas (LNG). The second aspect involves determining which customers should receive the gas that ultimately is provided.

This entire allocation problem is generally solved in our economy through the use of prices. The rate structure facing consumers of natural gas is, thus, the key to the question of determining and allocating available gas supplies at the state level. But economists have paid little attention to the problem of rate structure design for retail gas sales. Indeed, even with the drastic alteration in the relationship between sales and distribution capacity that has resulted from the recent curtailments, there has been no serious reexamination of retail gas pricing methodology. This lack of study contrasts sharply with the electric utility industry, which has made significant advances toward marginal-cost pricing through time-of-day rates.

We propose a methodology for retail gas rate design based on marginal cost pricing principles. The approach involves determining rates equal to marginal cost that clear gas demand with the available gas supplies and an adjustment to meet the revenue requirement. Only with price signals based on marginal cost can the most efficient use of a utility's gas supplies be obtained. When gas is underpriced, some consumers forego using alternative fuels, thereby depriving other customers of that gas, customers for whom there may exist only less suitable and more expensive alternatives and who would be willing to pay much more for gas than would the actual users. When gas is priced above its marginal cost, customers for whom gas should be the least-cost suitable source of energy are driven to a more costly alternative, such as propane or electricity. Rather than rely on marginal-cost-based rates, utilities commissions have relied on the administrative approach of priority systems to allocate gas to those customers who value it most highly, an approach that can only imperfectly accomplish the allocative function normally performed by prices.

Because marginal-cost pricing also conveys accurate information on the cost of supplemental supplies of gas, it is inconsistent with capital investment in new sources of supply, which entail a cost above the value of gas to consumers, and thus it reduces wasteful investments. Only under rolled-in prices that are below marginal cost, for example, could utilities expect to sell the large volumes of LNG that some are contemplating importing from Algeria.[1]

In many discussions of marginal-cost pricing, a state or a utility is advised to estimate the price of gas in a deregulated market and to base local gas rates on that estimate, thus pricing gas at the distribution level in a way that counters what is seen as the misallocation due to federal regulation. The approach we present here, however, accepts the constraints placed on the states by federal regulation of interstate gas prices. The perspective is that of the state or utility that is attempting to price its available supply of gas so as to achieve the optimal level of supply and the optimal distribution within its territory. As federal controls on interstate gas prices are loosened, this approach will continue to be applicable. The intrastate pricing mechanisms will then, moreover, be the primary determinants of allocative efficiency.

I. A Pricing Methodology

Criteria for Rate Design

Although good judgment must certainly be used in setting rates, the process is far from arbitrary. Rates serve two functions: they generate revenue, and they offer price signals to gas users that affect consumption decisions. Economists have agreed upon three primary criteria that should be used to judge how well these two functions are met by a set of rates: they must induce an economically efficient allocation, or use, of available gas supplies; the revenue requirement must be met; and rates should be fair in the sense of not being unduly discriminatory (Bonbright, 1961, pp. 287–316).

Economic efficiency requires that gas be purchased in that volume at which marginal cost equals marginal willingness to pay and that the gas purchased be distributed to those customers who most value it. Marginal costs provide a benchmark for setting rates. If rates need to be altered to meet the other criteria, then they should be varied in such a way as to cause the least distortion, or demand shifting, away from the economically efficient allocation. Like other public utilities, gas distribution companies must charge rates that will avoid undue or unjust discrimination; rates must be fair. Although some practitioners may argue, most economists agree that price discrimination occurs when different purchasers are charged prices that differ by varying proportions from the respective marginal costs of serving those customers (Kahn, 1970, 1:123). Thus setting rates equal to marginal cost is nondiscriminatory, and if rates must be modified from marginal cost to meet the revenue requirement, they should incorporate rate differentials generally reflective of differences in marginal cost.

The two primary criteria of economic efficiency and nondiscrimination imply that a gas utility's rates be based on marginal cost. We suggest using a rate design methodology based on three models: a supply model that determines marginal costs, a rate-setting model, and a demand model that allows adjustment to ensure that marginal-cost-based rates equate the supply and demand for gas.

The Supply Model

This model determines those quantities of supply and storage that minimize the cost of meeting seasonal demands for gas. This cost minimization is a principal objective of the state regulation of the gas utility. The year must be divided into multiple periods, where the simplest case would include a winter period (perhaps November—March) and a summer period (April–October). Demands in those two periods are provided by a demand model. Long-term contracts with a pipeline supplier would be expected to make up the bulk of gas supplies; however, most of these contracts are currently curtailed. The distribution companies take their maximum allowable contract volumes and then must either make emergency purchases of supplemental supplies in the intrastate markets or manufacture gas, such as SNG. In addition, they construct or contract for storage services that allow shifting of summer gas supplies to the winter period, when the shortage is most severe. The supply problem, then, is to minimize the cost of gas supplies (contract gas plus emergency purchases plus manufactured gas) and storage, subject to the constraints that demand must be met in each season. The particular advantage of this model, which represents the optimal planning decisions of a utility (given a set of demands), is that it directly identifies the marginal commodity costs of meeting seasonal demands: the cost of the least expensive method of supplying additional gas in each season.

Commodity cost (the cost incurred in obtaining and selling the gas itself, consisting primarily of the purchase price of gas) constitutes only one of the types of cost that can vary with the volume of gas supplied. Capacity cost (the cost of any new transmission and distribution capacity that a company would need to build in order to supply additional gas in any season) is also a component of the marginal cost of gas supply, as are operating costs that vary with the volume of gas distributed. In this period of extensive curtailments in purchased gas volumes, however, most companies are distributing substantially smaller volumes of gas than they were five years ago, and thus they have considerable excess capacity in their distribution network. For them, the marginal capacity cost is zero for a large range of additional gas volumes. In addition, operating costs, such as plant labor and energy that could vary with the volume of gas distributed, are essentially fixed over large ranges of supply volumes, resulting in a marginal operating cost that is insignificant.

It is thus evident that for most gas utilities, the only component of marginal cost based on volume as the marginal unit is the marginal commodity cost. The marginal cost generated by a supply model such as the one discussed above, and the example presented in appendix 6a, is the marginal commodity cost. In a situation where there is a positive marginal capacity cost, or the marginal operating cost is significant, the additional cost would need to be added to the marginal commodity cost to obtain the true marginal cost of satisfying an additional unit of demand. Determining marginal capacity cost in the case of no excess capacity requires determining the marginal cost of additional capacity for all those customers whom will ultimately be served. Although differences in marginal commodity cost exist only with respect to the period when the gas is demanded, marginal capacity cost may vary according to a customer's location and the geographical distribution of the company's customers in general. That issue is not addressed by the modeling of the supply problem presented here. When we use the term *marginal cost*, we refer to the marginal commodity cause, unless otherwise specified.

Some costs vary with the number of customers served rather than with the volume of gas distributed. Among them are costs such as those incurred in metering, billing, and the maintenance of the customers' individual service lines. These are called *customer costs* and are often billed to the customers in monthly fixed charges. They are truly marginal costs, where the marginal unit of analysis is the customer. Customer costs, however, being independent of gas volumes demanded or supplied, do not influence our rate-setting model and should be recovered through some charge completely independent of the amount of gas a customer consumes.

The Rate-Setting Model

The rate-setting model takes the marginal costs generated by the supply model and specifies a set of consumer prices, or rates, based on marginal costs. In the case where there are no marginal capacity costs or operating costs, the rates will be equal to the marginal commodity costs. The marginal commodity costs are given by the dual variables of the seasonal demand constraints in the supply model. They represent the minimum cost of supplying an additional unit of gas in the winter and in the summer.

The Demand Model

When solving the supply cost minimization problem, we assumed winter and summer demands to be fixed. Obviously winter and summer demands depend upon the rates charged, so the next step would be to estimate the demand functions for winter and summer demand.

There are two general approaches to this estimation problem. The engineering approach involves segmenting the market into customer groups with the same alternative fuel capabilities and determining the prices of gas equivalent to the prices of those alternative fuels. For example, the industrial market might be separated into those customers with no alternative fuel, those with propane as an alternative, those with number two fuel oil as an alternative, and those with heavy fuel oil as an alternative. Given the market segmentation, current demand for each segment, the prices of alternative fuels, and the capital investments needed to switch away from gas, the summer and winter demand curves can be estimated.[2] The second approach requires estimating an econometric model using time-series data on gas consumption within a state, cross-section data across states, or pooled time-series and cross-section data.

The Iterative Solution Process

To use the supply and demand models to set rates, an iterative procedure is needed to ensure that the summer and winter markets clear at the rates set by the rate model. First, current winter and summer consumption levels are used in the supply model to find the marginal costs associated with those demand levels. Then new demands are determined based on rates equal to those marginal costs. These new demand levels are substituted back into the supply model, and the entire process is repeated until rates are found that both clear the markets and equal marginal cost.[3]

Figure 6-1 illustrates this process. At the initial consumption level Q_o,

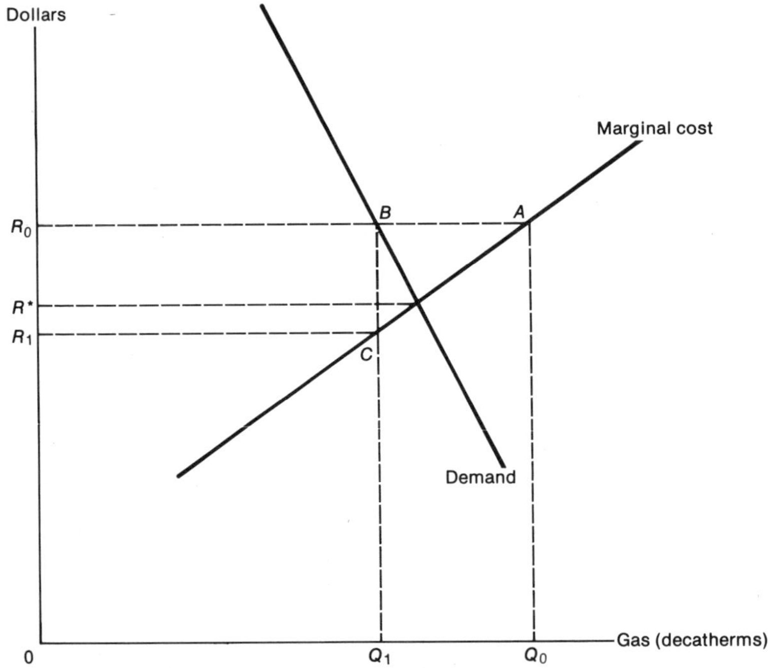

Figure 6-1. Price Determination

marginal cost is found to be AQ_o, so the rate R_o is set equal to AQ_o. At rate R_o demand equals Q_1, and marginal cost at this lower volume equals Q_1C. The new rate R_1 is set equal to Q_1C and the process iterates until at rate R^* demand equals the supply corresponding to a marginal cost of R^*.

The Structure of Marginal-Cost-Based Rates

Applying this methodology to the simplest case, the structure of the rates that result would consist of flat rates that are equal for all customer classes, a summer-winter differential, and a customer charge.[4]

Economic efficiency requires that all customers face the marginal cost of gas to the utility in making their consumption decisions. Marginal cost consists of the marginal commodity cost plus the marginal capacity cost plus the marginal operating cost. Since most gas utilities currently are supplying much less gas than they were selling five years ago before the massive curtailments of interstate shipments, they possess substantial excess capacity even in the winter, so no additional capacity need be built to supply more gas. In other words, if this situation does not change, the marginal capacity cost of the distribution system would be zero, as it is seen to be in the Piedmont Natural Gas Company example of the supply model in appendix 6A. Marginal operating costs are insignificant, so marginal cost is comprised only of the marginal commodity cost, and that does not vary between customers or with any customer's consumption level. Hence the rates should be flat and equal for all customer classes.[5]

As long as a utility must shift gas volumes from summer to winter through storage, the summer rates should be less than the winter rates by the amount of the marginal storage cost.[6] The Piedmont supply model (appendix 6A) illustrates such a differential. In that example, about two-thirds of the winter EP requirement must be purchased in the summer because of the uncertainty of EP gas availability in the winter and the need to match the schedule of daily supplies with daily demands. The cheapest way to meet an additional decatherm of winter demand is to store two-thirds of a decatherm of summer EP in WSS storage and to buy one-third of a decatherm of winter EP gas.[7] The marginal cost of gas in the winter is then the cost of EP gas plus two-thirds of the cost of WSS storage. Further, the cheapest way to meet an additional decatherm of summer demand is to store one less decatherm of the excess in summer supply (saving the WSS storage cost) and purchase one more decatherm of gas in the winter (at a cost equal to the EP price plus two-thirds the cost of WSS storage), for a net summer marginal cost of the EP price less one-third the cost of WSS storage. The resulting summer-winter differential is the marginal storage cost. For a proportion of summer EP purchases stored for winter use different from two-thirds of total winter EP needs, the summer-winter differential would still be equal to the marginal storage cost. Only the levels of the rates, not the differences between them, are affected by changes in that proportion in the case where there exists some excess gas supply in the summer, which is stored for winter use.

It is apparent that the proportion of EP gas that, to meet winter demand due to uncertainty, must be purchased in the summer and stored for winter use affects the relationship of marginal cost in the two periods, and thus, of rates, to the EP price. If this uncertainty did not exist under otherwise similar conditions, the cost of meeting an additional decatherm of winter demand would be the EP price. The cost of meeting an additional decatherm of summer demand would be the cost of storing one less decatherm of the excess in summer supply (a saving equal to the marginal storage cost) and purchasing one more decatherm of winter EP gas (a cost equal to the EP price). Adding those two components yields a summer marginal cost equal to the EP price less the marginal storage cost. The difference between that summer marginal cost and the winter marginal cost equal to the EP price is the marginal storage cost.

Finally, in the case where all emergency purchases of gas to meet winter demand must be made in the summer and stored, the winter marginal cost would be the EP price plus the marginal storage cost. The summer marginal cost would be the cost of supplying an additional decatherm in the winter—that is, the EP price plus marginal storage cost, less the savings realized from removing one decatherm of excess summer supply from storage—for a net summer marginal cost of the EP price and, again, a summer-winter differential equal to the marginal cost of storage.

This analysis depends on there being, as there was in the Piedmont example, an excess of summer gas supply over summer demand. When that is not the case, EP gas must be purchased to meet summer as well as winter demand, and all gas stored for winter use comes from emergency purchases in the summer. The marginal cost of summer gas would then be the EP price. The cost of an additional decatherm of winter gas would again be the EP price plus two-thirds (or three-fourths, or none or all, depending on what function of the winter EP requirement it is determined needs to be purchased in the summer and stored for winter use) of the marginal storage cost. The summer-winter differential in the case where there is no excess of summer supply over summer demand is dependent on the fraction of winter EP gas purchased in the summer and stored for winter use, and thus on the uncertainty in the EP market and the risk preferences of the decision makers.

Consider one final example of possible summer-winter differentials in marginal cost. In the case where there is no excess summer supply and no uncertainty over winter EP availability, the marginal costs in both the summer and winter would equal the EP price, and the differential would be zero.

In order to illustrate the customer charge component of the rate structure, we explicitly calculated the cost to Piedmont Natural Gas Company (exclusive of the cost of the gas) of serving an additional customer in each customer class. We found marginal customer costs of $4.01 per month for residential customers, $7.72 per month for general commercial and industrial customers, and $75.35 per month for industrial nonboiler customers.[8] In keeping with marginal cost pricing principles, these costs should be recovered in monthly customer charges.

II. Marginal-Cost-Based Rates and the Revenue Requirement

One approach to reconciling the revenue requirement with the revenues generated by marginal-cost-based rates is to use the inverse-elasticity rule, which is particularly easy to apply in the case of natural gas.[9] The rule dictates that rates be raised the most for those customer classes with the most inelastic demands, since the goal in modifying marginal-cost-based rates is to cause the smallest possible distortion in the gas allocation pattern. At prices that have prevailed historically, industrial and commercial demands have tended to be inelastic below the price of alternative fuels, at which point they can be expected to become highly elastic, while most studies have shown residential demand to be highly inelastic, at least in the short run. Thus a reasonable application of the rule would be to raise all rates equally, unless they reach the level of the equivalent price of alternative fuel for that customer class, in which case the rate would be set slightly below that alternative fuel cost.

Although not identifying their pricing policy as the inverse-elasticity rule, the American Gas Association (AGA) proposed the use of the "value of service" concept in rate making:

> Once the company has established the cost of serving a customer, the next consideration will be to determine the value of service to the customer, wherever possible, including the comparing of prices paid for competitive fuels, and giving consideration to certain inherent advantages of using gas. . . . Between the maximum level of value of service and the level of incremental cost of service, assuming the former is higher than the latter, is a so-called "zone of reasonableness." In practice, it is within this zone that rates are usually set. [AGA, 1969, p. 169]

Notice that the AGA agrees that if gas rates need to be raised above marginal (incremental) cost, they should be set below the elastic region of the demand curves (the maximum levels of value of service).

Setting rates that diverge from marginal cost in order to generate a particular amount of revenue requires an adaptation of the iterative solution process. The object becomes the maximization of the sum of consumer plus producer surpluses, subject to the constraint that costs are equal to the revenue recovered under the resulting rates. The extent to which the rates charged a particular customer class diverge from the marginal costs of supply will be seen to depend on the demand schedule of that group of customers, specifically on the price elasticity of their demand. At each iteration, the marginal costs would still be calculated for the given summer and winter demands; however, rates would be adjusted away from marginal costs using the inverse-elasticity rule. A less precise but simpler method of adjusting rates to meet the revenue requirement would be to allow the model to iterate to a set of rates based on marginal cost and then to adjust the rate faced by each class away from marginal cost according to the price elasticities of demand of the respective customer classes.

A second method of reconciling the revenue requirement with rates that face gas customers with the marginal cost of gas in making their purchase decisions is to use a block rate structure, fixing the tail blocks at marginal cost and raising or lowering the initial blocks. Since demand should respond primarily to the tail block rate (the customer's marginal cost), variations in the initial blocks would allow generation of more or less revenue with little change in sales.

In practice, this approach presents several problems. The block structure would have to be designed so that the first block for every customer would not exceed that customer's usage in any month, thus requiring many more rate schedules than currently exist. Residential heating customers might have to be classified under one schedule in the winter and a different one in the summer. Also this approach could lead to an unacceptable added revenue burden on some customer classes, since it would be difficult to spread the added revenue burden fairly across all customer classes and even within customer classes. In addition, distortions in usage would continue to exist if gas users base consumption decisions upon the average of the costs of gas purchased in all blocks rather than just on the tail block rate (the marginal cost).

A third approach would be to adjust customer charges away from the marginal customer cost. Consider the situation requiring an increase in customer charges. Aside from the problem of equitably spreading the burden of the extra customer charges across all customers, this approach exacerbates the often-observed consumer resistance to any form of a customer charge, even one based on marginal customer costs.

A final approach would be to close the revenue shortfall through some form of charge or subsidy, which would not be based on current consumption levels. This method should eliminate any distortion in consumption patterns. One proposal that has been suggested would be to base charges on consumption levels in some previous year. However, the inequities involved with such an approach would be prohibitive. The utilities commission would need to decide how to adjust charges for those families who were out of town during the base year, or whose family size changed, or who moved into another house or apartment. And there would be no easy method of revising the base year for the computation of charges without affecting current usage decisions, since consumers would quickly recognize that higher consumption in one period would result in higher charges in future periods.

III. Further Issues

Interruptible Sales

The temperature sensitivity of the winter demand for gas requires that in order to serve their customers with firm demand in colder than average winters, utilities purchase more gas than would be needed under normal weather conditions. These firm demand customers are defined for North Carolina as those in priorities 1 and 2 under the priority curtailment plan established by the state utilities commission.[10] The plan gives a higher priority of receiving gas in periods of limited supply to customers with limited alternative fuel capabilities. In North Carolina, gas companies are allowed to make commitments for sufficient gas to serve customers in priorities 1 and 2 in a winter that is a specified percentage colder than average (a design winter). These priorities include residential and commercial customers, as well as industrial process users. Customers in priorities 3–9 are classified as interruptible customers. Whereas service to any customer is potentially interruptible, customers in the lower priorities are, by definition, most likely to experience an interruption in their ability to purchase gas under the existing priority system. They have full alternative capabilities and are able to purchase gas only when firm customers do not demand the entire quantity of gas which was purchased for their possible use. Priorities 3–9 consist of those industrial customers with nonboiler uses of greater than fifty mcf per day and industrial customers who use gas as a boiler fuel.

The safety margin seen in the supply model would equal the amount of excess gas available for sale to these interruptible customers under less severe than design weather conditions. If by midwinter the utilities recognize that they will have excess gas available due to warmer than design weather, then they should sell the excess supplies to interruptible customers as long as they will receive more than the summer marginal cost of gas. The excess gas should be sold at a rate that maximizes the revenue from its sale. Because of the shape of industrial demand for these interruptible sales, this implies that the gas should be sold at a rate slightly below the cost of the alternative fuel. In this one-year model, if the summer marginal cost of gas exceeds the interruptible rate set in the above manner, then the gas should simply be stored because the savings from lower levels of gas purchases in the next year would exceed the revenues from the sale of the excess supply of gas.

Reflecting Peak Costs in Winter Rates

The supply model presented here differentiates between costs of supplying demand in different periods only to the extent of revealing a possible summer-winter differential in marginal cost. We have abstracted from a finer definition of peak periods out of the awareness that imposing a summer-winter rate differential would be a major institutional change in the structure of gas rates for most states and from a desire to propose a methodology entirely consistent with current metering technology. It is doubtful that differences in marginal cost among the seven summer months would justify a further differential within the summer period. Yet marginal costs do vary across the five winter months, and it is important to address the question of how those differences can be reflected in the winter rates so as to encourage the efficient usage of gas that results from rates reflecting differences in marginal cost.

A straightforward approach to achieving that efficiency, which is consistent with the preceding analysis, would be to confront customers in each subperiod within the winter period with the marginal cost of consuming in that subperiod. But this approach is currently infeasible because it would entail substantial changes in rate structure, metering, and billing practices. Such a set of rates might become feasible under a regulatory system that is comfortable with marginal cost pricing of gas and that had already instituted a summer–winter differential. Another constraining factor at this time is the fact that meters in most states are read on continuous and overlapping intervals. That is, different customers are under different billing cycles, so to institute one rate for, say, November, and a different one for December would mean that most customers would face more than one rate for one billing cycle. To devise a billing system under which they would be aware what rate they were facing on every day of the billing cycle would be a considerable task. We suggest, therefore, a methodology for computing a single winter rate that reflects differences in marginal cost during subperiods within the winter period.

The definition of the winter subperiods is based on temperature differences, not on time distinctions. Thus it is not necessary that the days within a subperiod follow continuously one after another. Noncontinuity of subperiod days poses no problem for a planning model such as this one, which combines the marginal costs of the respective subperiods into one winter rate. Such noncontinuity could, however, render the model invalid as an operating model, since not all sources of supply and storage can be utilized on a noncontinuous basis.

In formulating this winter rate, we are seeking to combine the marginal costs of supply during the subperiods in the way that will cause the least shifting from the levels of demand that would have prevailed had each subperiod been confronted with its marginal cost of supply. Turvey and Anderson, and Roberts have demonstrated that the optimal single winter price is obtained by weighting the marginal costs in the subperiods by the slopes of the respective demand schedules of the subperiods. These weights are equal to dQ_i/dP for each subperiod, where price P changes in each subperiod by the same amount dP and P is equal for all periods. This analysis assumes, as well, zero cross-elasticities of demand with respect to other goods. In the absence of information on the slopes of the subperiod demand schedules, we suggest approximating those slope weights by demand quantity weights for the different subperiods (Turvey and Anderson, 1977, pp. 338–339; Roberts, 1978, pp. 18–21). Since the ratio of slopes equals the product of the ratio of quantities times the ratio of elasticities, the accuracy of substituting quantity weights for slopes weights is dependent upon some stability across subperiods of the elasticity of demand. Unfortunately, an empirical measurement of the subperiod demand elasticities would be extremely difficult, so we have little choice other than using the ration of subperiod quantities to approximate the ratio of their demand function slopes.

Appendix 6B provides an example of the calculation of winter rates equal to the quantity-weighted average of the marginal costs during five subperiods of the winter period for the Public Service Company of North Carolina.

Multiyear Models

The supply models described in appendixes 6A and 6B consider only a one-year planning horizon, so they cannot prescribe investment decisions by the utilities. A multiyear model could examine relationships between the supply and demand conditions in different years and thus provide answers to questions regarding capital investments. Rather than simply determining the optimal use of an existing SNG plant or LNG plant, for example, it could determine the optimal level of investment in SNG production facilities and LNG storage plant for the distribution company over an extended planning horizon. Unfortunately, a multiyear model requires estimates of future supply prices and supply availability of all sources of gas, which are so highly uncertain that they severely limit the usefulness of this approach.

Pipeline Tracking Increases

The rate-setting methodology will work well in the design of rates for the test year; however, higher costs that the pipeline companies incur for gas are regularly passed on to the utilities through tracking increases, which raise their revenue requirements. In the next five years, contract gas supplies may increase, allowing the utilities to earn a higher profit margin on sales and helping to offset the effect of higher prices of contract gas. Even so, revenue requirements may rise faster than the marginal costs.

The net result could be that without rate cases, rates would be automatically adjusted upward to reflect the tracking increases for purchased gas. Typically utilities commissions allow the utilities to add a purchased gas adjustment to each decatherm of gas sold to recoup the tracking cost increases. This adjustment mechanism could raise rates above marginal cost. As long as demand is highly inelastic for all customer classes, these adjustments will cause little resource misallocation; however, continual increases could raise the small industrial rates above the equivalent cost or propane, causing a large reduction in demand. In addition, the rates for interruptible sales to nonboiler fuel industrial customers could be raised above the equivalent cost of number two fuel oil, making it impossible for the utilities to sell excess gas supplies in warmer than design weather years.

There is no easy answer to the problem of how to pass on tracking increases. At the current level of rates, the purchased gas adjustment surcharge probably will work reasonably well if rates are set in anticipation of expected tracking increases in the next couple of years. With the currently rapid state of change in the cost of purchased gas and the federal regulatory environment, utilities commissions will be forced to examine rate structures regularly to ensure that purchase of gas adjustments and changing supply conditions have not drastically altered the relationship among rates, marginal costs, and the equivalent costs of alternative fuels.

Notes

1. Here we are referring to LNG used to supplement normal supplies of gas during the entire winter period, and not to cheaper supplemental supplies, such as emergency purchase gas, currently available.

2. For two examples of the use of the engineering approach, see Glower, Goldstone, and Kelly, (1976), and Czamanski, Henderson, Kelly, and Detweiler (1977).

3. We are assuming that the process converges. A sufficient condition is that the elasticity of the marginal cost curve exceed the elasticity of the demand curve (in absolute value). Since we use a linear programming supply model, marginal cost is a step function, so along any segment the elasticity is infinite and convergence is guaranteed.

4. In this simple case, there are two seasons and only two available types of gas supplies—pipeline contract gas and emergency purchases.

5. It is not actually necessary that the rates be flat, provided that the rate faced by each customer for a marginal unit of consumption be equal to the marginal cost of gas. It may be desirable to have a block structure to adjust for a revenue requirement. It is, however, difficult to design nonflat rates that face everyone with price equal to marginal cost at their marginal units of consumption. Because of the wide variations in levels of consumption and usage patterns among customers, many rate schedules would be required.

6. This result of a summer-winter differential equal to the marginal storage cost agrees with the finding in Gravelle (1976).

7. WSS is a large storage field owned by Transcontinental Pipeline Company. See appendix 6A for more information.

8. See prepared testimony of Wesley A. Magat for North Carolina Utilities Commission (NCUC) Docket no. G-9, Sub 176, Exhibit I, for the assumptions underlying these calculations.

9. See, for example, Baumol and Bradford (1970), and Sherman and Visscher (chap. 7 to this book).

10. This plan is established under NCUC Rule No. R-6-19.2.

Appendix 6A The Supply Model: An Example

As an example of how the supply model is used to determine marginal costs, we include such a model of a North Carolina distribution company, the Piedmont Natural Gas Company. The Piedmont model is a planning model because it considers Piedmont's basic supply decisions to be made far enough in advance for the company to be able to vary its emergency gas purchase volumes and part of its storage contract volumes with changes in its expected demand and in its estimates of the supply conditions that it will face in the modeled year. This is, however, a one-period model, incapable of handling decisions such as investment in an SNG plant. Further, the model presented in this appendix assumes all sources of gas supply and storage classified as peaking sources to be fixed and solves for the volumes of other sources of gas supply and storage that meet the balances of winter and and summer demand. It is assumed that incremental changes in total winter demand do not require a change in the amount of peaking gas. Thus, the marginal costs of an additional decatherm of gas in the winter and in the summer can be determined without addressing the question of the cost-minimizing quantity of peaking storage capacity. This is a strong assumption, since an increase in demand in November might be met at a low marginal cost relative to the cost of supplying additional gas during a January cold spell when all the company's available sources of supply were being used. This assumption is relaxed in our peaking periods supply model in appendix 6B:

The Piedmont model is as follows:

Minimize

$E^W_W, E^W_S, E^S_S,$ $\quad P^W_E \cdot E^W_W + P^S_E \cdot E^W_S + P^S_E \cdot E^S_S \quad P_{WSS} \cdot WSS_N$

$WSS_N, WSS_E,$ $\quad + 0.02 \cdot WSS_N \cdot P^S_E + P_{WSS} \cdot WSS_E$

GSS_N, GSS_E $\quad + 0.02 \cdot WSS_E \cdot P^S_E + P_{GSS} \cdot GSS_N + P_{GSS} \cdot GSS_E$

subject to $\quad C^W + L^W + (E^W_W + E^W_S) + ED^W + LPG$

$$+ .995 \cdot WSS_N + GSS_N + LNG + LGA + PS$$

$$- 2 \geq X^W(1 + a) + U^W$$

$$C^S + L^S + E_S^S + ED^S - 1.015 \cdot WSS_N - GSS_N - - LNG - LGA \geq X^S + U^S$$

$$E_S^W = b(E_W^W + E_S^W)$$

$$.98 \cdot WSS_E + GSS_E = E_S^W$$

$$GSS_N + GSS_E \leq L_{GSS}$$

Definitions

P_E^W = price of *EP* gas in winter ($\$/Dt$)[= \$2.79 to \$3.34]

E_W^W = *EP* gas purchases in winter for winter use (Dt)

P_E^S = price of *EP* gas in summer ($\$/Dt$)[= \$2.79 to \$3.34]

E_S^W = gas available for winter use from *EP* purchases in summer (Dt)

E_S^S = *EP* gas purchases in summer for summer use (Dt)

P_{WSS} = yearly price of *WSS* storage ($\$/Dt$)[= \$0.42]

WSS_N = volume of *WSS* storage *not* used for storing E_S^W (Dt)

WSS_E = volume of *EP* gas used for injection of E_S^W into *WSS* storage (Dt)

P_{GSS} = yearly price of *GSS** storage (S/Dt)[= 0.02]

GSS_N = volume of *GSS* storage *not* used for storing E_S^W (Dt)

GSS_E = volume of *GSS* storage used for storing E_S^W (Dt)

C^W = winter *CD* – 2** supply (Dt)[= 10,358,065]

L^W = winter *LSS* – 1** supply (Dt)[= 2,319,135]

ED^W = winter gas supply from Piedmont Exploration and Development [= 92,702]

**WSS* and *GSS* are large storage fields owned by the Transcontinental Pipeline Company (Transco), which leases capacity in the fields to distribution companies such as Piedmont.

***CD*-2 and *LSS*-1 are contracts with Transco for flowing pipeline gas.

LPG = winter gas supply from propane–air plant (Dt)[= 51,250]

LNG = volume of LNG*** storage (Dt)[= 800,525]

LGA = volume of LGA*** storage (Dt)[= 56,841]

PS–2 = volume of PS–2**** storage (Dt)[= 140,425]

X^w = winter demand under normal weather (Dt)

a = fraction by which design weather demand exceeds normal demand [$X^w(I + a) = 17{,}989{,}824$]

U^w = company use and unaccounted for gas in winter (Dt)[= 520,157]

C^s = summer CD–2 supply (Dt)[= 8,658,373]

L^s = summer LSS–1 supply (Dt)[= 2,120,262]

ED^s = summer gas supply from Piedmont Exploration and Development (Dt)[= 124,395]

X^s = summer demand (Dt)[= 9,451,431]

U^s = company use and unaccounted for gas in summer (Dt)[= 9,451,431]

L_{GSS} = capacity limit for GSS storage contract (Dt)[= 3,157,940]

b = fraction of total winter EP gas supply that must be purchased in summer [= 2/3]

The objective function reflects the company's desire to supply whatever level of demand it might face with the least-cost combination of sources of gas supply and storage. The total commodity cost incurred by the distribution company depends on the volumes of each source of supply and storage, as well as their respective prices. The prices are exogenous to the company. Volumes of gas supply and storage classified as peaking sources are considered fixed in this model and thus do not enter the objective function. The

***LNG and LGA are peaking storages.

****PS–2 is a contract with Transco for flowing gas to meet peak winter demands.

severely curtailed sources of pipeline supply, CD-2 and LSS-1, are used by the company in the volumes for which they are available since they constitute the least expensive source of gas for the company. Because Piedmont is unable to purchase CD-2 and LSS-1 beyond the curtailed volumes, those sources do not appear in the objective function. Thus with volumes of peaking supply and storage, volumes of curtailed sources of supply, and all prices exogenous to the supply model, the company's minimization of commodity costs is dependent upon the volumes of the remaining sources of supply and storage chosen. The sources of supply are summer and winter purchases of emergency gas, and the storage sources consist of the WSS and GSS storage fields.

The first constraint requires that out of winter CD-2 and LSS-1 purchases, emergency gas purchased for winter use, winter supplies from Piedmont Exploration and Development, gas from the propane-air plant, and storage, Piedmont be able to meet its normal winter demand, plus an allowance for company use and unaccounted-for gas and a safety margin in the event of design weather. The second constraint requires that out of summer CD-2 and LSS-1 purchases, emergency gas purchased for summer use, and summer supplies from Piedmont Exploration and Development, Piedmont be capable of meeting its summer demand, plus an allowance for company use and unaccounted-for gas, plus volumes of WSS, GSS, LNG, and LGA gas injected into storage. No safety margin is needed because of the small degree of temperature sensitivity of summer demand. The third and fourth constraints require that a fraction of all emergency gas planned for use in the winter be purchased in the summer and stored until winter. For a utility such as Piedmont Natural Gas Company, which must purchase a significant portion of its winter gas needs in the EP market, the difficulties of guaranteeing a regular schedule of EP deliveries throughout the winter necessitate the purchase of some of its winter needs in the preceding summer and then storing this gas in either WSS or GSS storage until winter use. Due to the WSS fuel charges, only about 98 percent of the EP gas purchased for WSS_E storage is withdrawn for consumption. The fifth constraint recognizes that Piedmont cannot store more gas in the GSS field than permitted under its contract with Transco. Unlike the WSS field, Transco's GSS storage field is filled, so Piedmont cannot expand the level of its GSS storage contract.

CD-2 and LSS-1 gas supplies are drastically curtailed, so purchases beyond the summer and winter curtailed volumes are impossible. The company's estimates of supplies from Piedmont Exploration and Development are also assumed to be at maximum levels. LPG and PS-2 gas are used to meet the demand during a few peak days in the winter, so they are treated as fixed for the purpose of meeting total winter demand. In addition, LGA and LNG storage is purchased to meet peaking demand, not to transfer summer gas to the winter to meet the total winter demand, so this storage too is considered as fixed for the purpose of meeting total winter demand. Thus the only variables under the company's control to meet total summer demand and total winter demand are emergency gas purchases and WSS and GSS storage. The supply planning model determines those quantities of EP purchases and WSS and GSS storage that minimize the cost of meeting winter and summer demand.

This model is based on estimated demand for the year November 1978 through October 1979, as well as current best projections of CD–2 supplies, LSS–1 supplies, E and D supplies, LPG supply, LNG supply, LGA supply, PS–2 supply, current WSS and GSS storage costs, and best estimates of EP prices. Piedmont's gas supply volumes have been allocated in this problem on the basis of 77.3 percent to its North Carolina customers and 22.7 percent to South Carolina. Storage capacity has been allocated 78.11 percent and 21.89 percent for each type of storage to customers in North Carolina and South Carolina, respectively. Thus these calculations consider only 77.3 percent of the company's total supply volumes and 78.11 percent of its total storage.

WSS storage costs $0.45 per decatherm of storage per year. The full storage cost of having an additional decatherm available from WSS storage would, however, exceed $0.45 due to Transco's WSS fuel charge. Piedmont must purchase 101.5 percent of its WSS storage contract in order to cover a 1.5 percent fuel loss on injection. In addition, due to a 0.5 percent fuel loss on withdrawal, the company withdraws only 99.5 percent of its WSS storage. These two fuel losses require that Piedmont purchase an additional 2 percent of a decatherm of EP gas for each additional decatherm of WSS storage that it desires. Thus the full storage cost of WSS is $0.45/Dt, plus the cost of 2 percent of a decatherm of EP gas. At an EP price of about $3.00/Dt, that would be $0.45 plus $0.06, or $0.51/Dt. We are taking the GSS storage demand and storage capacity charges to be fixed costs at the 3,157,940 Dt contract level, so GSS storage up to this limit costs $0.02/Dt for injection and withdrawal. Each emergency gas purchase is made at a different price, but recent purchases have been in the range of $2.00/Dt to $2.50/Dt in the intrastate market, so after adding the transportation and fuel charges and the gross–receipts tax, EP gas can be expected to cost Piedmont between $2,79/Dt and $3.34/Dt.

The winter and summer levels of company use and unaccounted–for gas are calculated by prorating the total test–year level of company use and unaccounted–for gas by the length of the winter and summer periods. The safety margin for winter supply is designed to meet design weather. The determination of the optimal level of the safety constraint is a problem that has stimulated considerable discussion. We have abstracted in our model from making this difficult determination by using the margin adopted by the utilities commission in North Carolina. For an examination of the question of public utility pricing under uncertainty, see Crew and Kleindorfer (1976, 1978).

The summer demand constraint shows that the sum of summer CD-2 supply, summer LSS-1 supply, and summer E and D supply exceeds summer demand by 427,320 Dt. This amount is stored in the least-cost manner—in this case, in GSS storage—to be used to help meet winter demand. The winter demand constraint requires that EP gas be purchased to fill the 5,007,337 Dt shortfall between the available supply from CD-2 gas, LSS-1, E and D gas, LPG gas, LNG storage, LGA storage, the 427,320 Dt of gas stored in GSS from excess summer supply, and the winter demand.

Since about two-thirds of this winter EP requirement must be available from summer EP purchases, all of the remaining GSS storage capacity and a significant volume of WSS storage are needed to store this EP gas until the winter. For every additional decatherm of winter demand, summer EP purchases yielding two-thirds of a decatherm of gas will have to be stored in WSS until the winter. The marginal cost of gas in the winter, therefore, is the cost of EP gas, plus two-thirds of the full cost of WSS storage ($0.34). The cheapest way to meet an additional decatherm of summer demand is to store one less decatherm of the excess in summer supply (saving the full WSS storage cost of $0.51) and purchase one more decatherm of gas in the winter (at a cost equal to the EP price plus $0.34), for a net cost of the EP price less about $0.17. Thus the marginal cost of winter gas exceeds the marginal cost of summer gas by $0.51.

Since the nonenergy operating costs of supplying gas are fixed within a range of test-year demands, no additional operating cost need be included in marginal commodity cost. Given the range of EP gas costs, in the summer marginal commodity cost ranges from $2.62/Dt to $3.17/Dt and the winter marginal commodity cost ranges from $3.13/Dt to $3.68/Dt. If we were to take the middle price in the range of likely EP gas prices, the summer marginal commodity cost would be $2.89/Dt, and the winter marginal commodity cost would be $3.40/Dt.

Appendix 6B Another Supply Model Incorporating Peaking Supply Decisions

For public Service Company of North Carolina, we have constructed a supply model of the winter period 1977–1978 from which to obtain the respective marginal costs of supplying gas in the different subperiods. The breakdown into five subperiods was chosen after examination of the load duration curve for Public Service Company, which reveals five relatively homogeneous subperiods. The periods are as follows, ranging from coldest needle-peak days to the least cold—period 1, 5 coldest days; period 2, 5 next-coldest days; period 3, 15 next-coldest days; period 4, 25 next-coldest days; and period 5, 101 next coldest days—for a total of 151 days in the winter period. The model is described in detail in appendix II of Blaydon, Magat, and Thomas (1978).

The model yields the following marginal costs in the five subperiods: subperiod 1, \$3.88/Dt; subperiod 2, \$3.88/Dt; subperiod 3, \$3.88/Dt; subperiod 4, \$3.72/Dt; and subperiod 5, \$3.27/Dt. The marginal cost is highest in the three coldest subperiods because the most expensive sources of supply and storage are needed to meet those peak demands. One might expect to be able to determine the marginal cost of a subperiod directly by observing what source of supply or storage would be needed to meet the marginal unit of demand in that subperiod. For example, LNG storage would be used to obtain additional gas supplies in subperiods 1, 2, and 3. The nature of the constraints of this particular model, however, prevents the observation of marginal cost by rudimentary inspection. By constraining gas from WSS storage to be consumed evenly over all but the peak five winter days and constraining winter EP purchases to be equal to one-half of summer EP purchases stored for winter use, our model requires that for a decatherm of EP gas purchased to meet marginal demand in the 101-day winter subperiod, two decatherms of EP gas be purchased in the summer and stored for winter use. Part of the gas stored in WSS will be available for consumption in three colder subperiods. The model thus finds a marginal cost for the 101-day subperiod that reflects the cost of making summer as well as winter emergency purchases and reflects the cost savings in the colder subperiods that result from replacing more expensive marginal sources of supply with the gas that is necessarily made available from supplying marginal units in the 101-day subperiod.

The five marginal costs determined by the model must be weighted by the relative demands of the respective subperiods to achieve an average rate that can be charged for the entire winter period. These weightings were obtained for Public Service Company's load duration curve (Blaydon, Magat, and Thomas, 1978, p. 50). In determining one winter rate for all customers, the following weights were used—subperiod 1, 950,000/16,205,000 = 0.059; subperiod 2, 806,250/16,205,000 = 0.505; subperiod 3, 3,168,750/16,205,000 = 0.135; subperiod 4, 3,168,750/16,205,500 = 0.196; and subperiod 5, 9.077,375/16,205,000 = 0.560—where 950,000 is the total number of decatherms demanded in subperiod 1, 806,250 is the total number of decatherms demanded in subperiod 2, and so forth. The number of decatherms demanded in the entire winter period is 16,205,500. The average winter rate is thus 0.059($3.88) + 0.050($3.88) + 0.135 ($3.88) + 0.196($3.27) + 0.560($3.27) = $3.42/Dt. It is interesting to compare this rate with the winter rate of $3.41/Dt that would be calculated for Public Service Company without considering the subperiods separately. Thus for this example (only), the incorporation of peaking supply decisions into the supply planning model did not significantly affect the winter rate.

Inspection of the load duration curve of Public Service Company reveals that the percentage of consumption in different subperiods varies across customer classes. Even accepting the constraint that the winter rate cannot vary within the winter period, the inefficiency caused by this constraint can be reduced by allowing the winter rates for each customer class to differ. One does, therefore, more fully capture the efficient consumption signals of marginal-cost pricing by setting different rates for the different customer classes, based on their relative levels of consumption during the five subperiods. If the marginal cost of serving customers during the winter period varies across classes because some classes of customers demand a higher proportion of their gas during peak periods when marginal cost is higher, then their rates would reflect their more costly consumption pattern.

Applying the same procedure to each of three customer classes separately produces the following set of rates:

Residential: 0.061(3.88) + 0.050(3.88) + 0.131(3.88) + 0.184(3.27) + 0.574(3.27) = $3.42/Dt.

Commercial and small industrial: 0.058(3.88) + 0.050(3.88) + 0.141 (3.88) + 0.212(3.27) + 0.539(3.27) = $3.42/Dt.

Process industrial: 0.020(3.88) + 0.023(3.88) + 0.061(3.88) + 0.097 (3.72) + 0.799(3.27) = $3.33/Dt.

This method results in a slight decrease in the rate charged to industrial users. A model such as this would be most needed in the case where there exists substantial differentiation among the marginal costs of serving customers in different subperiods during the winter, a situation that does not occur in the Public Service example. However, only from an analysis of the supply and demand conditions of the individual subperiods, such as is obtained with this model, can the proper degree of differentiation be determined.

This example contradicts the finding in the text of this chapter that rates should not differ across customer classes, which was based on a simpler model with only two seasons and fixed peaking supplies. Our previous result is still correct. In general, rates should be equal for all customer classes because the marginal customer costs are equal. However, if the limitations of metering technology require that rates be calculated using a weighted average of several different subperiod marginal costs, then the criterion of economic efficiency suggests that rates vary across customer classes when the classes' load factors are different.

7 Rate-of-Return Regulation and Price Structure

Roger Sherman and
Michael L. Visscher

For two main reasons, rate-of-return regulation has not been much concerned with the structure of prices. First, in the history of regulation, the dominant question for many years was whether the state could intervene to control prices, rates, or fees charged, not how it should be done.[1] When attention was turned to the question of how to regulate price, the main issue was that of limiting monopoly profit, so allowing an overall fair rate of return was set out as guideline for the level of price, without regard for rate structure.[2] Second, economic theory would not reject out of hand as undesirable the result of all monopolistic urges where the rate structure is concerned. A monopolist can be very efficient in raising money from consumers, and that skill might be used in rate design to benefit society. Specifically, in those natural-monopoly circumstances of decreasing average cost, a multiproduct monopoly would set relative unit prices by roughly the same considerations as a budget-constrained, welfare-maximizing public enterprise (that is, where profit margins are inversely related to demand elasticities).[3] The monopoly would set all rates higher, to be sure, but the ideal prices would be some constant fraction of the monopolist's prices. Thus the monopolist tends to depart from marginal cost in a socially desirable way, and one might think that tendency could be harnessed by allowing the monopoly discretion in proposing the structure of rates.

A little more than fifteen years ago, the motives of regulated firms were shown to be distorted by the process of rate-of-return regulation. Although most attention has been focused on the input inefficiency they diagnosed, Averch and Johnson (1962) pointed out that the rate-of-return regulated producer of two (or more) products or services could have perverse incentives to expand into other industries. Wellisz (1963) illustrated the same inefficiency consequences at about the same time and noted that rate-of-return regulation could discourage peak-load pricing. There may be scope for even more serious distortions where complicated multipart tariffs are concerned. An overall profit limit thus may not adequately constrain the firm to price optimally, in part because the rate-of-return regulation intended to effect that limit may at the same time invite distortions in price structures. Lack of attention to price structure may have permitted important economic inefficiencies to be introduced in regulation and to persist.

Of course, other theories, about rate structure which are more political than economic, stress the regulator's aims. For example, Stigler (1971) has argued, with some empirical supports, that regulators choose rates to maximize political support. By this argument, they set low rates that will affect consumers who are likely to be most vocal in protest and they set high the rates that impinge on more passive and powerless consumers.[4] On the other hand, Posner (1971) has described regulators as redistributors of income, taxing some users with high rates and subsidizing others in turn with low rates. That institutions which guide public utility regulation today allow scope for such outcomes is owed partly to the fact that little attention has been given to rate structure itself.

We shall confine our attention here to the narrower economic treatment of rate-of-return regulation and its implications. The situations we examine are kept simple. Rigidities in law or regulatory institutions that prevent better pricing incentives or controls are not examined. The allowed rate of return is assumed always to be above the cost of capital but below the monopoly rate of return as in earlier studies in the Averch-Johnson mold. And regulation is assumed to be continuous, without the problems and opportunities that arise with regulatory lag.

Our aim is to review principles of rate structure efficiency and observe whether firms subject to rate of regulation are motivated to serve efficiency through their price choices. We shall look at three categories of pricing: relative prices (really profit margins) in multiproduct firms, peak and off-peak prices, and two-part prices. We shall also look at implications of the rate structure for the form and nature of a public utility service to illustrate the importance of price structure itself beyond the question of market-by-market efficiency.

I. A Single Price for Each Product in the Rate-of-Return Regulated Multiproduct Firm

A well-established benchmark for optimal prices in the multiproduct firm comes from Marcel Boiteux's early analysis of the public enterprise that faces decreasing average costs in producing its products but must still break even (or is subject to some other profit or loss constraint) and so cannot price at marginal cost.[5] The enterprise, in an abstract representation of a static economy, chooses optimal profit margins that are inversely proportional to demand elasticities for its various products. Such prices cause the smallest possible amount of inefficiency, compared with prices that equal marginal costs. A rate-of-return regulated firm is similar to this public enterprise insofar as the firm faces decreasing average costs and is constrained to cover cost, where the allowed rate of return represents capital cost. Ideally the public utility would follow similar pricing rules. For each of i products or services, the pricing rule would be $(p_i - mc_i)/p_i = A/\eta_i$ for all i, where p_i is price, mc is marginal cost, $\eta_i = -(dx_i/dp_i)p_i/x_i$ is elasticity of demand for the product or service (cross-elasticities are assumed to be zero),[6] and A is a constant between 0 and 1 that will allow the firm to satisfy its budget constraint.[7]

It is easy to derive the above pricing rule from a simple model that can indicate economic welfare in some way. Suppose the regulated enterprise produces only two goods in quantities x_1 and x_2. Let us assume that production and consumption of other goods in the economy will not be much affected by outputs of x_1 and x_2, so we may focus on social welfare as if it stemmed only from the regulated firm's production, everything else remaining the same. Then social welfare, W, from production of x_1 and x_2, can be represented as consumer willingness to pay from each good less the cost of producing each good—$W = S(x_1, x_2) - \beta(k_1x_1 + k_2x_2)$—where S is total consumer willingness to pay, k_i $(i = 1,2)$ is the amount of the sole input, capital, and β is the cost per unit of capital needed per unit of x_i produced. Such a measure as W is widely used to represent welfare (Baumol and Bradford, 1970). Willingness to pay less cost essentially captures the sum of consumer surplus and producer surplus. In addition to the independence of x_1 and x_2 from each other and the rest of the economy in their effects, this welfare measure requires an assumption about income distribution: changes in income distribution do not matter; any gain in money benefits is counted the same, no matter who receives it. That assumption yields $\partial S/\partial x_i = p_i$ (Mohring, 1970), and thus the simple marginal effect of x_i on welfare, $\partial W/\partial x_i = p_i - \beta k_i$.

Now consider the problem of maximizing welfare, W, subject to the constraint that the firm's revenues exceed costs by an amount C (which may be zero or negative). To find a rule that will solve this problem, construct the Lagrangian function G: $G = W + \lambda[p_1x_1 + p_2x_2 - \beta(k_1x_1 + k_2x_2) - C]$. And on maximizing G with respect to x_i, we can obtain,

$$\frac{p_i - \beta k_i}{p_i} = \left[\frac{\lambda}{1 + \lambda}\right]\frac{1}{\eta_i}, \qquad i = 1, 2, \qquad (7.1)$$

which is equivalent to the rule above; βk_i is now the marginal cost of production mc_i, and the ratio involving the Lagrange multiplier, $\lambda/(1 + \lambda)$, now replaces the constant, A.

Let us inquire whether rate-of-return regulation of a profit-maximizing monopolist will reach the ideal set of prices revealed in expression 7.1. We can form the monopolist's constrained profit maximizing Lagrangian, *M*, as

$$M = p_1x_1 + p_2x_2 - \beta(k_1x_1 + k_2x_2) + \mu[p_1x_1 + p_2x_2 - \beta(k_1x_1 + k_2x_2) - B],$$

where *B* is the allowed return to capital and μ is the Lagrange multiplier attached to the constraint that limits profit to that rate of return. On maximizing *M* with respect to x_i we obtain,

$$\frac{p_i - \beta k_i}{p_i} = \frac{1}{\eta_i} - \frac{\mu}{1 - \mu} \cdot \frac{(B - \beta)k_i}{p_i}. \quad (7.2)$$

This equation obviously differs in form from 7.1. The equations are difficult to compare, of course, because the Lagrange multipliers λ and μ differ, but we can see that the rate-of-return regulated firm will not satisfy the welfare-maximizing pricing rule in equation 7.1. In equation 7.2, rather than depending on elasticity alone (plus the constant), the markup $(p_i - \beta k_i)/p_i$ will vary also with $(B - \beta)k_i/p_i$. Goods requiring more capital per unit of output price will be favored with lower markups as long as $B > \beta$.[8] Further, a positive constant term, $\mu/(1 - \mu)$, is applied to this adjustment-for-capital term in 7.2, and no such factor is applied to the inverse of demand elasticity as it was in 7.1. Thus, rate-of-return regulation interferes with the otherwise desirable efficiency of monopolists in extracting payments from consumers.

Besides this distorting effect of rate-of-return regulation on efficient pricing, there is another reason why regulation might be extended to the design of rate structure. Our welfare pricing rule in equation 7.1 is derived from a static certainty model in which markets can always be cleared. When uncertainty is present and prices must be chosen before demand is known, as they must be in virtually all regulated industries, the static rule that shows monopoly incentives to be socially useful is no longer entirely applicable.[9] If uncertainty is present, the monopoly remains indifference about who is served in those inevitable instances when demand exceeds capacity. Yet social welfare calls for some effort to distinguish among consumers to accomodate those who value the service most. Even if making such distinctions among consumers is not possible, the optimal welfare maximizing prices will reflect the role of price in partly sorting out consumers who value the good or service most. The monopolists who can charge only one price will not attempt such distinctions (Sherman and Visscher, 1978a). Furthermore, the optimal reliability of service will not be chosen either (see Crew and Kleindorfer, chapter 9 to this book).

Since the motives of the regulated firm will not lead reliably to optimal prices, one wonders how effectively regulators can insist on socially desirable rate structures. Here we encounter the same problem that receives inadequate attention in the regulation of profit level. The capacity of the regulator either to know and control cost or to design incentive schemes under rate-of-return regulation that lead the firm to minimize cost at optimal output levels is not great. Not only is the detection of inefficient factor utilization inherently difficult, as Crew and Kleindorfer (chapter 9) show, but the rate-of-return regulated firm has little incentive to correct a factor or output bias. With its control over the definition of cost, the firm can achieve its preferred rate structure even if the regulator prescribes relations between prices and costs. By choosing cost definitions, the firm preserves enough discretion to obtain its desired rate structure.

II. Peak-Load Pricing in the Rate-of-Return Regulated Firm

We know that where capacity is scarce, prices should generally be higher in periods of high demands and lower in periods of low demands.[10] To reflect marginal cost, the prices should vary with demand in this way because those who combine their demands together at the peak time determine the maximum level of capacity, and so they should bear the cost of marginal capacity additions. Those who use capacity at off-peak times make no such marginal demand on capacity. When a range of technologies exists—some appropriate for peak times only, some appropriate at all times, and some appropriate when demands are uncertain so that peak and off-peak demands cannot be predicted perfectly—Crew and Kleindorfer (1975a, 1976) have shown that such simple pricing rules will not be adequate. But even with this modification for realistic technology and uncertainty, the ideal prices will still reflect the added marginal cost in higher prices in peak times than in off-peak times.

An example will show how rate-of-return regulation can lead the firm away from peak-load pricing. Consider a simple case in which demands in peak and off-peak periods are independent. The peak demand is so much greater that even when price is set to recover all capacity cost from peak users (so no capacity cost is assessed off-peak users), the off-peak users still would not use all capacity. This is what Steiner (1957) would call the "firm-peak" case, the case that Davidson (1955) originally analyzed.

We use subscript 1 to identify peak price, p_1, and rate of output, x_1. The fraction of time over the cycle during which peak demand is in effect of a, b i marginal cost, k is the capacity limit in either period, and β is the cost of the capital. The appropriate Lagrangian H for the profit maximization problem is then $H = ap_1x_1 + (1 - a)p_2x_2 - b(ax_1 + (1 - a)x_2)\ \beta k + \Psi_1(k - ax_1) + \Psi_2(k - (1 - a)x_2)$, where Ψ_1 and Ψ_2 are Lagrange multipliers on the peak and off-peak capacity constraints. (We already noted that we expect $\Psi_2 = 0$ because off-peak demand will not be limited by capacity.) The profit-maximizing monopolist would set p_i so that

$$\frac{p_i - b - \Psi_i}{p_i} = \frac{1}{\eta_i}, \tag{7.3}$$

where η_i is price elasticity of demand in the ith period. At the peak, when capacity is limited, the multiplier Ψ_1 would equal the cost of capacity β, so the monopoly solution would reflect long-run marginal cost; at off-peak times, with $\Psi_2 = 0$, only short-run profit maximizing would occur. Monopolistic pricing occurs at both peak and off-peak times, for expression 7.3 sets the profit margin (price minus marginal cost over price) equal to the reciprocal of demand elasticity. The marginal cost in peak periods is $b + \beta$, and price then will be $p_1 = (b + \beta)\eta_1/(\eta_1 - 1)$. At off-peak times the capacity limit is not binding, so $\Psi_2 = 0$. Thus, long-run capacity cost can be ignored by the monopolist at off-peak times, when it will choose the price $p_2 = b\eta_2/(\eta_2 - 1)$.

Turning to the task of finding prices to maximize social welfare as depending only on the goods x_1 and x_2—in this case, peak and off-peak consumption of the good or service under consideration. Welfare can be pursued by maximizing the sum of consumer surplus and producer surplus for those two goods. For maximizing consumer surplus plus producer surplus by choice of prices and capacity, it is easy to find ideal peak and off-peak prices in this situation (Williamson, 1966). The peak price will equal the sum of operating and capacity cost. The off-peak price will equal only b, the operating cost. Thus welfare-maximizing prices will be $p_1 = b + \beta$ and $p_2 = b$. These ideal prices reflect marginal costs at peak and off-peak times.

The rate-of-return regulated firm would try to maximize profit as in Lagrangian H above but would be subject to the added constraint, $\alpha p_1 x_1 + (1 - \alpha)p_2 x_2 - b(\alpha x_1 + (1 - \alpha)x_2) \leq Bk$, where B is the allowed rate of return on capital. Differentiating the resulting problem (with Φ the Lagrange multiplier on this latter constraint) with respect to prices and capacity we find the regulated firm's pricing rule for the peak times to be

$$\frac{p_1 - b - \beta}{p_1} = \frac{1}{\eta_1} - \frac{\Phi}{1 - \Phi}\,\frac{(B - \beta)}{p_1}. \tag{7.4}$$

The off-peak price remains as in 7.3 with $\Psi_2 = 0$, which yields the short-run profit maximum. The derivative of this problem with respect to capacity, when set equal to zero, implies that $\Phi = \beta/B - \Psi_1/B$. Since we know $\Phi > 0$ and $\Psi_1 > 0$, we therefore know that $\Phi < \beta/B$ (and we also know that $\Psi_1 = \beta - \Phi B < \beta$). With the allowed rate of return exceeding the cost of capital, or $B > \beta$, this means $\Phi < 1$ so the last term that is subtracted on the right in 7.4 is positive, and the peak-load price therefore will be reduced by rate-of-return regulation. The regulated firm thus takes the full effect of rate-of-return regulation at peak times, when its added customers will justify more capacity, and behaves just like an unregulated monopolist at off-peak times to earn profit that its large peak capacity will entitle it to keep.

Thus the rate-of-return regulated firm is not motivated to adopt welfare-maximizing, peak-load pricing. This lack of socially desirable motivation was described clearly by Wellisz (1963) and elaborated also by Bailey (1972), so we shall not pursue it further here. Let us simply note that because the profit of the rate-of-return regulated firm is limited according to the capital it uses, an allowed rate of return set above the cost of capital can invite use of large amounts of capital to justify keeping profit earned at off-peak times. A rate-of-return regulated firm facing peak and off-peak demands may simply set a monopoly price at off-peak periods to earn high profit and in order to be allowed to keep that profit will expand peak capacity while keeping the peak price low enough to warrant the expansion. A single price often is in effect at both peak and off-peak times, especially in the electric utility industry. That result is consistent with these distorted peak-load pricing incentives created by rate-of-return regulation that call for a higher-than-optimal off-peak price and a lower-than-optimal peak price.

III. Two-part Tariffs in the Rate-of-Return Regulated Firm

Relatively little attention has been given to the way that regulation may effect the most obvious monopoly abuses of rate structure: two-part (or multipart) tariffs and declining block rates. It is well known that a monopoly will be tempted to employ such rate structures in order to raise more revenue from consumers than would otherwise be possible. Such rate structures are common in electricity, communications, and other industries where rate-of-return regulation is in effect, so the lack of attention to possible abuses is surprising.

The analysis of complex rate structures is not easy because consumer responses to two or more prices, including the decision whether to be a consumer of a service, are hard to represent. Oi (1971) presented a very useful analysis.[11] More general nonlinear rate structures, called nonlinear outlay schedules, have also been carefully examined.[12] Optimal two-part tariffs for budget-constrained enterprises have even been provided (Ng and Weisser, 1974). But no general treatment of how rate-of-return regulation might affect such rate structures is currently available.

As a simple illustration, consider the case of only one consumer, who is choosing between a service x and an alternative good, c, where the firm supplying x charges a fixed fee p_0 plus a fee per unit of x consumed, p_1. Profit, π, is $p_0 + p_1x - \beta x$, where β is the cost of producing x, represented entirely as capital cost. As Oi has shown (1971), the firm maximizing profit will set $p_1 = \beta$ and collect all of the single consumer's surplus through p_0. The firm realizes that it cannot push the consumer to a lower level of satisfaction than he can reach by spending all of his income on the other good, c. Thus the monopolist wants to adjust p_1 and p_0 in order to maximize profit while keeping the consumer buying x.

Keeping the consumer buying x requires that as p_1 is varied, p_0 be adjusted also, so that in buying x, the consumer will not be expected to move to an indifference curve, or level of utility, lower than the one he can achieve by spending all of his income on c. Then for a profit maximum, we must have

$$\partial \pi / \partial x = \frac{dp_0}{dp_1} \cdot \frac{dp_1}{dx} + p_1 + x\frac{dp_1}{dx} - \beta = 0.$$

Because p_0 is a lump sum payment, we can expect $dp_0/dp_1 = -x$, just as the derivative of the income constraint with respect to p_1 would be $-x$. The result that $p_1 = \beta$ then follows directly from the necessary condition immediately above.

Now let us introduce regulation that will limit the monopolist's profit, to obtain the regulated firm's prices so we can compare them with what we know of the requirements for welfare maximization. Suppose profit is limited by a constraint of the form

$$p_0 + p_1x \leq Bx. \tag{7.5}$$

Since producing x requires only capital, the constraint limit profit to the amount B per unit of x is like setting an allowed rate-of-return constraint. When constraint 7.5 is added to form a Lagrangian with multiplier ω, on maximizing it with respect to x, we find the rule for p_1 to be

$$\frac{p_1 - \beta}{p_1} = - \frac{\omega}{1 - \omega} \cdot \frac{(B - \beta)}{p_1}. \tag{7.6}$$

Since $\omega/(1 - \omega)$ is positive (see Bailey, 1972), $B - \beta > 0$ implies that p_1 will be set less than β, or below marginal cost. In that way, the firm can collect profit through a higher fixed price p_0 and be entitled to keep it by expanding output, x, thereby raising its allowed profit.

Some effects of rate-of-return regulation on two-part tariffs are evident from this example. If the allowed rate of return exceeds the cost of capital, which in this example is represented by $B > \beta$, the firm will wish to exaggerate that aspect of consumption that requires the most capital. If as in this example above, more capital per dollar of revenue is needed to produce marginal units of the service (where the variable charge p_1 is relevant) than is needed to connect a consumer for service (where the fixed charge p_0 is relevant), the regulated firm can be expected to set a relatively lower variable fee; more consumtion per consumer will be encouraged. This case could induce the firm to offer declining block rates even in the absence of the genuine decreasing-average-cost technologies that could justify their use. On the other hand, if less capital per dollar of revenue is needed to produce electricity than to add another customer, then we should expect the fixed fee to be biased downward and the variable fee to be biased upward. More complicated block-rate structures also could lead to the same kinds of effects, of course, over more than the two prices we have used here for simplicity.

Causal empirical evidence is not clear on this point. Block rate structures that are common in electric utilities would be more profitable if capital were associated primarily with service. However, considering total accounts for all private U.S. electric utilities, the book value of capital that is devoted to electricity generation actually is less than the book value of capital devoted to transmission and distribution. If the latter is taken to imply a high marginal capital need per customer, we might expect a bias toward low fixed fees. It is difficult to estimate generally the marginal capital requirement for a customer, however, because transmission or distribution equipment is not always limiting. Indeed, the marginal capital cost may differ markedly from the average capital cost per customer. Any predictions about specific pricing distortions therefore must await further analysis of the capital needed for a marginal unit of electricity or an added customer.

When a complex rate structure is available for adjustment by the firm, it is evident that rate-of-return regulation gives much less control to the regulator than might appear. The main problem is that the firm can put monopolistic ingredients in its price structure merely by having freedom to design a multipart rate structure. In the multiproduct case when there was only one price for each product, there was an argument that this monopolistic instinct could serve society, for then, if uncertainty of demand could be ignored, the monopolist's pricing rule was a constant multiple of the socially optimal rule. With two-part tariffs, the monopoly solution and the social optimum are also related in a simple way (Sherman and Visscher, 1978b). But as in the case of the multiproduct firm, rate-of-return regulation will distort the pricing rules of the firm away from the ideal ones. In keeping with the capital needs traceable as consequences of the different elements of the rate structure, the firm will modify optimal pricing rules in an effort to increase its allowed profit. In the end, a rate structure with monopolistic elements will be used to raise more money from consumers, money that can be kept in part as allowed profit by the firm clever enough to choose a rate structure that increases the amount of capital it uses.

Effects of regulatory lag have been omitted from our analysis here. We should not, however, that Joskow (1974) has pointed out how the presence of rapid inflation might lead electric utilities to alter multipart price structures so they yield more revenue from usage is increasing more with time than is the number of customers. He observed a trend toward "flatter" rate structures, where "average revenue should decline more slowly over time as average consumption per customer increases" (ibid., p. 322). Therefore, an effect of rate-of-return regulation we have not considered may be influencing the relative prices charged per customer and per unit of output.

Although the role of two-part tariffs (or more complicated tariffs) can be important, the effect that rate-of-return regulation may have on them remains largely unexplored. The problem of determining such tariffs is serious, of course, especially for a firm kept by regulation from experimenting freely, so actual profit gains through the manipulations we sketch here may be small. Political considerations also may weigh more heavily in the design of complex rate structures than profit considerations. On the other hand, the industry's reluctance to abandon declining block rates might still be due to rate-of-return regulation. More work is clearly needed to uncover unwanted perverse incentives in rate structure design that rate-of-return regulation may cause.

IV. The Rate Structure Defines the Product

This discussion about possible effects of rate-of-return regulation on price structure has so far been concerned with whether each product or service of a regulated firm is priced efficiently. We have asked whether prices represent true marginal opportunity costs or, if they do not, whether departures from marginal cost are chosen in keeping with some social goal. Rate-of-return regulation can interfere with such pricing goals because capital intensity can be influenced by price structure choices and rate-of-return regulation invites capital intensity. Thus, by failing to deal with rate structure, rate-of-return regulation does not provide adequate control over firm performance.

The price structure problem is not confined to welfare losses caused by simple pricing inefficiencies of well-defined products or services, however. In some cases the right product or service characteristics may not even be priced, because a rate-of-return regulated firm will emphasize certain elements that might be priced and will deemphasize others. For instance, the regulated firm's lack of incentive to conserve capital will discourage it from peak-load pricing. Indeed, the firm may not even introduce pricing by time periods. What is called interruptible service may be an even better way to deal with peaking problems than peak-load pricing.[13] It allows consumers to indicate, and pay for, the maximum level of service they wish to be assured. Then when demand is strong, the consumers will have their usage levels cut back to the maximum levels for which they contracted. The rate-of-return constrained, profit-maximizing monopoly does not have great incentive to distinguish among consumers efficiently like this to conserve scarce capacity, however, and so interruptible service is another possible choice that may be denied us.

Price structures may not portray for consumers the full range of opportunities available. The consumer simply is not asked to make some choices, and by that fact alone the range of consumer choice is cut. This is so because the shape of the service can be seriously affected by the aspects of choice in which it is expressed and offered to consumers. Any failure of regulation to deal with the question of price structure is important, then, not simply because prices may be set at levels that are not optimal but also because the elements of products or services that are priced may not be the best ones. So products and services can be defined inadequately for ideal pricing, before the pricing task itself is even undertaken.

Pricing is combined with other decisions that affect the situation we observed, and wrong pricing may make the ideal solution unobservable. By failing to offer peak and off-peak prices, for example, a regulated firm also will experience a different demand load during the typical day or year. As a result, the particular combination of equipment that is chosen is not likely to be the same as the optimal equipment combination. Marginal costs at peak and off-peak times ordinarily will be affected by the technical choices, so marginal cost calculations cannot yield truly correct answers. A similar problem can arise with two-part tariffs, when the number of customers and the usage per customer both differ from choices that would follow under ideal pricing. When wrong prices are joined with wrong facilities, it is impossible to see what genuine ideal prices would be because observed costs are not those that would result with an optimal choice of production and other facilities.

Remedies for this problem of product quality definition by price structure are not easy to find, for distortions in product or service definition can be caused by too much, as well as too little, oversight of price structure. Airline rates were set over many years by a systematic Civil Aeronautics Board procedure, for example, which required all airlines connecting any two cities to charge the same fare.[14] Apart from whether the resulting single price might be judged either too high or too low, the single price led to a single quality level, and that itself had drawbacks. Some consumers might happily fly in a slower airplane, without a meal, and even without a confirmed reservation, if the fare was sufficiently reduced. The responses to Freddy Laker's Skytrain service and to the recent flexible pricing policies of the Civil Aeronautics Board indicate that many air-travel consumers actually are interested in lower-priced, lower-quality options, but they had been denied them for years by regulatory policies.

All we can do here is point out that when rate-of-return regulation brings inefficient pricing structures, the consequences are not simply wrong prices but also wrong production and other facilities, wrong service qualities, or wrong bundles of product characteristics in the services offered. There is a qualitative aspect to the problem that goes beyond effects of the price levels and feeds back to affect the definitions of products or services, the technologies chosen, and thus the very determinants of costs and prices.

V. Conclusion

We have reviewed here the major categories of price structures to observe effects of rate-of-return regulation. All are based on the assumption that the allowed rate of return exceeds the firm's cost of capital. When single prices are charged for separate multiple products or services of the regulated firm, there arises a bias favoring lower prices for the more capital-intensive products or services. In cases where peak-load pricing would improve efficiency, the rate-of-return regulated firm may not employ it because the firm prefers a low price at peak times to justify the use of more capital. The rate-of-return regulated firm also can adjust multipart tariffs in subtle ways to induce a greater use of capital per dollar of revenue in the production process. In all of these cases, socially optimal pricing rules are modified. The rules that result under rate-of-return regulation are given in equations 7.2, 7.4, and 7.6. The modified rules give a role to the excess of the allowed rate of return over the cost of capital that socially optimal pricing rules would ignore. And these pricing distortions, which may be sizable in individual cases, have an effect beyond price alone. They can alter the definition of what is offered to consumers as a service. The design of a service and the shape it finally takes depend very much on what aspects of it are priced and thus what choices the consumer is allowed to make. Prices also influence technological choices, which in turn affect costs and definitions of service in ways that make remedies difficult.

Our analyses have used simple models of continous regulation and assumed throughout that the allowed rate of return exceeded the cost of capital, and constant-returns-to-scale technology was assumed. In actuality, the regulatory process is far more complex than such portrayals will allow. Although some of these complexities, like the lag in reaching regulatory decisions, may augment incentives to operate efficiently and to price efficiently, many others are apt to introduce still more distortions of price structure away from true costs. Costs are recorded in accounting rather than economic terms (like current market value), for instance, and inflation quickly makes the accounting terms faulty as true economic cost measures for regulation. But how these practices affect price structure can vary from circumstance to circumstance, so we have not examined them. The influences we have reviewed are systematic, uniform in favoring higher capital, and almost certainly unfair as well as costly in efficiency. Remedies will not be easy to find, but we should at least be looking.

Notes

1. See Munn v. Illinois, 94 U.S. 133 (1877), which established the right of a state government to intervene and set prices where the public interest warranted.

2. The fair return aim was set out initially in Smyth v. Ames, 169 U.S. 466 (1898) and put into the rate-of-return form that is still the guideline today in Federal Power Commission v. Hope Natural Gas Co., 320 U.S. 591 (1944).

3. For a review of these pricing principles, see Baumol and Bradford (1970).

4. See also Peltzman's (1976) analysis of political influence on rate structure.

5. A translation by Baumol and Bradford of Boiteux's 1956 paper is available as Boiteux (1971).

6. For analysis of nonzero cross-elasticities among products of the regulated industry and also with products in unregulated industries, see Sherman and George (1979).

7. At $A = 0$, we should have marginal cost pricing, the standard presumably achieved by a competitive economy; at $A = 1$, we should have a monopolist's solution to the pricing problem.

8. Averch and Johnson (1962, pp. 1058–1067) described a possibly perverse result using a telephone and telegraph example. But instead of looking directly at pricing, they stressed how the regulated firm would be tempted to expand into other markets, perhaps even at a loss, so the capital base could be increased and the original market exploited further. The same kind of analysis was examined in more detail by Needy (1975) and by Peles and Sheshinski (1976).

9. Regulation tends to force this result by requiring that prices be

approved in advance and then adhered to in all transactions. But even without regulation, the prices for many services such as electricity, communications, and transportation could not easily be adjusted quickly in response to current conditions. Consumers simply cannot be informed of unpredictable price changes, and even when that would be possible, they often cannot make short-run responses to the changed prices.

10. This result is demonstrated for stochastic demand in Sherman and Visscher (1978a). See Williamson (1966) for an exposition of the peak-load problem under static certainty conditions. For a thorough description of peak-load pricing principles and applications, see Mitchell, Manning, and Acton (1978).

11. See also Buchanan (1953).

12. See Willig (1978) and Brito and Oakland (1978).

13. Pricing rules for firms offering interruptible service are given in Marchand (1974).

14. For a critical analysis of this regulatory practice, see Douglas and Miller (1974). A more general analysis is provided by Sheshinski (1976). Recent developments in CAB policy are described by Bailey (chapter 2 of this book).

8 Peak-Load Pricing and Regulatory Accountability

Gerald R. Faulhaber

The social desirability of pervasive regulation of the traditional public utilities has recently been called into serious question. Economists and others argue that the competitive marketplace can act as a much more effective spur to efficient, innovative, and customer-responsive supply than the cumbersome process of regulation. Other, more cynical observers question whether regulatory-sanctioned competition, as we have observed in the motor and rail freight industry under Interstate Commerce Commission jurisdiction, will result in any benefits. In counterpoint to this theme of increased competition, we also hear the tune of increased accountability on the part of established utilities, particularly in the Federal Communications Commission's (FCC) regulation of interstate telecommunications. In principle, increased accountability is an important complement to increased competition. The rates of established carriers must be monitored by regulators to ensure that franchised services are not subsidizing carrier services subject to competition, thereby ensuring new entrants a fair shake.

This goal is certainly laudable, but what has it meant in practice? As a result of the FCC's findings in docket 18128, Bell is required to produce on an annual basis realized revenues and costs for its services and to calculate rates of return for each service. The earnings ratios of each service could be compared and services earning more or less than their fair share can be identified. But what are these costs used in calculating these alleged earnings ratio? First, the costs involved are historical ones. Second, the nature of the technology for the provision of communications dictates that much of the costs are common or joint among a number of services; the procedures applicable to these costs for report card purposes are to allocate these common costs, or overhead costs, to each service. In short, were this process used by the FCC to prescribe rates explicitly or implicitly, there is no reason to suspect that the resulting rates would reflect any economic reality whatsoever. Hence the ability of the established carriers to compete in a dynamic, responsive marketplace may be seriously hampered.

This problem is not unique to the telecommunications industry. Any industry subject to price regulation and pervasive product-by-product ex

This chapter reflects the views and opinions of only the author, and not the views of the American Telephone and Telegraph Company or the Bell system.

post accountability faces the possibility of serious price distortions. Without the spur of competition, however, such distortions tend to go undetected (but nevertheless incur welfare loss). In the presence of competition, the perceived need of accountability is greater and its difficulties more obvious.

My purpose here is not to analyze whether lowering entry barriers is a good idea but to explore whether firms can meet the requirements of both the marketplace and of accountability and how the public fares as a result. I explore these questions within the context of a specific problem—peak-load pricing—which highlights the difficulties in handling common costs. Specifically, this paper is organized as:

1. reiteration of the welfare result of the classic peak-load model;
2. analysis of the competitive equilibrium in this model;
3. demonstration that in principle the utility can be held accountable *ex post* for efficient pricing, using observables only;
4. discussion of cost allocation and accountability in practice, and what distortions are likely to result;
5. analysis of a dynamic instability which can arise with a naive regulatory price adjustment mechanism, with any allocation method.

I. The Classic Peak-Load Solution

The basic peak-load pricing problem was analyzed by Steiner (1957) over twenty years ago, and its solution is well known.[1] To review the Steiner assumptions,

1. The demand function for a nonstorable commodity varies over the time period (day, month, year).
2. The time period can be divided into subperiods (hours, days, weeks) within which the demand function does not vary.
3. A different price can be charged for each of the subperiods.
4. The technology of supply is fixed proportions, constant returns to scale, with capacity (≡ capital) fixed over the time period; that is,

$$C(q_1, \ldots, q_T) = \beta \cdot \max\{q_1, \ldots, q_T\} + b \sum_{i=1} q_i.$$

5. Pareto-efficient prices are characterized by $p_i = b$ when i = off-peak hour ($q_i < q_{max}$), $p_j > b$ when j = peak hour ($q_j = q_{max}$), and $\Sigma(p_j - b) = \beta$ when $q_j = q_{max}$ and j = peak.

In other words, efficient time-of-day (assuming the full day is the relevant time period) prices have off-peak prices at variable costs and on-peak prices individually covering variable costs and in aggregate covering capacity costs.

To many observers, peak pricing appears to be rather drastic. In capacity-intensive industries such as telecommunications, a large fraction of the costs are loaded to the peak user, while the off-peak user enjoys the benefit of the capacity while bearing none of the cost. Hence, the peak-load pricing role is seen by the practitioner as both drastic and unfair.

The key to understanding the pricing rule is to bear in mind that demand in each subperiod is responsive to price, generally more than we think. As peak prices are increased and off-peak prices are decreased (thinking of a price change from uniform to peak prices as a continuous process), peak demand shrinks and off-peak demand increases, ultimately resulting in more hours becoming peak hours and thus spreading those capacity costs over more consumers. However, the rationale that I find most appealing is that peak pricing exerts maximum pressure to level the load across times of the day and thus make the maximum use of the capacity. Therefore, peak pricing leads to the most efficient use of resources. The recent energy shortage has made regulatory commissions more amenable to such arguments for electricity rates.

Steiner's work limits itself to a public monopoly situation, however, with no consideration of competitive entry. Furthermore, he ignores the peculiar regulatory fantasy of basing prices on fully allocated costs, but for those who must operate in the regulated sector, these are issues that must be dealt with. I therefore extend the Steiner model to include the possibility of competitive entry, analyzing the sustainability of time-of-day pricing. Simultaneously, I examine the prices achievable through cost allocation methods. I then examine whether a carrier can be held accountable ex post by the allocation process, using observables only. Surprisingly, accountability is indeed possible but not with currently popular allocation methods. In fact, this scenario could lead to serious price instabilities of a long-run nature.

Entry and Sustainability

For ease of exposition, the discussion is limited to a two-subperiod model; each period is of equal length. The demands in subperiods 1 and 2 are q_1 and q_2, respectively, with demand in each subperiod dependent upon both prices, p_1 and p_2. The results for an arbitrary number of subperiods are identical. I maintain the assumption of the Steiner technology—$C(q_1,q_2)$ =

$\beta \cdot \max(q_1, q_2) + b \cdot (q_1 + q_2)$—although some important caveats should be noted. The Steiner technology is at best only a poor first-order approximation to the realities of telecommunications and probably an even poorer approximation for electricity generation. I use it here as the simplest model that reflects the key aspects of time-of-day pricing. Even given the Steiner technology, the observed values of capacity cost β and operating costs b may be seriously distorted from the economic costs by certain regulatory conventions. For example, the separations process in common carrier communications assigns certain state jurisdiction costs to interstate operations, primarily on the basis of total usage. As such, these separations costs appear as variable costs. This convention has the result of understating capacity costs and overstating variable costs, perhaps by significant amounts.[2]

The utility here supplies service at prices p_1, p_2, which yield demands of q_1 and q_2 (the subscripting convention is $q_1 \geq q_2$; if prices are such that the peak shifts, so do the subscripts), operates efficiently, meets all demands at that price, and just realizes zero economic profit, thus meeting its revenue requirement.

$$\sum p_i q_i = \beta \cdot q_i + b \cdot \sum q_i \tag{8.1}$$

Suppose another firm were contemplating market entry, and its capacity and operating costs were β' and b', respectively. It can choose to enter one or both markets (say, the set S of subperiods, $S \subseteq \{1,2\}$), and choose its prices in those markets. We shall assume that the necessary and sufficient conditions for entry to occur are:

There exists an $S \subseteq \{1,2\}$, a p_i', $i \in S$, and a $\bar{q}_i \leq q_i'$, $i \in S$, such that

$$p_i' \leq p_i \tag{8.2}$$

for all $i \in S$, with strict inequality for at least one $i \in S$, and

$$\sum_{i \in S} p_i' \cdot \bar{q}_i \geqq \beta' \cdot \max_{S} \{\bar{q}_i\} + b' \cdot \sum_{S} \bar{q}_i . \tag{8.3}$$

The firm can successfully enter if and only if it can underprice the utility in at least one of its markets (subperiods) and serve some or all of the demand thus generated profitably.

Under what circumstances will successful entry take place? First, suppose the utility chooses an off-peak price strictly less than variable costs: $p_2 < b$, in order to meet the revenue requirement, $p_1 > b + \beta$. An entrant could then choose to compete only during the peak hour with a price $p_1' < p_1$, and the operation would be profitable if and only if $p_1' \geqq b' + \beta'$. In other words, successful entry would occur whenever $\beta' + b' < p_1$.

Clearly, this situation could encourage wasteful entry in two ways: a producer with higher unit costs could be encouraged to enter if $p_1 > \beta' + b' > \beta + b$, and even if the entrant had the same costs, the selective entry would result in duplication of capacity, with the entrant building capacity to handle peak demand and the utility maintaining at least some of its capacity to handle off-peak demand.

Clearly, $p_2 < b$ and $p_1 > b + \beta$ is a strategy that is detrimental to both the utility and to society as a whole. This pricing strategy is neither sustainable nor welfare optimal. Suppose the utility adopted a strategy of $p_2 > b$ and, consequently, $p_1 < b + \beta$. The potential entrant could then build capacity to handle a demand of q_2 (in either hour, of course); set $p_2' = p_2 - \epsilon$ by pricing slightly below the off-peak price of the utility in order to obtain all of the utility's off-peak demand (our assumption is that consumers will switch for any price difference; thus we may assume that the price difference is effectively zero); or set p_1' to ensure nonnegative profits for the entrant:

$$p_1' \geqq \beta' + b' - (p_2' - b') = \beta' + b' - (p_2 - b') \tag{8.4}$$

and serve $\bar{q}_1 = q_2$, thus utilitzing fully in both hours the entrants' capacity for q_2 calls. Of course, this would result in an unmet peak-hour demand of $q_1 - \bar{q}_1$, which the entrant leaves for the utility to supply.

This pricing strategy of the entrant firm will be successful only if its peak-hour price, p_1', is less than the utility's peak-hour price, p_1, thereby permitting the entrant firm to capture the base demand, $\bar{q}_1 = q_2$. This will only be possible if (from equations 8.1 and 8.4)

$$\beta' + b' - (p_2 - b') < p_1 = \beta + b - (p_2 - b) \cdot \left[{}^{q_2}/_{q_1} \right].$$

By hypothesis, $p_2 > b$, and hence $p_1 < \beta + b$. Let us further assume that at these prices, the utility does not have a joint peak ($q_1 > q_2$). Then successful entry can occur if

$$\beta' - \beta + 2b' - \left[1 + {}^{q_2}/_{q_1} \right] \cdot b < p_2 \left[1 - {}^{q_2}/_{q_1} \right]. \tag{8.5}$$

Since $q_2/q_1 < 1$, the right-hand side of expression 8.5 is strictly positive, which suggests that an entrant with a less efficient technology ($\beta' > \beta$ and $b' > b$) could find it profitable to enter at lower prices, using this base demand strategy.

Any price strategy by the utility that is not peak-load pricing leaves the utility vulnerable to wasteful entry. Conversely, an examination of equation 8.5 shows that if the utility adopts the Steiner peak-load price strategy, then entry can occur only if the new firm has lower costs.[3] Therefore, the utility that foregoes the use of peak pricing not only leaves itself open to losing profitable business, it also encourages wasteful use of economic resources.

The intuitive reason for this result is clear. If the utility does not use a price structure that results in the most efficient use of its capacity, a potential entrant may be able to compensate for its more costly capacity by filling up that capacity more effectively than the utility.[4]

II. Cost Allocation and Accountability

Given the regulatory penchant for reflecting pricing methods in cost allocations, is there an allocation method that supports peak-load pricing? In this time-o.-day pricing problem, the common costs are the capacity costs (which capacity is used by all subperiods).

The analysis suggests that all capacity costs be allocated to the peak subperiods and none to the off-peak subperiods. If there is more than one peak hour, then demands in all such hours are equal, and the appropriate allocation of capacity costs among the joint peak subperiod is that allocation which leads to prices for the different subperiods, resulting in equal demand across the subperiods. However, the service that causes the peak demand on capacity is the joint peak subperiods, taken collectively, and any attempt to further disaggregate the allocation to individual joint peak subperiods is bootless.

Can the utility be held accountable by its regulators to peak pricing? If the firm can identify its per unit operating costs (costs per unit of off-peak demand), then it can be held accountable on a historical basis. The firm can measure actual usage on its facility by time of day and indentify the peak subperiods. In practice, of course, joint peaks will not have exactly the same demand because of forecasting errors, day-to-day variation, and sampling errors. A simple rule of thumb may be used to identify the effective joint peak subperiods, such as all subperiods whose demand is within some small percentage of the realized peak demand. Having identified the joint peak subperiods, if the price of the off-peak subperiods is equal to unit operating costs, and, overall, revenues just cover total costs, then the firm is pricing efficiently.

In principle, it would appear that the time-of-day pricing problem is well in hand. The Steiner peak-load price structure is Pareto optimal in both the regulated monopoly environment, as well as competitive environment. Further, utilities would have positive incentives to adopt such a price structure, and regulatory commissions have the means to hold utilities accountable ex post for efficient pricing. In spite of the apparent advantages of this method, there are many obstacles to the instant application of this theoretical solution.

III. Traditional Cost Allocation Methods

The time-honored method of allocating common costs is relative use. In the context of the time-of-day model, this method leads to equal prices for all subperiods. To see this, the price equation for subperiod i is $p_i q_i = bq_i + (q_i/\Sigma q_j) \cdot \beta \cdot q_1$ so that $p_i = b + (q_1/\Sigma q_1) \cdot \beta$. Since the right-hand side does not depend on the subperiod i, then the price p_i for each subperiod must be the same. This appealing but simplistic allocation rule leads to the very opposite of peak pricing—uniform pricing throughout the period. Were capacity costs a reasonable fraction of running costs, say, $\beta = b$, then the efficient competitive peak-hour price would be twice the off-peak price. The relative use method would yield equal prices. Thus, consumers would be strongly encouraged (via prices) to treat peak-hour capacity as if it were free.

Other cost allocation methods used or suggested for use are based on revenues. It is not generally recognized that an allocation based on relative revenues is, in the long run, equivalent to a relative use method. To see this, let Θ_i be the proportion of revenues collected in subperiod i: $\Theta_i = p_i q_i / \Sigma p_j q_j$. The long-run price equation is then $p_i q_i = bq_i + \Theta_i \,.\, \beta \,.\, q_1$; and so,

$$\Theta_i = \frac{p_i q_i}{\Sigma p_j q_j} = \frac{bq_i + \Theta_i \beta q_1}{b\Sigma q_j + \beta q_1 \Sigma \Theta_i}.$$

Therefore, as $\Sigma\Theta_j = 1$, $\Theta_i b\Sigma q_j + \Theta_i \beta q_1 = bq_i + \Theta_i \beta q_1$, or $\Theta_i = q_i/\Sigma q_j$, which is the relative use method, yielding uniform prices throughout the day.

Another revenue method occasionally suggested is to allocate costs on the basis of revenues less operating costs. Amazingly, it is not generally understood that this is not an allocation mechanism, but a mathematical tautology, at least in the long run. In other words, any arbitrary allocation device will result in relative revenues less direct cost being driven to equal the allocator. To see this, let Θ_i be any allocator, $\Sigma\, \Theta_j = 1$. The price equation is then $p_i q_i = bq_i + \Theta_i \beta \cdot q_1$ or $(p_i - b)q_i = \Theta_i \beta q_i$. Total revenues less direct cost is $\Sigma(p_j - b) \,.\, q_j$, and if total revenues cover total costs, $\Sigma(p_j - b)q_j = \beta q_1$. Hence,

$$\frac{(p_i - b)q_i}{\Sigma(p_j - b)q_j} = \frac{\Theta_i \beta q_1}{\beta q_1} = \Theta_i \,.$$

Thus any arbitrary allocator will drive prices to the point where relative revenues less direct costs are equal to the allocator, no matter what the allocator.

IV. Accountability by Earning Ratio.

The current thrust in FCC regulation is to compute an earnings ratio for each priced good (subperiod), equal to revenues for that good divided by the cost of that good, including its allocated share of common costs. The implication is that unequal earnings ratios among subperiods is at the very least questionable. Even if all capacity costs are properly allocated to the joint peak subperiods collectively, this earnings ratio approach will be seriously misleading if applied to each of the joint peak subperiods. In our two-period model, suppose that peak prices result in a joint peak, $q_1 = q_2$. Since demands are equal in the two subperiods, common costs might be allocated equally to the two periods. Thus, costs for each subperiod would appear to be equal if the firm is pricing efficiently. Hence, the earnings ratios for the two subperiods will in general be different if the firm is pricing efficiently, and equal earnings ratios in this context should be viewed with great suspicion.

Regulatory Process Instabilities

The discussion so far has focused on the equilibrium price–cost relationship and has ignored the path to equilibrium taken by the utility and its regulators. The usual treatment of dynamics is that no matter what the initial conditions, any reasonable adjustment process will lead to the right steady-state prices. Unfortunately, the easy way out is not available in the peak pricing problem. Even if the problems already discussed can be resolved, the traditional regulatory adjustment processes remain unstable.

A quite popular regulatory adjustment rule is to examine recent accounting costs (test year costs), including allocated common costs, and to determine unit costs. Prices for the next year may then be set on the basis of last year's fully distributed cost per unit. This process is repeated every year, with blind faith that eventually, price will approach fully distributed unit cost. Unfortunately, blind faith will not do it in this case. Suppose that initially prices are such that the first subperiod is peak, but prices are considerably below capital plus operating cost. In the first year, the regulators allocate all capacity costs to the peak subperiod. They insist that the price of service in the first subperiod be raised substantially and the price of service in the second subperiod be lowered substantially. As a result, in the second year the second subperiod becomes the peak. Upon receipt of the second-year data, the regulators now allocate all capital costs to subperiod 2, resulting in a major swing for the third year, resulting in a large demand swing, ans so forth. In general, if the optimal price structure leads to a joint peak, then this test-year adjustment process will never converge. Instead it will oscillate year by year. The more capacity intensive the technology, the wilder will be the oscillations.

This shifting-peak problem can occur in practice if the peak period depends upon prices. Perhaps the best-known case of this peak shifting occured in the early 1960s, when the telephone industry's "after 9 P.M." discount rates went into effect, and many parts of the country experienced a shift from the day peak to an "after 9" peak.

V. More Caveats

In practice, the time-of-day pricing problem cannot be considered in isolation from the rest of the firm or industry. In telecommunications, the separations process can seriously distort peak pricing, which could easily invalidate the conclusions of this simple model. This is a special case of the more general theorem that optimizing a piece of a system that is otherwise not optimal is not necessarily beneficial. Hence, implementation of peak pricing must account for these other factors. Further, the model discussed in this chapter (and the Steiner paper as well) implicitly assumes that every capacity-constrained facility managed by the firm has a separate time-of-day price structure. Typically utility customers face a price structure for a service, such as calls of a certain distance, which uses many facilities in tandem, each of which is used in common with other services and other customers, and each of which may have a different time-of-day demand profile. Clearly, an implementable model would have to take this into account. The present model does not.

VI. Conclusions

Despite the warnings concerning this model's applicability, we can still glean some useful though limited conclusions from this model. Were the model to be representative of the supply of services by a public utility and were we able to consider the time-of-day pricing problem in isolation, then in principle peak-load pricing can achieve Pareto efficiency in both a regulated monopoly and a competitive environment. The firm has positive incentive to move to a peak-load prices, and regulators can hold firms accountable ex post for efficient pricing. But it is very easy to make serious mistakes. Inappropriate cost allocation standards applied by the regulator or the firm will almost certainly lead to an inefficient use of resources. Further, application of an equal earnings ratio standard in the peak pricing context will almost certainly be quite misleading, and any adjustment process based on test-year cost allocations will almost certainly be unstable.

Therefore present trends in regulator accountability may need to be reconsidered and redirected in order to ensure that capital resources are used most effectively.

Notes

1. Much of the literature since Steiner has been concerned with the relaxation of these rather stringent assumptions, including stochastic demand, substitutability of capital and labor, and the existence of scale economies, all of which would make this analysis more realistic as well as longer. I choose this rather simplistic model to bring out the difficulties more clearly that regulatory accountability raises. A more realistic treatment would no doubt raise more difficulties.

2. This is not intended to be a treatise on the separations process, of which I disclaim any expertise. The example illustrates two points: observed costs of a carrier may differ significantly from economic costs, and an arbitrary cost allocation such as separations can distort our view of economic costs. For further discussion of the separations process, see *Separations Manual,* NARUC–FCC Cooperative Committee on Communications, February 1971, available from National Association of Regulatory Utility Commissions, P.O. Box 684, Washington, D.C., 20044.

3. This conclusion is dependent upon the assumption that the utility's economic capacity and operating costs are reflected in the analysis. Regulatory practices such as separations can seriously distort these costs, leaving room for wasteful entry with any feasible price structure of the utility.

4. My colleague, J.H. Rohlfs of Bell Laboratories, contributed the key results of this section.

9 Some Elementary Considerations of Reliability and Regulation

Michael A. Crew and
Paul R. Kleindorfer

This chapter examines the relationship between reliability and regulation in public utilities. In section I we introduce the problem, briefly describe some recent developments in the economic analysis of regulation, and suggest how these affect the issue of reliability. In section II we discuss the so-called welfare maximizing approach to reliability, particularly in relation to the problem of rationing schemes in the event of scarcity. We examine the problem of rate-of-return regulation in section III, discussing its relation to the familiar regulatory models of Averch-Johnson and Bailey. Finally, in section IV we discuss briefly some of the implications of this analysis for regulatory policy regarding reliability.

I. Introduction to the Problems of Reliability and Regulation

Rate-of-return regulation is well established in the United States, as is its study by economists. We follow the recent developments of Harris and Raviv (1976, 1978), Ross (1973) and Williamson (1975) in analyzing the theory of regulation as a problem in the theory of agency.[1] The theory of agency is concerned with situations where a principal desires to accomplish a task but must rely on an agent to perform it because of asymmetrical resource or information endowments. This situation presents the principal with a problem of how to choose appropriate incentives and set behavioral limits for the agent in an attempt to balance the agent's better knowledge of uncertain states of the world against divergences in preferences between principal and agent. Williamson is concerned with the implications of such divergences in preferences and different endowments of information for the efficient operation of institutions and organizations. His approach emphasizes the limited capacity of the human mind for rational problem solving (bounded rationality) and the potential for opportunism within organizations. It involves analyzing organizations for their ability to economize on bounded rationality and to attenuate opportunism.

Regulation of utilities can be examined in this framework. The regulatory commission might be seen as the principal requiring the agent (the utility) to provide a vector of public utility services.[2] Much of the existing economics of regulation provides predictions that are consistent with the theory of agency. As an example, consider the classic Averch–Johnson (A–J) framework where the utility is characterized as a profit maximizer subject to rate-of-return regulation. The utility proceeds to maximize profits subject to the regulatory constraint and the implicit informational asymmetries between the regulatory commission and the utility. This results in the A–J effect where the firm uses an inefficient amount of capital. Generalizations to other classes of utility objective (such as expense-preference maximization) and regulatory constraints, notably Bailey (1973), fall within the same general class of agency problems.[3] The underlying message of all of this literature is that the regulatory process may entail nontrivial social costs in promoting its intended benefits of limiting monopoly power while achieving the economies of scale inherent in the technologies of most public utilities. These costs of regulation include the costs of inefficiencies of supply (such as the A–J effect) and the transaction costs (see Williamson, 1975) of monitoring and enforcement involved in the process. To these inefficiencies on the supply side may be added further inefficiencies when we introduce considerations of uncertainty in demand, the major focus of this chapter.

Essentially we aim to show that additional, sometimes gross, inefficiencies can result from rate-of-return regulation when demand is uncertain. These inefficiencies arise because demand uncertainty makes the detection of inefficient factor utilization more difficult. This is particularly so in the case of capacity and reserve margins since, arguably, a high reserve margin is in the consumers' interest to the extent that it provides more reliable service. Additionally, characterizing welfare-optimal pricing and investment policies under uncertainty is compounded with the problem of rationing excess demand and evaluating the social costs of doing so. Thus, under uncertainty there are problems both in characterizing the welfare benchmarks for policy as well as problems of achieving these benchmarks via rate-of-return regulation.

II. Summary and Synthesis of Welfare Optimal Pricing under Uncertainty

We restrict our attention to a simple case that enables us to abstract from problems of peak loads and technology.[4]

The Welfare Optimal Model

Our model has one type of plant with capacity costs given by β per unit, and running cost of b per unit. Capacity itself is represented by the variable z.

We will typically assume that demand is of one of the following forms, having either an additive or multiplicative disturbance term:

$$D(p,\tilde{u}) = X(p) + \tilde{u} \tag{9.1}$$

or

$$D(p,\tilde{v}) = \tilde{v}X(p), \tag{9.2}$$

where $X(p)$ represents mean demand, and $\tilde{u}$ (resp., $\tilde{v}$) is a disturbance term with $E(\tilde{u}) = 0$ (resp., $\tilde{v} \geq 0$ and $E(\tilde{v}) = 1$). We assume X to be continuously differentiable, with $dX/dp = X'(p) < 0$, and to have an inverse denoted by $P(x)$. We assume $\tilde{u}$ and $\tilde{v}$ to be continuous random variables. The probability density functions (*pdf*) and cumulative distribution functions (*cdf*) of the disturbance term, whether this be $\tilde{u}$ or $\tilde{v}$, are denoted respectively by $g(.)$ and $G(.)$.

We employ the following social welfare function, $W = TR + CS - TC - R$, where TR = total revenue, CS = consumer's surplus, TC = total cost, and R = rationing costs.

Rationing costs are included because of the possibility that quantity demanded may exceed capacity, thus creating a rationing problem. To understand the nature of the costs associated with rationing, consider the following scenario. Suppose demand is given by expression 9.1 where $D(p,u)$ is such that quantity demanded ($x = X(p) + u$) exceeds capacity z. Then there will be losses in consumers' surplus from unsatisfied demand, and there may be costs of operating and administering the procedures used to shed the excess demand. The losses in consumers' surplus and any rationing costs implied by the excess demand $x - z$ clearly depend upon the rationing scheme employed. For example, in rationing, consumers may be serviced randomly, or they may be serviced according to marginal willingness to pay. The former would presumably have greater expected losses in consumers' surplus and lower rationing costs than the latter.

Our general approach to studying these problems may be posed as the problem of maximizing a welfare function of the form,

$$W(p,r) = E\{W(\tilde{u},p,z) - r(D(p,\tilde{u}), z)\} \tag{9.3}$$

where W represents welfare returns under perfect rationing (costless rationing according to willingness to pay) and where $r(x, z)$ represents additional surplus losses and administrative costs associated with the rationing scheme in actual use. To illustrate, let us consider the case where demands are additive as in expression 3.1 and where r is the form $r(D - z)$, depending only on excess demand. In fact, let us assume that $r(D,z) = r(D - z) =$

$c \cdot \max[D - z,0]$—costs beyond perfect rationing are proportional to excess demand. To obtain the welfare function for this case, note that the actual output, when demand is $D(p,u)$ and capacity is z, is given by

$$S(p,u,z) = \min[D(p,u),z]. \tag{9.4}$$

This implies that the revenue plus consumers' surplus is

$$TR + CS = \int_o^{S(p,u,z)} P(x - u)dx, \tag{9.5}$$

when rationing is according to marginal willingness to pay. Subtracting operating expenses, capacity costs, and rationing costs from this and taking expected values, we obtain the following expression for 9.3:

$$\overline{W}_c\,(p,z) = E\{\int_o^{S(p,\tilde{u},z)} P(x - \tilde{u})dx - \tag{9.6}$$

$$bS(p,\tilde{u},z) - \beta z + c \cdot \max[D(p,\tilde{u}) - z,0]\}.$$

The first-order conditions for optimal price and capacity have been derived elsewhere (Crew and Kleindorfer 1976, 1979b) and are

$$\frac{\partial \overline{W}}{\partial p} = [(p - b)G(z - X(p)) - c(1 - G(z - X(p)))]X'(p) = 0; \tag{9.7}$$

$$\frac{\partial \overline{W}}{\partial z} = \int_{z - X(p)}^{\infty} [P(z - u) - b]dG(u) +$$

$$+ c[1 - G(z - X(p))] - \beta = 0, \tag{9.8}$$

where $G(u) = Pr\{\tilde{u} \leq u\}$ is the *cdf* of the disturbance term in expression 9.1, so that $G(z - X(p))$ is just the reliability $= Pr\{D(p,\tilde{u}) \leq z\}$.

We may interpret expressions 9.7 and 9.8 as follows. When reliability is nonzero at optimum, we may divide by G in expressions 9.7 to obtain

$$p = b + c(1 - G)/G, \tag{9.9}$$

where $G = G(z - X(p))$. Thus, price is set equal to the sum of marginal operating and rationing costs but is also a function of reliability. To determine the optimal reliability level, we need expression 9.8, which indicates that the reserve margin $z - X(p)$ is to be set so as to equate the marginal cost of capacity with the sum of expected marginal rationing and surplus losses.

It is interesting to note that, when $c > 0$, G must be an interval $0 < G < 1$ to satisfy expressions 9.7 and 9.8. Thus, neither complete unreliability nor complete reliability is welfare optimal when $c > 0$. Comparative statics also verifies that as c increases, price and capacity both increase, where always $b \leq p \leq b + \beta$, and where for c sufficiently high, price is close to the deterministic optimal price $b + \beta$ and capacity is close to the right-most fractile of the demand distribution at price $b + \beta$.[5]

The above should give a flavor for the welfare-optimal pricing and capacity strategies and their interaction with rationing. Additional results of this genre have been derived by Brown and Johnson (1969), Visscher (1973), and Carlton (1977). We summarize the pricing and profitability aspects of these results in table 9-1. The rationing schemes listed in it are these:

B-J: Costless rationing according to willingness-to-pay, perfect rationing as originally assumed by Brown and Johnson (1969).

CED: Rationing whose costs above B-J rationing depend only on excess demand (as we have dealt with to this point).

RAN: Random rationing, in which consumers are served randomly in the event of excess demand until capacity is exhausted.

LWP: Rationing in order of lowest willingness to pay until capacity is exhausted.

Gross profit refers to expected revenues minus expected operating and capacity costs and excludes any rationing costs or surplus losses. The additive and multiplicative disturbance specifications are those given by expressions 9.1 and 9.2, respectively.

The results on RAN and LWP are due to Visscher (additive disturbance) and Carlton (multiplicative disturbance). The results on B-J and CED rationing are derived in Crew and Kleindorfer (1979b). A detailed dis-

Table 9-1
Comparison of Rationing Schemes

	Additive Disturbance		*Multiplicative Disturbance*	
Rationing Scheme	*Price*	*Gross Profit*	*Price*	*Gross Profit*
B-J	$b \leq p < b + \beta$	Negative	$b \leq p < b + \beta$	Negative
CED ($c > o$)	$b < p < b + \beta$	Negative($>B-J$)	$b < p < b + \beta$	Negative ($>B-J$)
RAN	$b < p < b + \beta$	Negative	$p < b + \beta$	Zero
LWP	$b + \beta$	Negative	$p > b + \beta$	Positive
Deterministic	$b + \beta$	Zero	$b + \beta$	Zero

cussion of the additive case is also contained in Sherman and Visscher (1978).

If we think of rationing inefficiency as increasing in the order B–J, RAN, LWP, then we see reflected in table 9–1 the following conclusion, which we hinted at earlier for the class of CED rationing schemes: as rationing becomes less efficient, the welfare optimal solution entails increased prices, capacity, reliability, (gross) profit, and, of course, decreasing welfare.

Thus table 9–1 provides some confirmation of the general principle that the more inefficient the rationing scheme, the more reliance will have to be placed on normal price rationing to clear the market (the higher will be the welfare-optimal price and profits). In addition, welfare-optimal prices (and profits) are higher under multiplicative demand uncertainty than under additive uncertainty. This is doubtless because under multiplicative uncertainty, price and uncertainty interact, with the consequence that random outcomes on the high side are magnified by price effects, lending greater importance to the rationing effects of price in avoiding excess demand.

Welfare-optimal pricing is indeed a complex matter, requiring an integrated analysis of rationing, demand uncertainty specification, and capacity planning. Practical matters, such as second-best considerations, would require further analysis along the lines of the well-known inverse-elasticity rule as examined by Sherman and Vissher (1978a). Another issue of importance is the appropriate modification of the above results when price discrimination is possible among different consumer groups.

Multiple Consumer Groups

The issue of charging different prices to different groups, according to their demand patterns and rationing costs, has been ignored in the literature.[6] To model this situation, we assume there are two consumer groups with demand functions specified as follows:

$$D_i(p_i,\tilde{u}_i) = X_i(p_i) + \tilde{u}_i\,, \qquad i = 1,2, \tag{9.10}$$

where the random variables $\tilde{u}_i$ are assumed continuous, with compact range, and with mean zero.

When demand exceeds capacity, rationing occurs. A key question in this case is how excess deman is apportioned among the two consumer groups. We assume here that each group bears a constant share of excess demand, so that output to group $i = 1,2$ is

$$S_i(\mathbf{p},\tilde{\mathbf{u}},z) = D_i(p_i,\tilde{u}_i) - \gamma_i[D_1(p_1,\tilde{u}_1) + + D_2(p_2,\tilde{u}_2) - z]^+, \tag{9.11}$$

where $\gamma_1 + \gamma_2 = 1, \gamma_i \geq 0$, where $y^+ = \max(y,0)$ for any real number y, and where we assume that optimal prices and capacity satisfy

$$z \geq \max[D_1(p_1, \widetilde{u}_1),\ D_2(p_2, \widetilde{u}_2)] \tag{9.12}$$

with probability one, so that expression 9.11 implies, always, that

$$S_1(\mathbf{p}, \widetilde{\mathbf{u}}, z) + S_2(\mathbf{p}, \widetilde{\mathbf{u}}, z) \leq z, \tag{9.13}$$

with equality holding in the event of excess demand.

Note that when $\gamma_1 = 0$, group 1 always has all its demand met; any excess demand is carried by group 2. More generally, the γ_i represent the relative portions of excess demand borne by the respective groups.

In framing our welfare function we assume, as a generalization of expression 9.6, that excess demand within each consumer group is rationed according to marginal willingness to pay, with costs of doing this proportional to each group's excess demand, with per unit costs $c_i \geq 0$, $i = 1,2$. This lead to the following welfare function:

$$\overline{W} = E\{ \sum_{i=1}^{2} \int_{o}^{S_i(\mathbf{p}, \widetilde{\mathbf{u}}, z)} [P_i(x - \widetilde{u}_i) - b]dx - \tag{9.14}$$

$$- \beta z - \sum_{i=1}^{2} c_i \gamma_i [D_1(p_1, \widetilde{u}_1) + D_2(p_2, \widetilde{u}_1) - z]^+\},$$

where $\gamma_i [\widetilde{D}_1 + \widetilde{D}_2 - z]^+$ is just excess demand, and where p_i is the inverse of the mean demand function X in expression 9.10.

Substituting 9.11 in 9.14 and taking first-order conditions,[7] we obtain

$$\frac{\partial \overline{W}}{\partial p_i} = (p_i - b)X_i'(p_i)G[M(\mathbf{p}, z] +$$

$$+ \gamma_j X_i'(p_i) \int_{M(\mathbf{p},z)}^{\infty} [P_i(X_i(p_i) + \gamma_i M(\mathbf{p}, z) \quad \gamma_i u) \quad b]dG(u)$$

$$- \gamma_j X_i'(p_i] \int_{M(\mathbf{p},z)}^{\infty} [P_j(X_j(p_j) + \gamma M(\mathbf{p}, z) - \gamma_j u) - b]dG(u) -$$

$$- cX_i'(p_i)(1 - G[M(\mathbf{p}, z)]), \qquad (i,j \in \{1,2\}, \qquad i \neq j), \tag{9.15}$$

and

$$\frac{\partial \overline{W}}{\partial z} = \sum_{k=1}^{2} \gamma_k \int_{M(\mathbf{p},z)}^{\infty} [P_k(X_k(p_k) + \gamma_k M(\mathbf{p}, z) - \gamma_k u) - \mathrm{b}]dG(u) +$$

$$+ c(1 - G[M(\mathbf{p}, z)]) - \beta, \tag{9.16}$$

where $c = c_1\gamma_1 + c_2\gamma_2$, where G is the cumulative distribution function (cdf) of the random variable $\tilde{u} = \tilde{u}_1 + \tilde{u}_2$, and where the mean reserve margin $M(\mathbf{p},z)$ is defined as

$$M(\mathbf{p},z) = z - X_1(p_1) - X_2(p_2). \tag{9.17}$$

With this definition, readers should note that $G[M(\mathbf{p},z)] = Pr\{\tilde{u}_1 + \tilde{u}_2 \leq M(\mathbf{p},z)\}$ is just system reliability.

The first-order conditions 9.15 and 9.16 are similar to 9.7 and 9.8 for the case of a single consumer group, and they indicate that price and capacity should be set to equate expected marginal surplus gains to expected marginal (rationing and operating) costs. Regarding 9.15, for example, the expression

$$-X_i'(p_i) \int_{M(\mathbf{p},z)}^{\infty} [P_i(X_i(p_i) + \gamma_i M(\mathbf{p},z) - \gamma_i(u) - b]dG(u) \tag{9.18}$$

represents the expected marginal increase in consumer surplus over running cost for group i from lowering price p_i slightly when excess demand exists, provided that group i is supplied with the additional quantity demanded. In fact, however, given the rationing scheme embodied in expressions 9.11–9.13, group i will enjoy a marginal increase in supply of only $-(1 - \gamma_i)X_i'(p_i) = -\gamma_j X_i'(p_i)$, $j \neq i$, X from a price reduction. A corresponding reduction in group j's supply would accompany this, of course. Thus, the second and third terms in expression 9.15 represent the difference in net benefits and costs accruing to groups i and j from a price reduction to group i. The first and fourth terms in the equation represent the difference between marginal surplus gains and marginal rationing costs. The sum of these marginal benefits and costs must balance to zero at optimum.

Further insights into optimal pricing may be obtained by canceling $X_i'(p_i)$ in expression 9.15, adding the result to $\partial \overline{W}/\partial z$ in 9.16 and setting this sum equal to zero. Doing so we obtain the following conditions for the optimal prices,

$$(p_i - b)G[M(\mathbf{p},z)] - \beta + \tag{9.19}$$

$$+ \int_{\infty}^{M(\mathbf{p},z)} [P_i(X_i(p_i) + \gamma_i M(\mathbf{p},z) - \gamma_i u) - b]dG(u) = 0,$$

where we have used $\gamma_1 + \gamma_2 = 1$. From this we see that as long as optimal system reilability $G[M(p,z)] > 0$, optimal prices satisfy

$$p_i = b + \frac{\beta - \int_{\infty}^{M(p,z)} [P_i(X_i(p_i) + \gamma_i M(\mathbf{p},z) - \gamma_i u) - b]dG(u)}{G[M(\mathbf{p},z)]}, \tag{9.20}$$

with optimal capacity determined conjointly through 9.16 evaluated at 0.

It is interesting to note that if one eliminates the term $c(1 - G)$ from equations 9.7 and 9.8, an expression very similar to 9.20 results for the optimal price with a single group of consumers. Thus, the optimal price (and capacity) specification does not change much when multiple consumer groups are present.

The case where $\gamma_i = 0$ is of special interest. When $\gamma_i = 0$ (the case where all shortages are borne by the other group $j \neq i$), the integral in 9.20 reduces to

$$\int_{M(\mathbf{p},z)}^{\infty} [P_i(X_i(p_i)) - b] dG(u) = (p_i - b)(1 - G[M(\mathbf{p},z)]). \quad (9.21)$$

From this, we see that $\gamma_i = 0$ implies from 9.20 that $p_i = b + \beta$. More generally, the monotonicity of P_i implies for any $u > M(\mathbf{p},z)$ that $P_i(X_i(p_i) + \gamma_i M(\mathbf{p},z) - \gamma_i u) \geq P_i(X_i(p_i)) = p_i$, so that the integral in 9.20 is always greater than or equal to $(p_i - b)[1 - G(M(\mathbf{p},z))]$. From this price is always less than or equal to $b + \beta$.

We can also note that $\gamma_i = 0$ implies from 9.15 that

$$p_j = b + c(1 - G)/G, \quad (9.22)$$

as in expression 9.9, where $G = G(M(\mathbf{p},z))$ is system reliability. In general, we would expect that, at optimum, $dp_i/d\gamma_i \leq 0$ and $dp_i/d\gamma_j \geq 0$, so that, as a function of rationing priority weight $\gamma = \gamma_1 = 1 - \gamma_2$, optimal prices would behave as illustrated in figure 9-1. However, we have not verified the indicated monotonicity.

It is also possible to derive an optimal uniform price for the class of rationing schemes discussed here by adding the constraint $p_1 - p_2 = 0$ to the problem of mazimizing expression 9.14. Doing so leads to the following first-order condition in place of 9.20:

$$\begin{aligned} 0 = \Theta[\bar{p} - b) G(M(\bar{\mathbf{p}},z)) - (\beta - \\ \int_{M(\mathbf{p},z)}^{\infty} [P_1(X_1(\bar{p}) + \gamma_1 M(\bar{\mathbf{p}},z) - \gamma_1 u) - b] \, dG(u)] \\ + (1 - \Theta)[(\bar{p} - b) G(M(\bar{\mathbf{p}},z)) - (\beta - \\ \int_{M(\mathbf{p},z)}^{\infty} [P_2(X_2(\bar{p}) - \gamma_2 M(\bar{\mathbf{p}},z) - \gamma_2 u) - b[dG(u)], \end{aligned} \quad (9.23)$$

where $\bar{\mathbf{p}} = (\bar{p},\bar{p})$ and

$$\Theta = \frac{X_1'(\bar{p})}{X_1'(\bar{p}) + X_2'(\bar{p})}, \quad (9.24)$$

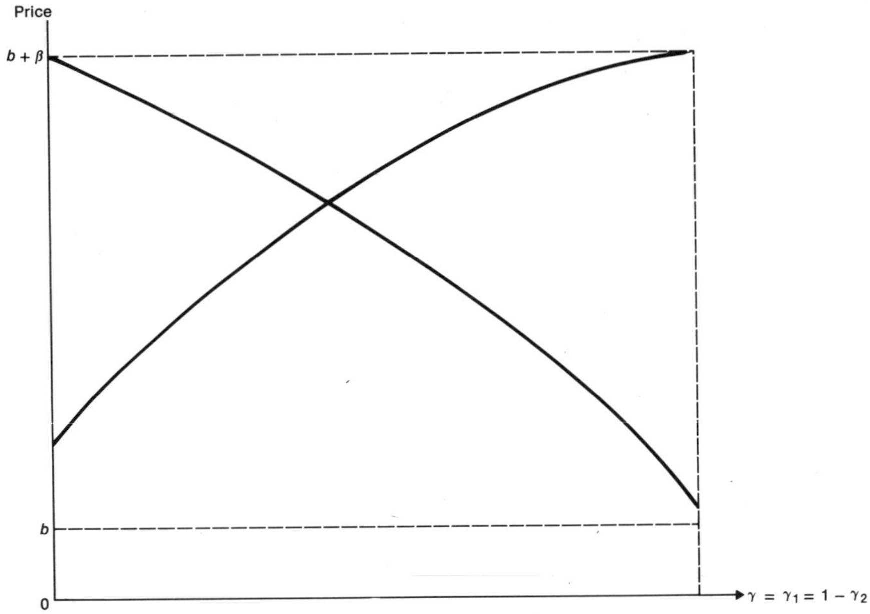

Figure 9–1. Pricing According to Rationing Priorities

so that 9.23 represents a convex combination of the first-order conditions that would obtain for the individual prices p_1 and p_2 (compare expressions 9.20 and 9.23). The weight $\Theta \in (0,1)$ indicates the relative importance of each of these first-order conditions, along the expected lines of a least-distortion principle.

A host of other issues could be discussed in relation to multiple consumer groups. These would include characterizing optimal rationing between groups (the choice of γ_1, γ_2) and a study of the price and profitability effects of alternative rationing policies within groups (such as random rationing). Given the above analysis, we may aniticipate that the general conclusions of these studies will be similar to those for single consumer groups outlined in section II. The only difference is that intergroup interactions and surplus losses through rationing have to be considered in the optimal pricing policy.

Summary of Welfare Optimal Results

Welfare-optimal pricing under uncertainty entails marginal-cost pricing rules similar to those obtaining under certainty. However, determining and quantifying the appropriate marginal costs requires that rationing and excess demand conditions be explicitly considered. Optimal capacity should be set so that losses in consumer surplus net of operating costs (as determined by the rationing scheme in use) are just equal to the LRMC of increasing capacity, all of this to take place at optimal prices. The optimal prices are complicated (although they typically may be expected to be close to deterministic optimal prices when reliability is high), but essentially they are obtained by equating expected benefits from the actual marginal unit of demand met to expected SRMC. Given the above capacity rule, this amounts to determining price by maximizing expected consumer surplus (given the rationing scheme or load-shedding procedure used), subject to optimal reliability levels.

III. Rate-of-Return Regulation and Reliability

The Averch-Johnson Model under Uncertainty

The A-J model under certainty envisages a profit-maximizing firm subject to the constraint that the rate-of-return the firm earns on its capital stock be no greater than some prespecified level set by the regulatory commission. The basic results obtained for this case (see, for example, Bailey, 1973) are that such a regulated firm will use an inefficiently large amount of capital at the output level it chooses. However, even so, for some allowed rates of return, social welfare increases over the unregulated monopoly situation. Indeed, as the allowed rate of return decreases from the unregulated monopoly level, output increases while the magnitude of factor input distortions from cost-minimizing levels increases. Finding an optimal allowed rate of return then consists of weighing consumer benefits from increased output against the social costs of increased supply inefficiencies.

Under uncertainty, there are a number of possibilities for extending the A-J model, and several sets of assumptions have been examined in the literature to date. The major differences in assumptions used can be classified as follows:

1. Does the regulator set price (consistent with the preestablished fair rate of return), or may the regulated firm set any price it wishes consistent with the allowed rate of return (as A-J originally assumed)?
2. Is price set before or after demand uncertainty is revealed?
3. Various technology specifications and forms of uncertainty have been used.
4. Is the rate-of-return constraint required to hold with certainty ex post, or is it required to hold in an expected value sense ex ante?
5. Finally, must demand be met or is excess demand allowed?

The results of the various assumptions can be strikingly different. For example, Leland (1974) has shown that when price is set ex ante by the regulator to achieve a fair return, the firm can be induced to choose inputs efficiently. We show below that this result does not hold when the firm sets the price. Similarly, assuming output must exactly equal demand (that is, short-run factors are varied to absorb random fluctuations), Peles and Stein (1976) and Perrakis (1976a) have shown that when price is adjusted ex post by the regulated firm, there are cases where restricting the allowed rate of return may lead to decreased capital stock.[8] We show below that this does not hold when price is adjusted ex ante and excess demand is allowed. Baron and Taggart (1978) have shown that if the regulator sets price, the behavior of the regulated firm depends on whether that price is (known to be) affected by the firm's choice of capital stock. If the firm knows that price will be set to earn a fair return on its capital stock, whatever that might be, then incentives toward overcapitalization occur. But when the price does not depend on the firm's actual capital stock, efficient factor proportions will obtain.

A large number of possibilities exist for modeling rate-of-return regulation under uncertainty. One aspect common to all of these previous approaches, however, is their neglect of reliability. The issue of reliability does not arise in any of this earlier work since output is always assumed to be equal to demand; reliability is always unity. We now formulate a model that relaxes the assumption that output equals demands. We employ the following notation:

π	= profit.
x	= output (measured in physical units).
K	= capital.
L	= labor.
r	= firm's cost of capital.
w	= unit cost of labor (wage rate).
$s(>r)$	= rate of return allowed by regulatory commission.
$x = F(K,L)$	= where F is a quasi-concave, neoclassical production function with positive marginal products denoted F_K and F_L and for which $F(0,L) = F(K,0) = 0$ for all K,L.
$D(p,\tilde{u})$	= $X(p) + \tilde{u}$ = demand function as in 9.9 (results for 9.2 are entirely analogous).
$P = P(x)$	= inverse demand function, $P(X(p)) = p$.
$R = P.x$	= revenue.
h	= cost of a physical unit of capital; henceforth we assume $h = 1$.
β	= rh.

The firm is assumed to maximize expected profit subject to the regulatory constraint that its ex ante expected rate of return does not exceed the allowed rate, s:

$$\max E\{\widetilde{\pi}\} = E\{pS(D(p,\widetilde{u}), F(K,L)) - wL - \beta K\}, \tag{9.25}$$

subject to:

$$E\{pS(D(p,\widetilde{u}), F(K,L)) - wL - \beta K\} \leq (s - \beta)K, \tag{9.26}$$

where $S(\widetilde{D},x) = \min(\widetilde{D},x)$.

Assuming $s > r = \beta$ and forming the Lagrangian,

$$£ = E\{\widetilde{\pi}\} - \lambda[E\{\widetilde{\pi}\} - (s - \beta)K], \tag{9.27}$$

we obtain the following first-order conditions:

$$\frac{\partial £}{\partial p} = (1 - \lambda)\{[X(p) + pX'(p)]G[F(K,L) - X(p)] + \tag{9.28}$$

$$+ \int_{-\infty}^{F(K,L) - X(p)} udG(u) + F(K,L)(1 - G[F(K,L) - X(p)])\} = 0;$$

$$\frac{\partial £}{\partial K} = (1 - \lambda)(pF_K(1 - G[F(K,L) - X(p)]) - \beta) + \lambda(s - \beta) = 0; \tag{9.29}$$

$$\frac{\partial £}{\partial L} = (1 - \lambda)(pF_L(1 - G[F(K,L) - X(p)]) - w) = 0 \tag{9.30}$$

Readers will have no difficulty establishing for this case the usual theorem that $0 \leq \lambda < 1$, where $\lambda = 0$ obtains only when regulation is inconsequential; that is, the allowed rate(s) is no less than the monopoly rate.[9] When $\lambda = 0$, it follows from expressions 9.29 and 9.30 that efficient factor combinations obtain ($\beta/w = F_K/F_L$). When $\lambda > 0$ we obtain from 9.29 and 9.30,

$$\frac{F_K}{F_L} = \frac{\beta}{w} - \frac{\lambda}{1 - \lambda}\frac{s - \beta}{w} > \frac{\beta}{w}, \tag{9.31}$$

so that, just as in the deterministic case, the A–J overcapitalization effect obtains for the model 9.25 and 9.26.

We have treated all variables above (p, K, and L) as adjustable only in the long run and before demand uncertainty resolves itself. The recent literature on rate-of-return regulation under uncertainty implies that if price or labor were variable in the short run, different results might obtain, though this remains an open question for the case treated here where some excess demand is allowable. One would expect, however, that the basic incentive toward overcapitalization inherent in expressions 9.25 and 9.26 would persist even if L were adjustable in the short run. We will leave these matters for future research in order to pursue here in more depth the issue of reliability.

Regulation and Reliability with a Fixed Proportions Technology

Readers can easily verify from 9.28, 9.30, and $0 \le \lambda < 1$ that $G[F(K,L) - X(p)] =$ reliability $= Pr\{D(p,\tilde{u}) \le F(K,L)\}$ always satisfies $0 < G < 1$, no matter what s is. Of interest, of course, is how reliability or its surrogate, reserve margin $= F(K,L) - X(p)$, varies as s changes. Such comparative statics results turn out to be immensely complicated for the model 9.25–9.26, however, and so we must consider a somewhat simpler model whose comparative statics properties are analytically tractable. Retaining earlier notation, the model we study follows:

$$\max E\{(p - b)S(D(p,\tilde{u}),z) - \beta z\}, \tag{9.32}$$

subject to

$$E\{(p - b)S(D(p,\tilde{u}), z) - \beta z\} \le (s - \beta)z, \tag{9.33}$$

where we assume the additive demand specification 9.1. We also assume here that the expected net-revenue function $(p - b)X(p)$ is concave for $p \ge b$. Forming the Lagrangian analogous to expressions 9.28–9.30 and taking first-order conditions, we obtain,

$$[(p - b)X'(p) + X(p)]\,G(M)p,z)) + \int_{-\infty}^{M(p,z)} u dG(u) + z[1 - G(M(p,z))] = 0, \tag{9.34}$$

and

$$(1 - \lambda)(p - b)[1 - G(M(p,z))] - \beta + \lambda s = 0, \tag{9.35}$$

where the reserve margin $M(p,z)$ is

$$M(p,z) = z - X(p). \tag{9.36}$$

$G(M) > 0$ must always hold since 9.34 reduces to $z = 0$ when $G(M) = 0$. Note also that when $\lambda = 0$, the profit-maximizing case—9.35—implies that $1 - G(M) > 0$. Thus, reliability is strictly between 0 and 1 for the expected profit-maximizing monopolist.

Using comparative statics in appendix 9A, we verify for the system of equations 9.33–9.35 (assumed to hold as an equality) that at optimum

$$\frac{dz}{ds} < 0 \text{ and } \quad \frac{dM(p,z)}{ds} = \frac{dz}{ds} - X'(p)\frac{dp}{ds} < 0. \tag{9.37}$$

Thus, capacity and reserve margin both increase as the regulated return is lowered. We also discuss conditions in the appendix under which, as we would expect from deterministic theory, price decreases and welfare increases as the allowed rate of return is decreased from the monopoly level.

To illustrate 9.37, as well as to point out some of the problems of rate-of-return regulation under uncertainty, consider the following example, which is specialization of a similar result for a peak-load case in Crew and Kleindorfer (1978). Suppose that the disturbance term $\tilde{u}$ is bounded—that is, there is some bounded interval $[u_1, u_2]$ such that $Pr\{\tilde{u} \in [u_1, u_2]\} = 1$—and let the maximum expected net revenue obtainable when capacity is effectively a free good be denoted by R^*. When capacity z is a free good, the monopolist will set z high enough to insure that demand is always less than z. Thus

$$R^* = \max_{p \geq 0} \; E\{(p - b)(X(p) + \tilde{u})\} \tag{9.38}$$

or, since $E\{\tilde{u}\} = 0$, R^* reduces to the maximum obtainable deterministic net revenue with capacity unconstrained,

$$R^* = \max_{p \geq 0} \; (p - b)X(p). \tag{9.39}$$

Letting p^* be the optimal pricing solution to 9.34, it is straightforward to show that if

$$R^*/s \geq X(p^*) + u_2, \tag{9.40}$$

then the regulated monopolist will set price equal to p^* and $z^* = R^*/s$, thus achieving equality in the regulatory constraint.[10] This being so, we see from 9.40 and the definition of u_2 that a reliability level of unity will be optimal for such a monopolist. Note that the optimal policy in this case satisfies the monotonicity property noted above and summarized in 9.37. Note also that if strict inequality holds in 9.40, then the monopolist will set z^* larger than what would be required to meet the maximum conceivable demand at his chosen price, p^*. Any attempts to decrease this socially wasteful margin would require slackening the rate-of-return constraint.

These results underscore the complexity of the relationship between reliability and regulation. Of course, we have dealt with a very simple model and with only one set of assumptions concerning the timing of the various decisions and random events involved. Thus, testing the robustness of the above propositions on reliability and reserve margin to more general assumptions is required before we place too much faith in these results. Nonetheless, the inverse relationship between reliability and allowed rate of return discovered above, though tentative, is sufficiently intriguing to prompt brief speculations on the policy implications.

IV. Discussion and Implications for Policy

Even if reserve margins increase as regulation becomes tighter, such increases may not be undesirable from a welfare point of view. Indeed, as rationing becomes more costly or more inefficient (for example, the rationing cost parameter c it (t) becomes large), it is clear that welfare optimal reliability approaches unity, and this is so for any fixed price. Since the unregulated firm sets reliability strictly between 0 and 1, we see that, for sufficiently high rationing or shortage costs, the unregulated monopoly will have a lower reserve margin than is socially desirable. Thus, the increases in reserve margin occasioned by decreasing the allowed rate of return below that which an unregulated monopoly would achieve may be all to the good.

Suppose, however, that a regulatory commission is faced with an excess capacity problem in that there is a gross divergence between actual reserve margin and the reserve margin, which, at current prices, would be implied by the welfare optimal capacity condition (see expression 9.8). It is tempting to argue that the commission should simply attempt to restrict (regulate) reliability level or reserve margin in this case. However, the problems with this are legion. First and foremost, there are severe informational difficulties in translating an allowed reliability level or reserve margin constraint into an actual capacity and operating regime because of the problem of maintenance and availability of plants. Specifically, if commissions employed a "used-and-useful" criterion to say that particular plants were in excess of what was required to provide a regulated level of reliability, the utilities could overcome this by reducing maintenance, causing more plant downtime and therefore more use of previously "unused and unuseful" plants. The only cure for this scenario would appear to be more regulation, now of maintenance.

Somewhere in this increasing spiral of regulatory intervention, one would expect the social costs of regulation to exceed its benefits. At the risk of contributing to this spiral, the results of this paper would seem nevertheless to call for a more explicit treatment of reliability and reserve margin in regulatory proceedings. This will require a more positive approach to reliability than has been apparent in theory or practice to date.

The first element of a positive approach to reliability and regulation would be the recognition by both the industry and commissions of the importance of developing benchmarks for reliability and reserve margins. This is not likely to be an easy task, even given our trust in the theoretical models addressed to this issue. One problem is that we have very little experience in assessing the rationing costs and surplus losses associated with excess demand; these data are required for any of the welfare-optimal benchmarks developed to date.[11] A detailed comparison could be made of the reliability, reserve margins, maintenance of companies and power interchanges within the United States and compared with some European counterparts, both regulated utility companies (in Germany, for example) and publicly owned utilities in France and the United Kingdom. Some rough figures cited by Telson (1975) indicate that reliability is higher in the United States and in France or Britain. In 1969 the U.S. reliability was 99.98 percent, and the French and U.K. reliabilities were, respectively, 99.93 percent and 99.8 percent, which, measured in terms of loss per customer year, amounted to 1.75 hours, 6 hours, and 17.5 hours, respectively.

There are also substantial differences in reserve margins among public utilities within the United States, suggesting that a closer scrutiny of reliability and reserve margins by commissions is called for. A very simple proposal would be for commissions, when they have reason to believe that reserve margins of a particular company are excessive, to move to exclude some plant from the rate base. Clearly the process by which these moves and supporting audits are undertaken must be structured with great care. Some considerations affecting the design of such procedures may be drawn from the results of this chapter.

Taking account of the incentives toward increasing reserve margins as rate of return is reduced, which the theoretical model above suggests, one would expect that social optimality might dictate some inverse relationship between allowed rate of return and reserve margin, both as a descriptive and normative proposition. Devising practical schemes that reflect these incentives and account for related welfare-optimal benchmarks seems to us to be a very promising area of research and policy development.

Notes

1. For more details see our book, Crew and Kleindorfer (1979b).

2. An alternative might be to envisage the consumers as principal and the commission as agent. This would be, arguably, more reasonable to the extent that regulatory commissions develop motivation and objectives of their own diverging from consumer interests.

3. The issues of expense preferences are analyzed in Williamson (1964) and in more detail for public utilities in Crew and Kleindorfer (1979a).

4. We provide a detailed discussion of these issues elsewhere. See Crew and Kleindorfer (1976, 1979b).

5. See chapter 5 of Crew and Kleindorfer (1979b).

6. This issue has been raised by Meyer (1975) and Carlton (1977). In this regard, Mayer's claim that his framework accommodates multiple groups of users making demands on a common facility at a singel point in time is evidently flase. For this to be so, his capacity constraints would have to read $\Sigma D_i(p_i) \leq z$, whereas his are always of the form $D_i(p_i) \leq z$ (no summation).

7. See the appendix to Crew and Kleindorfer (1976) for details and methods of obtaining first-order conditions to welfare-maximization problems of the form of expression 9.14.

8. See also Perrakis (1976b) for the case where price is adjusted ex ante by the firm and where ex post output must equal demand and the regulatory constraint must be satisfied.

9. See Bailey (1973) for a formal proof in the certainty case. The easiest way to see that $0 \leq \lambda < 1$ is as follows. First note that $\lambda \geq 0$ by the Kuhn-Tucker conditions. Moreover, by the implicit function theorem (applied to expressions 9.28–9.30 and to 9.26 when $\lambda > 0$), λ varies continuously as s varies. Finally, $\lambda = 0$ for the unregulated monopoly return, and $\lambda = 1$ is impossible by 9.29 as long as $s > \beta$. Thus, $\lambda < 1$ must hold whenever $s > \beta$.

10. Let $z^* = R^*/s$ and suppose 9.40 holds. If the optimal capacity z is assumed less than z^*, we have $E\{\pi(p,z,u)\} \leq (s - \beta)z < (s - \beta)z^* = E\{\pi(p^*,z^*,\tilde{u})\}$, where the first inequality holds since any optimal solution (p,z) must satisfy 9.33, the strict inequality follows from $(s - \beta) > 0$, and the final equality holds by 9.40 and the definition of z^*. Thus, for any feasible price p, z cannot be optimal. Suppose, also, that $z > z^*$. Then $E\{\pi(p,z,\tilde{u}\} = E\{\text{Rev}(p,z,u)\} - \beta z < R^* - \beta z^* = E\{\pi(p^*,z^*,\tilde{u})\}$, where the inequality follows by definition of R^* as the maximum obtainable revenue. We see again that z is nonoptimal. Clearly z is the optimal capacity and, since 9.40 holds, p^* is feasible and also optimal in expressions 9.32 and 9.33.

11. See Munasinghe and Gellerson (1977) for a case study and background literature on assessing curtailment costs and welfare-optimal reliability levels.

Appendix 9A Comparative Statics of the Regulated Firm

This appendix verifies for the model of section IIIB the asserted monotonicity of the regulated firm's optimal capacity z and reserve margina $M(p,z)$, as the allowed rate-of-return s varies. We show that dz/ds and dM/ds are both negative. We also discuss other comparative statics properties of the regulated firm under uncertainty.

From the first-order conditions 9.34 and 9.35 and the constraint 9.33, the relevant equations for a comparative statics analysis may be written thus:

$$H_1(p,z,s,\lambda) = \int_{-\infty}^{M(p,z)} [(p - b)X'(p) - M(p,z) + u]dG(u) + z = 0; \tag{9a.1}$$

$$H_2(p,z,s,\lambda) = (p - b)(1 - \lambda)[1 - G(M(p,z))] - \beta + \lambda s = 0; \tag{9a.2}$$

$$H_3(p,z,s,\lambda) = \int_{-\infty}^{M(p,z)} (p - b)(u - M(p,z))dG(u) + (p - b - s)z = 0. \tag{9a.3}$$

Using the implicit function theorem we have for $i = 1,2,3$,

$$\frac{\partial H_i}{\partial p}\frac{dp}{ds} + \frac{\partial H_i}{\partial z}\frac{dz}{ds} + \frac{\partial H_i}{\partial \lambda}\frac{d\lambda}{ds} = -\frac{\partial H_i}{\partial s}$$

This yields from 9a.1–9a.3 the following conditions:

$$([(p - b)X'' + 2X']G(M) - (p - b)(X')^2g(M))\frac{dp}{ds} + ((p - b\,X'g(M) + (1 - G(M)))\frac{dz}{ds} = 0; \tag{9a.4}$$

$$(1 - \lambda)[(p - b)X'g(m) + (1 - G(M))]\frac{dp}{ds} - (1 - \lambda)(p - b)g(m)\frac{dz}{ds} + [s - (p - b)(1 - G(M))]\frac{d\lambda}{ds} = -\lambda; \tag{9a.5}$$

$$\frac{\partial H_3}{\partial p}\frac{dp}{ds} + [(p - b)(1 - G(M)) - s]\frac{dz}{ds} = z; \tag{9a.6}$$

where $M = M(p,z)$, $X' = X'(p)$, and $X'' = X''(p)$.

We now note from 9.33 that $\partial H_3/\partial pH_1 = 0$, from 9a.1 so that 9a.6 implies

$$\frac{dz}{ds} = \frac{z}{[(p - b)(1 - G(M)) - s]} \cdot \tag{9a.7}$$

Moreover, the denominator in 9a.7 is easily seen to be negative whenever $s > \beta$ from 9a.2 and $0 \leq \lambda < 1$. Thus, $dz/ds < 0$.

Next, solving 9a.4 for dp/ds in terms of dz/ds, we have

$$\frac{dM}{ds} = \frac{dz}{ds} - X'(p)\frac{dp}{ds}$$

$$= \frac{dz}{ds}[1 + X'\frac{(p - b)X'g(M) + (1 - G(M))}{[(p - b)X'' + 2X']G(M) - (p - b)(X')^2g(M)}] \tag{9a.8}$$

$$= \frac{dz}{ds}\left[\frac{(p - b)X'' + 2X']G(M) + [1 - G(M)]X'}{[(p - b)X'' + 2X']G(M) - (p - b)(X')^2g(M)}\right].$$

Now the denominator in 9a.8 is negative since clearly $p - b >$ and since we assumed the expected net-revenue function $(p - b)X(p)$ to be concave (so that its second derivative $[(p - b)X'' + 2X'] \leq 0$).

The numerator in 9a.8 is also negative since by 9.34, $G(M) > 0$, $X' < 0$ and $[(p - b)X'' + 2X'] \leq 0$. Thus, dM/ds has the same sign as dz/ds—negative.

Several other matters of interest are now sketched. First, note from 9a.6 and 9a.8 that

$$\frac{\partial \overline{W}}{\partial z} = \int_{M(p,z)}^{\infty} [P(z - u) - b + c]dG(u) - \beta. \tag{9a.9}$$

Also, $P' < 0$ so, for $u > M(p,z)$, $P(z - u) > P(z - m) = P(X(p)) = p$. Thus 9a.9 implies

$$\frac{\partial \overline{W}}{\partial z} > (p - b + c)(1 - G(M)) - \beta. \tag{9a.10}$$

Now at the unregulated monopoly solution, whose rate of return we denote s_m we have $\lambda = 0$ so 9.35 implies

$$(p - b)(1 - G(M)) = \beta. \tag{9a.11}$$

From 9a.10 and 9a.11 we have

$$\left.\frac{\partial \overline{W}}{\partial z}\right|_{s = s_m} > 0, \tag{9a.12}$$

so that expected welfare increases as capacity increases from the unregulated monopoly solution (with price held fixed at the profit-maximizing level).

A further result, which is entirely intuitive and easily obtainable from 9a.7, and the fact that $\partial \bar{\pi}/\partial p = 0$ is

$$\frac{d\bar{\pi}}{ds} = \frac{\partial \bar{\pi}}{\partial p}\frac{dp}{ds} + \frac{\partial \bar{\pi}}{\partial z}\frac{dz}{ds} = \lambda z, \tag{9a.13}$$

which is positive whenever regulation is effective ($\lambda > 0$).[1]

Perhaps the most perplexing aspect of this comparative statics analysis concerns dp/ds. From 9a.4 and the fact noted above that

$$([(p - b)X'' + 2X']G(M) - (p - b)(X')^2 g(M)) < 0, \tag{9a.14}$$

we see that, since $dz/ds < 0$, dp/ds has the opposite sign of

$$[(p - b)X'g(M) + 1 - G(M)] = \frac{\partial}{\partial p}[(p - b)(1 - G(M))]. \tag{9a.15}$$

One would expect from the deterministic case that $dp/ds \geq 0$, but we have been unable to establish this except under strong assumptions. Assuming $dp/ds \geq 0$ for the moment, we can also show that some regulation is desirable; that is, $d\overline{W}/ds$, evaluated at $s = s_m$, is negative. To see this, note that from 9a.6–9a.8 that

$$\frac{d\overline{W}}{ds} = \frac{\partial \overline{W}}{\partial p}\frac{dp}{ds} + \frac{\partial \overline{W}}{\partial z}\frac{dz}{ds} = [(p - b)G(M) - c(1 - G(M))]$$

$$X'(p)\frac{dp}{ds} + [\int_M^\infty (P(z - u) - b)dG(u) + c(1 - G(M)) - \beta]\frac{dz}{ds}. \tag{9a.16}$$

Thus rearranging,

$$\frac{d\overline{W}}{ds} = X'(p)(p - b)G(M)\frac{dp}{ds} + [\int_M^\infty (P(z - u) - b)dG(u) - \beta]\frac{dz}{ds} +$$

$$+ c(1 - G(M))[\frac{dz}{ds} - X'(p)\frac{dp}{ds}]. \tag{9a.17}$$

The first term in 9a.17 is nonnegative whenever $dp/ds \leq 0$. The term in brackets in the second term in 9a.17 is positive at $s = s_m$ by the same argument used in obtaining 9a.12. Moreover, $dz/ds < 0$, so the entire second term is negative. Finally the third term in 9a.17 is negative because the bracketed is just dM/ds. Altogether we see that

$$\left.\frac{d\bar{W}}{ds}\right|_{s = s_m} < 0, \tag{9a.18}$$

provided that $dp/ds \geq 0$ at $s = s_m$.

As our final task we provide one condition insuring $dp/ds \geq 0$. Since

$$\frac{\partial \bar{\pi}}{\partial p} = \frac{\partial}{\partial p}[(p - b)\int_{-\infty}^{M}(X(p) + u)dG(u) + \tag{9a.19}$$

$$+ (p - b)z(1 - G(M)) - \beta z] = 0$$

at the regulated optimum, we have

$$\Lambda = \frac{\partial}{\partial p}[(p - b)\int_{-\infty}^{M}(X(p) + u)dG(u) = \tag{9a.20}$$

$$- \frac{\partial}{\partial p}[(p - b)z(1 - G(M))].$$

Thus, from 9a.15, dp/ds has the sign of the left-hand side of 9a.20—that is, the sign of

$$\Lambda = \int_{-\infty}^{M}(X(p) + u) + (p - b(X'(p)[G(M) - zg(M)]. \tag{9a.21}$$

Since $X(p) + u \geq 0$ for all (p,u), and since $X'(p) < 0$, we see that a sufficient condition that $dp/ds \geq 0$ is that, at optimum, $G(M) \leq zg(M)$. One special case of this is the uniform distribution where $g(x) = ½\gamma$ for $-\gamma \leq x \leq \gamma$ and $g(x) = 0$ elsewhere. In this case

$$G(M) - zg(M) = \frac{1}{2\gamma}[\gamma - X(p)] \tag{9a.22}$$

which is negative since $X(p) + u \geq 0$ (over the feasible range of prices) for all $u \epsilon [-\gamma,\gamma]$. Thus, $G(M) \leq zg(M)$ for every feasible M in this case.

Notes

The derivation of 9a.13, is straightforward. From 9.34, we have $H_1 = \partial \bar{\pi} / \partial p = 0$, as repeated in 9a.1. Thus

$$\frac{\partial \bar{\pi}}{\partial p} \frac{dp}{ds} + \frac{\partial \bar{\pi}}{\partial z} \frac{dz}{ds} = \frac{\partial \bar{\pi}}{\partial s} \frac{dz}{ds}.$$

But $\partial \bar{\pi} / \partial$ is easily seen to be

$$\frac{\partial \bar{\pi}}{\partial z} = (p - b)(1 - G(M)) - \beta,$$

and dz/ds is given in 9a.7, so that

(*) $$\frac{\partial \bar{\pi}}{\partial z} \frac{dz}{ds} = \frac{z((p - b)(1 - G(M)) - \beta)}{(p - b)(1 - G(M)) - s}.$$

Finally 9a.2 implies (after some manipulation)

$$(p - b)(1 - G(M)) - \beta = \frac{\lambda(\beta - s)}{1 - \lambda}$$

$$(p - b)(1 - G(M)) - s = \frac{\beta - s}{1 - \lambda}$$

so that from (*)

$$\frac{\partial \bar{\pi}}{\partial z} \frac{dz}{ds} = \frac{\partial \bar{\pi}}{\partial p} \frac{dp}{ds} + \frac{\partial \bar{\pi}}{\partial z} \frac{dz}{ds} = \lambda z$$

as asserted.

References

Alchian, A., and R.A. Kessel. 1962. "Competition, Monopoly and the Pursuit of Money." In *Aspects of Labor Economics,* National Bureau of Economic Research, Princeton: Princeton University Press.

American Gas Association Rate Committee. 1969. *Gas Rate Fundamentals.* Arlington, Va.: American Gas Association.

Averch, H., and L.L. Johnson. 1962. "Behavior of the Firm under Regulatory Constraint." *American Economic Review* 52 (December): 1052–1069.

Backman, J., and J.B. Kirsten. 1974. "Comprehensive Adjustment Clause for Telephone Companies." *Public Utilities Fortnightly* (March 28): 3–8.

Bailey, E.E. 1972. "Peak Load Pricing under Regulatory Constraint." *Journal of Political Economy* 80 (July–August): 662–679.

———. 1973. *Economic Theory of Regulatory Constraint.* Lexington, Mass.: D.C. Heath.

Bailey, E.E., and J.C. Malone. 1970. "Resources Allocation in the Regulated Firm." *Bell Journal of Economics and Management Sciences* 1 (Spring): 129–142.

Baron, D.P., and R.A. Taggart, Jr. 1978. "Regulatory Pricing Policies and Input Choices under Uncertainty." Northwestern University Discussion Paper No. 315, February.

Baumol, W.J. 1977. "On the Proper Test of Natural Monopoly in a Multiproduct Industry." *American Economic Review* 67 (December): 809–822.

Baumol, W.J., and D.F. Bradford. 1970. "Optimal Departure from Marginal Cost Prices." *American Economic Review* 60 (June): 265–283.

Blaydon, Colin, C.; Wesley Magat; and Celia Thomas. 1978. "Marginal Cost and Rate Structure Design for Retail Sales of Natural Gas: An Applied Study." Graduate School of Business Administration (GSBA) Paper No. 232, Duke University, August.

Boiteux, M. 1949. "La tarification des demandes en point: Application de la théorie de la vente au cout marginal." *Revue Générale de l'électricité* 58 (August): 321–240. Translated as "Peak Load Pricing," *Journal of Business* 33 (April 1960): 157–198.

———. 1971. "On Management of Public Monopolies Subject to Budgetary Constraints." *Journal of Economic Theory* 3 (December): 219–240.

Bonbright, James C. 1961. *Principles of Public Utility Rates.* New York: Columbia University Press.

Brito, D., and W.H. Oakland. 1978. "Nonlinear Price Schedule for Public Goods." Unpublished manuscript, Ohio State University, 1978.

Brown, G., and Johnson, M.B. 1969. "Public Utility Pricing and Output under Risk." *American Economic Review* 59 (March): 119–129.

Buchanan, J.M. 1953. "Theory of Monopolistic Quantity Discounts." *Review of Economic Studies* 20: 199–208.

Carlton, D.W. 1977. "Peak Load Pricing with Stochastic Demand." *American Economic Review* 67 (December): 1006–1010.

Christensen, J.R.; D.W. Jorgenson; and T.J. Larrs. 1973. "Transcendental Logarithmic Production Frontiers." *Review of Economics and Statistics* 55 (February): 53–74.

Courville, L. 1974. "Regulation and Efficiency in the Electric Utility Industry." *Bell Journal of Economics and Management Sciences* 5 (Spring): 53–74.

Crew, M.A., and P.R. Kleindorfer. 1971. "Marshall and Turvey on Peak Loads or Joint Product Pricing." *Journal of Political Economy* 79 (November–December): 1369–1377.

———. 1975a. "On Off-Peak Pricing: An Alternative Technological Solution." *Kyklos* 28: 80–93.

———. 1975b. "Optimal Plant Mix in Peak Load Pricing." *Scottish Journal of Political Economy* 22 (November): 277–291.

———. 1976. "Peak Load Pricing with a Diverse Technology." *Bell Journal of Economics* 7 (Spring): 207–231.

———. 1978. "Reliability and Public Utility Pricing." *American Economic Review* 68 (March): 31–40.

———. 1979a. "Managerial Discretion and Public Utility Regulation." *Southern Economic Journal* 46 (January): 696–709.

———. 1979b. *Public Utility Economics.* New York: St. Martins Press.

Czamanski, Daniel Z.; J. Stephen Henderson; Kevin A. Kelley; and James S. Detweiler. 1977. "Benefits and Costs of Gas Storage Development in Ohio." Columbus: Public Utilities Commission of Ohio.

Dansby, R.E. 1975. "We Have Optimal Peak Load Pricing with Time Varying Demand." Holmdel, N.J.: Bell Laboratories.

———. 1978. "Interruptible Service Options." Murrayhill, N.J.: Bell Laboratories.

Data Resources, Inc. 1978. "The Impact of Marginal Cost Pricing in the State of Maryland Power Plant Siting Program." Baltimore: Maryland Department of Natural Resources.

Davidson, R.K. 1955. *Price Discrimination in Selling Gas and Electricity.* Baltimore: Johns Hopkins University Press.

Diewert, W.G. 1976. "Exact and Superlative Index Numbers." *Journal of Econometrics* 4: (May): 115–145.

Douglas, G., and J.C. Miller III. 1974. *Economic Regulation of Domestic Air Transport.* Washington, D.C.: Brookings Institution.

Edwards, F.R. 1977. "Managerial Objectives in Regulated Industries: Expense-Preference Behavior in Banking." *Journal of Political Economy* 85 (February): 147-162.

Elliot, J.W. 1972. "Control, Size, Growth and Financial Performance in the Firm." *Journal of Financial Quantitative Analysis* 7 (January): 1309-1320.

Fisher, I. 1922. *The Making of Index Numbers.* Boston: Houghton Mifflin.

Glower, Donald D.; Seymour E. Goldstone; and Kevin A. Kelly. 1976. "Alternative Policies for Pricing Non-Historical Gas with Implications for Conservation and Shortage Management." Columbus: Ohio Public Utility Commission.

Gravelle, H.S.E. 1976. "The Peak Load Problem with Feasible Storage." *Economic Journal* 86 (June): 250-277.

Harris, M., and A. Raviv. 1976. "Optimal Incentive Contracts with Imperfect Information." Unpublished manuscript, Carnegie-Mellon Institute.

———. 1978. "Some Results of Incentive Contracts with Application to Education and Employment, Health Insurance and Law Enforcement." *American Economic Review* 68 (March): 20-30.

Hatta, T. 1977. "A Theory of Piecemeal Policy Recommendations." *Review of Economic Studies* 44: 1-21.

Hirshleifer, J. 1978. "Peak Loads and Efficient Pricing: Comment." *Quarterly Journal of Economics* 72 (August): 451-462.

Houthhakker, H.S. 1951. "Electricity Tariffs in Theory and Practice." *Economic Journal* 61 (March): 1-25.

Hulten, R.C. 1973. "Divisia Index Numbers." *Econometrica* 41 (November): 1017-1025.

ICF, Inc. 1978. "Report to Department of Energy." DOE Contract CA-04-70228-00.

Jensen, M.C., and W.H. Meckling. 1976. "Theory of the Firm: Managerial Behavior Agency Costs and Ownership Structure." *Journal of Financial Economics* 3 (October): 305-360.

Jorgenson, J.W., and Z. Griliches. 1967. "The Explanation of Productivity Change." *Review of Economic Studies* 34 (July): 249-283.

Joskow, Paul L. 1974. "Inflation and Environmental Concern: Structural Changes in the Process of Public Utility Price Regulation." *Journal of Law and Economics* 17 (October): 291-327.

Joskow, Paul L., and Roger G. Noll. 1978. "Regulation in Theory and Practice: An Overview." Working Paper Number 218. Cambridge: MIT Department of Economics.

Kahn, Alfred E. 1970. *The Economics of Regulation.* New York: Wiley.
Kamerschen, D.R. 1968. "The Influence of Ownership and Control on Profit Rates." *American Economic Review* 58 (June): 432–447.
Kamien, M.I., and N.L. Schwartz. 1975. "Market structure and Innovation: A Survey." *Journal of Economic Literature* 13 (March): 1–37.
Kendrick, J.W. 1973. *Postwar Productivity Trends in the U.S., 1948–1969.* New York: National Bureau of Economic Research.
———. 1975. "Efficiency Incentives and Cost Factors in Public Utility Automatic Revenue Adjustment Clauses." *Bell Journal of Economics* 6 (Spring): 299–313.
Larner, R.J. 1970. *Management Control and the Large Corporation.* New York: Dunellen.
Latimer, H.A. 1974. "The Cost and Efficiency Revenue Adjustment Clause." *Public Utilities Fortnightly* (August 15): 19–24.
Leibenstein, H. 1966. "Allocative vs. X-Efficiency." *American Economic Review* 56 (June): 392–415.
Leibenstein, H. 1975. "Aspects of the X-Efficiency Theory of the Firm." *Bell Journal of Economics* 6 (Autumn): 580–606.
Leland, H.E. 1974. "Regulation of Natural Monopolies and the Fair Rate of Return." *Bell Journal of Economics* 5 (Spring): 3–15.
Levine, Michael E. 1965. "Is Regulation Necessary? California Air Transportation and National Regulatory Policy." *Yale Law Journal* 74 (July): 1416–1447.
Lewis, W.A. 1941. "The Two-Part Tariff." *Economica* 8 (August): 249–270.
Little, I.M.D. 1953. *The Price of Fuel.* New York: Oxford University Press.
Magat, W.A. 1976. "Regulation and the Rate and Direction of Induced Technical Change." *Bell Journal of Economics* 7 (Autumn): 478–498.
Marchand, M. 1974. "Pricing Power Supplied on an Interruptible Basis." *European Economic Review* 5 (July): 273–274.
Meyer, R.A. 1975. "Monopoly Pricing and Capacity Choice under Uncertainty." *American Economic Review* 65 (June): 326–337.
Mitchell, B.M.; W.G. Manning, Jr.; and J.P. Acton. 1978. *Peak Load Pricing: European Lessons for U.S. Energy Policy.* Cambridge, Mass.: Ballinger.
Mohring, H. 1970. "The Peak Load Problem with Increasing Returns and Pricing Constraints." *American Economic Review* 60 (September): 693–705.
Monsen, R.T.; T.S.Y. Chiu; and E.E. Cooley. 1968. "The Effect of Separation of Ownership and Control on the Performance of Large Firms." *Quarterly Journal of Economics* 82 (August): 435–451.
Mount, T.D., and L.D. Chapman. 1976. "Effects of Increasing the Use of Electricity on Environmental Quality in the U.S.: A Model of Power Generation and Policy Issues Raised by Its Applications." In *Proceedings of the Workshop on Energy Demand,* edited by W.D. Nordhaus.

Loxenburg, Austria: International Institute for Applied Systems Analysis.

Munasinghe, M., and M. Gellerson. 1977. "Economic Criteria for Optimizing Power System Reliability Levels." Washington, D.C.: World Bank.

National Economic Research Associates, Inc. 1977. "How to Quantify Marginal Costs." Topic 4, Electric Utility Rate Design Study. Palo Alto, Cal.: Electric Power Research Institute.

Needy, C. 1975. *Regulation-induced Distortions.* Lexington, Mass.: D.C. Heath.

Ng, Y., and M. Weisser. 1974. "Optimal Pricing with a Budget Constraint—The Case of the Two-Part Tariff." *Review of Economic Studies* 41 (July): 337–345.

Oi, W.Y. 1971. "Two Part Tariffs for a Mickey Mouse Monopoly." *Quarterly Journal of Economics* 85 (February): 77–96.

Okuguchi, K. 1975. "The Implications of Regulation for Induced Technical Change: A Comment." *Bell Journal of Economics* 6 (Autumn): 703–705.

Palmer, J. 1973. "The Profit-Performance Effects of the Separation of Ownership from Control in Large U.S. Industrial Corporations." *Bell Journal of Economics and Management Science* 4 (Spring): 293–303.

Panzar, J.C., and D.S. Sibley. 1978. "Public Utility Pricing under Risk: The Care of Self-Rationing." *American Economic Review* 68 (December): 888–895.

Panzar, J.C., and R.D. Willig. 1977. "Free Entry and the Sustainability of Natural Monopoly." *Bell Journal of Economics* 8 (Spring): 1–22.

Peles, Y., and J.L. Stein. 1976. "The Effect of Rate-of-Return Regulation Is Highly Sensitive to the Nature of Uncertainty." *American Economic Review* 66 (June): 278–289.

Peles, Y., and E. Sheshinski. 1976. "Integration Effects of Firms Subject to Regulation." *Bell Journal of Economics* 7 (Spring): 308–313.

Peltzman, S. 1976. "Toward a More General Theory of Regulation." *Journal of Law and Economics* 19 (August): 211–240.

Perrakis, S. 1976a. "Rate-of-Return of a Monopoly Firm with Random Demand." *International Economic Review* 17 (February): 149–161.

———. 1976b. "On the Regulated Price Setting Monopoly Firm with a Random Demand." *American Economic Review* 66 (June): 410–416.

Posner, R. 1971. "Taxation by Regulation." *Bell Journal of Economics* 2 (Spring): 28–50.

Public Service Company of New Mexico. 1977. Electrical Marginal Cost Study: Base Year 1977. Case No. 1419, Exhibit DME-1. Santa Fe: New Mexico Public Service Commission.

Pustay, Michael W. 1978. "Industry Efficiency under Regulatory Surveillance." *Journal of Industrial Economics* 27 (September): 49–68.

Ramanathan, Ramu. 1977. "Comments in Electric Power Research Institute, Forecasting and Modeling Time-of-Day and Seasonal Electricity Demands.'' Special Report EA-578-SR. Palo Alto, Calif.: EPPI.

Rees, R. 1974. "A Reconsideration of Expense-Preference Theory of the Firm.'' *Economica* 41 (August): 295-307.

Roberts, Kevin W.S. 1978. "Welfare Considerations of Nonlinear Pricing.'' Working Paper. Cambridge: MIT.

Ross, S.A. 1973. "The Economic Theory of Agency: The Principal's Problem.'' *American Economic Review* 63 (May): 134-139.

Sherman, R., and A. George. 1979. "Second-Best Pricing for the U.S. Postal Service.'' *Southern Economic Journal* 45 (January): 685-695.

Sherman, R., and M. Visscher. 1978a. "Second-Best Pricing with Stochastic Demand.'' *American Economic Review* 68 (March): 41-53.

———. 1978b. "Rate-of-Return Regulation and Multi-part Pricing.'' Unpublished manuscript, University of Virginia.

Shesinski, E. 1976. "Price Quality and Quantity Regulation in Monopoly Situations.'' *Economica* 43 (May): 127-137.

Smith, V.H. 1974. "The Implications of Regulation for Induced Technical Change.'' *Bell Journal of Economics and Management Science* 5 (Autumn): 623-632.

Sorenson, R. 1974. "The Separation of Ownership and Control and Firm Performance: An Empirical Analysis.'' *Southern Economic Journal* 40 (July): 145-148.

Spann, R.M. 1974. "Rate-of-Return Regulation and Efficiency in Production: An Empirical Test of the Averch-Johnson Thesis.'' *Bell Journal of Economics and Management Science* 5 (Spring): 38-52.

Stano, M. 1976. "Monopoly Power, Ownership Control, and Corporate Performance.'' *Bell Journal of Economics* 7 (Autumn): 672-679.

Star, S., and R.E. Hall. 1976. "An Approximate Divisia Index of Total Factor Productivity.'' *Econometrica* 44 (March): 257-263.

Steiner, P.O. 1957. "Peak Loads and Efficiency-Pricing.'' *Quarterly Journal of Economics* 71 (November): 585-610.

Stigler, G.J. 1971. "The Theory of Regulation.'' *Bell Journal of Economics* 2 (Spring): 3-21.

Stigler, G.J., and C. Friedland. 1962. "What Can Regulation Regulate? The Case of Electricy.'' *Journal of Law and Economics* 5 (October): 1-16.

Sudit, E.F. 1977. "Alternative Measures of Total Factor Productivity.'' *Total Factor Productivity Symposium I,* Teleglobe, Montreal, Canada, May 1977.

Taylor, Lester D. 1975. "The Demand for Electricity: A Survey.'' *Bell Journal of Economics* 6 (Spring): 74-110.

Telson, M.L. 1975. "The Economics of Alternative Levels of Reliability for Elective Power Generation System.'' *Bell Journal of Economics* 6 (Autumn): 679-694.

Turvey, R., and Dennis Anderson. 1977. *Electricity Economics.* Baltimore: Johns Hopkins University Press.

Vinod, H.D. 1972. "Nonhomogenous Production Functions and Applications to Telecommunications." *Bell Journal of Economics and Management Science* (Autumn): 531-543.

Visscher, M. 1973. "Welfare-Maximizing Price and Output with Stochastic Demand: Comment." *American Economic Review* 63 (March): 224-229.

Webb, Michael. 1978. "Policy on Energy Pricing." *Energy Policy* (March): 53-65.

Wellisz, S.H. 1963. "Regulation of Natural Gas Pipeline Companies: An Economic Analysis." *Journal of Political Economy* 71 (February): 30-43.

Wenders, John T. 1976. "Peak Load Pricing in the Electricity Industry." *Bell Journal of Economics* 7 (Spring): 232-241.

Wenders, John T., and R. Ashley Lyman. 1977. "A Benefit/Cost Analysis of Peak Load Pricing of Electricity to Large Residential Users." Electric Power Research Institute, *Forecasting and Modeling Time-of-day and Seasonal Electricity Demands,* Special Report EA-578-SR. Palo Alto, Calif.: EPRI.

Wenders, John T., and Lester D. Taylor. 1976. "Experiments in Seasonal Time-of-Day Pricing of Electricity to Residential Users." *Bell Journal of Economics* 7 (Autumn): 531-552.

Werner, M. 1977. "An Integrated Total Factor Productivity-Financial Based Corporate Planning Model." *Total Factor Productivity, Symposium I,* Teleglobe, Montreal, Canada, May.

Williamson, O.E. 1964. "The Economics of Discretionary Behavior: Managerial *Objectives in a Theory of the Firm.* Englewood Cliffs: Prentice-Hall.

———. 1966. "Peak Load Pricing and Optimal Capacity." *American Economic Review* 56 (September): 810-827.

———. 1968. "Economics as an Anti-trust Defense: The Welfare Tradeoffs." *American Economic Review* 58 (March): 18-36.

———. 1963. "Managerial Discretion and Business Behavior." *American Economic Review* 53 (December): 1032-1057.

———. 1975. *Markets and Hierarchies: Analysis and Antitrust Implications.* New York: Free Press.

Williamson, O.E. 1976. "Franchise Bidding for Natural Monopolies and with respect to CATV." *Bell Journal of Economics* 7 (Spring): 73-104.

Willig, R.D. 1978. "Pareto Superior Nonlinear Outlay Schedules." *Bell Journal of Economics* 9 (Spring): 56-69.

Seminar Participants

Enrique Arzac
Associate Professor Graduate School or Business
Columbia University

The Honorable Elizabeth E. Bailey
Member, Civil Aeronautics Board

Bert Blewitt
Corporate Economist
Public Service Electric and Gas Company

John Bonin
Associate Professor
Wesleyan University

Frank Cassidy
Engineering Economist
Public Service Electric and Gas Company

George Clarkson
Manager
Rates and Load Management
Public Service Electric and Gas Company

Michael A. Crew
Associate Professor and Director of the Business Research Center
Graduate School of Business Administration
Rutgers University

Robert E. Dansby
Supervisor
American Telephone and Telegraph

Horace J. De Podwin
Dean
Graduate School of Business Administration
Rutgers University

Franklin R. Edwards
Professor
Graduate School of Business
Columbia University

Gerald R. Faulhaber
Director
Pricing and Economics
American Telephone and Telegraph Company

Fred S. Grygiel
Chief Economist
New Jersey Board of Public Utilities

H.E. Harvey, Jr.
General Rate Manager
New Jersey Bell Telephone Company

Paul R. Kleindorfer
Professor
Wharton School, University of Pennsylvania and Research Fellow
International Institute of Management

Harvey Leibenstein
Andelot Professor of Economics and Population
Harvard University

Wesley A. Magat
Associate Professor of Business Administration
Duke University

Everett L. Morris
Senior Vice-President, Customer Operations
Public Service Electric and Gas Company

Glenn Myers
Senior Economist
Horace J. De Podwin Associates Inc.

Roger Sherman
Professor
Department of Economics
University of Virginia

Thomas K. Standish
Commissioner
Public Utilities Control Authority
Hartford, Connecticut

Rodney Stevenson
Assistant Professor
Madison School of Business
University of Wisconsin

E. Fred Sudit
Assistant Professor
Graduate School of Business Administration
Rutgers University

Michael L. Visscher
Assistant Professor
Department of Economics
Ohio State University

Richard E. Weber
Executive Director
Human Resources Development Authority
Feasibility Study
Rutgers University

John T. Wenders
Professor
Department of Economics
University of Arizona

James E. Young
Provost
Newark Campus, Rutgers University

About the Editor

Michael A. Crew was educated in England, receiving the B. Com. and Ph.D. degrees from the University of Birmingham and University of Bradford respectively. He has taught economics at universities in the United Kingdom and the United States. He has published several articles on public utility economics, monopoly, and antitrust in the leading professional journals as well as two books. His latest book is *Public Utility Economics* (with Paul R. Kleindorfer). He is currently associate professor and director of the Business Research Center, Graduate School of Business Administration, Rutgers University.